Editor's Note

Jonathan Wilson, Editor

I'm writing this on the way to Zagreb for the second leg of Croatia's World Cup play-off against Iceland. Last week I was in Amman for Jordan's first-leg defeat to Uruguay. When it comes to games at this stage of the process, when you see what the proximity of the World Cup means to nations like Jordan and Iceland who have never been there before, who have probably never dreamed of being there, it's hard not to be contemptuous of those who roll their eyes at the very notion of international breaks. Yet in the juxtaposition of the yawning English or Spanish fan and the excitement of the Jordanian or Icelander lies the main problem facing the World Cup.

On the one hand it is too big. The tournament itself drags on for a full month, featuring 64 games of which, in a good year, perhaps 10 or 12 are meaningful in terms of deciding who wins. It can now only be hosted by a tiny handful of wealthy and/or vast nations, and even they find their infrastructure creaking under the strain of hundreds of thousands of additional visitors and face being left with white elephant stadiums. For the bigger nations, qualifying is a dull slog round increasingly familiar outposts, and tends to end up being decided by a pair of games against the next biggest side in the group (England's campaign this time was rare in featuring three other decent sides, and even that ended up being settled, if not comfortably, then at least without England ever having to produce a genuinely top-class performance). If many fans are bored by international football, it's not without reason.

And yet, the World Cup also seems too small. There are constant complaints from the African and Asian confederations that they should have greater representation. The argument that it's not fair that only a tenth of their members qualify when half of Conmebol does is ludicrous, an embarrassing special pleading that ignores how utterly Conmebol nations have outperformed CAF and the AFC at every tournament — and the World Cup is, ultimately, a competition, not a charitable centre for football education. But it probably is true that playing better sides will help a team develop (up to a point; there's no evidence San Marino have developed at all with their regular hammerings — there has to be at least some equivalence of ability). That said, playing in a World Cup, for all it may do in offering experience and raising profile and interest is only part of the issue. CAF and AFC evangelists like to point to the example of the USA's development since 1990, as though that tournament magically transformed them from minnows to being in the world's top 20. It may have helped, but MLS and associated infrastructure development has far more to do with it. Togo, Trinidad & Tobago, UAE and China provide equally compelling arguments that a World Cup qualification does next to nothing to improve the standard in the long-term.

So there are three basic issues: a bloated finals format, weariness at the familiarity of qualification, and an impetus to spread to joy a little. There is a solution, one that could have profound benefits for everybody other than those who have a vested interest in milking the finals tournament for every penny. Which is to say, there is no chance of this happening, however much sense it may make from a purely footballing point of view.

It is possible to both spread the tournament wider while at the same time streamlining the finals tournament. A 16-team finals works, as the Euros have proved (even if Uefa are now ruining it). Quality is concentrated, almost every game matters and even relatively small nations can put on a three-week tournament. Reducing the length of the tournament by a fortnight would give national managers an additional week to prepare and give players an extra week's break before the new season. It benefits national team and clubs.

So that's the making it smaller. The making it larger comes at the previous stage. Run qualifying over two phases: the first regional, the second global. That would have two advantages: firstly, that the 16 teams at the finals would all have earned their right in a global market over the previous two years. They would be, as far as possible, the host plus the best 15 of the rest. And secondly, it would provide far more of those games that are supposedly so key in the educational process to twice as many teams. Not only that, but half those games would be played at home: it would genuinely take the game to fans everywhere. There may be an increase in travel costs and there may need to

be some stadium redevelopment, but neither of those are insurmountable issues: Fifa, after all, has enormous cash reserves. And, besides, how much better for the development of the global game to develop one stadium in a number of nations rather than 12 in the same country, of which the majority are wholly unnecessary?

Stage one is to select a host. This has not proved entirely simple in the past, but if the IOC can reform itself, so too can Fifa. Let's, for the sake of argument, go with Russia.

Stage two: regional qualifying to get down to 60 nations. You can quibble over how exactly they would be distributed among the confederations, but let's, for the sake of argument, amalgamate Conmebol and Concacaf into a confederation of the Americas, and merge the OFC and AFC. Roughly doubling the present allocation, that would give 24 teams from Europe, and 12 each from the Americas, Africa and Asia/Oceania – although it would probably be wise to adopt some sort of coefficient system, similar to that Uefa uses for club competition, to maintain a balance that reflects the present actuality.

Stage three: form one pot from the top 15 sides in the Fifa rankings as seeds. At the moment that would be: Spain, Germany, Argentina, Colombia, Belgium, Uruguay, Switzerland, Netherlands, Italy, England, Brazil, Chile, USA, Portugal, Greece. Form another pot from the remaining 15 European sides; by Fifa ranking, that would be: Bosnia, Croatia, Ukraine, France, Sweden, Denmark, Czech Republic, Serbia, Romania, Scotland, Armenia, Turkey, Hungary,

Wales, Iceland (with Russia as hosts). Form a third pot from the six remaining teams from the Americas, plus nine from Africa (Ecuador, Mexico, Costa Rica, Honduras, Panama, Venezuela; Côte d'Ivoire, Ghana, Algeria, Nigeria, Mali, Cape Verde, Tunisia, Egypt, Burkina Faso). Form a fourth pot of the remaining three African sides and the 12 AFC/OFC teams (Cameroon, Libya, South Africa; Japan, Iran, Uzbekistan, South Korea, Australia, Jordan, UAE, New Zealand, Oman, China, Saudi Arabia, Iraq). Draw 15 groups – keeping American seeds apart from American sides in Pot 3, and the CAF sides in Pot 4 away from those in Pot 3, to produce something like this:

Everybody plays everybody home and away, with the group winners going on to the finals in Russia, and the second-placed side guaranteeing some sort of seeding for their regional qualifying the next time round. Yes, some groups are tougher than others — you wouldn't fancy Oman's hopes playing Germany, France and Nigeria — but which Welshman wouldn't relish the trips to Bogota, Praia and Tashkent? Imagine the impact of Lionel Messi arriving for a game in Algiers or Arjen Robben in Wellington or Cristiano Ronaldo in Panama City, something now that could happen on only the wackiest pre-season tour.

It's fun, it's fair and it's genuinely global. And it will never, ever happen.

December 2013

Brazil	Greece	Portugal	Colombia	Belgium
Armenia	Scotland	Ukraine	Wales	Sweden
Egypt	Venezuela	Panama	Cape Verde	Costa Rica
South Korea	UAE	Libya	Uzbekistan	Cameroon

Argentina	Netherlands	Switzerland	Spain	USA
Denmark	Hungary	Romania	Turkey	Croatia
Algeria	Ghana	Mexico	Honduras	Côte d'Ivoire
Australia	New Zealand	Jordan	South Africa	Iran

Uruguay	Italy	Chile	England	Germany
Bosnia	Iceland	Serbia	Czech Republic	France
Tunisia	Ecuador	Burkina Faso	Mali	Nigeria
Saudi Arabia	Iraq	China	Japan	Oman

Contents

The Blizzard, Issue Eleven

FSC
www.fsc.org
MIX
Paper from responsible sources
FSC® C008152

8

African Champions League

"Armoured cars would roll in and circle around the
athletics track outside the pitch, with president Mobutu
in the central one, waving to the crowd, with the
guards pointing guns."

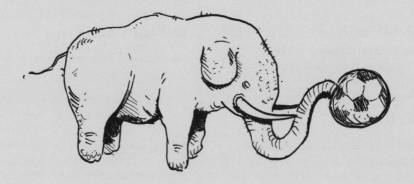

A Voyage under Jolly Roger

*Following Orlando Pirates' run to the final of the
African Champions League*

By Firdose Moonda

**Only once has a South African side
won the African Champions League,
when Orlando Pirates lifted the trophy
in 1995. They played in a semi-final in
2006, and Mamelodi Sundowns reached
the final in 2001, but South African
sides have traditionally placed little
importance on continental competition,
seeing games in less than hospitable
destinations interfere too much with
their domestic schedule. This time it
would be different.**

Roger de Sá, the Pirates coach, began his
second season with an additional task.
He was told the Champions League was
not a tournament to be taken lightly.
In his previous role with university club
Bidvest Wits, who only ever qualified for
the Confederations' Cup, De Sá used the
continental tournament to experiment and
fielded fringe players. The message from
the Pirates' management was that he was
to do no such thing with this competition.

"They see this as a challenge and they
always want to go as far as possible. With
that one star on their badge, they want
a second one and to prove they can win
on the continent," he said.

The Pirates captain Lucky Lekgwati
started the campaign bullishly and with

a promise about his own future. "We
have a team that is capable of beating
anybody on the continent if we stay
focused," he said. "I have also made it
clear I will quit soccer if I lead Pirates to
Champions League success."

**Preliminary qualifying round
16 February 2013, Orlando Stadium,
Johannesburg
Orland Pirates 5 Djabal Club 0**

"We will beat them with an avalanche
of goals," Lekgwati said before the tie
against a team from the Comoros made
up of amateurs. Lekgwati also thought
it was a good omen that Pirates had
drawn an offshore side because "when
we reached the semi-finals in 2006, we
started the preliminaries with another
team from an Indian Ocean island, AS
Port Louis from Mauritius."

The biggest challenge was the fact that
Pirates had never seen the team from
the Comoros before. But that did not
matter — they beat Djabal 5-0, thanks to
four goals from the Zimbabwean striker
Takesure Chinyama. Sifiso Myeni opened
the scoring and Chinyama did the rest,
taking advantage of the opposition's
fragile defence. It could have been more,
and Pirates had two goals ruled out for
offside. Despite being in complete control,
De Sá said Pirates were surprised by the

quality of their opposition. "We didn't really know how they were going to play and they frustrated us at times," he said. "We wanted more goals but we got the result. I just hope this lead will be enough."

De Sá seemed oddly irritated by what had been a comfortable win, and two days after the game he was still criticising the standard of the officiating, commenting specifically on the number of times his players were caught offside. "At least now we've had a taste of the refereeing," he said. "Only a handful of our players have been in this competition before and I warned them what to expect. I told them it's going to get a lot worse. They've got to get mentally strong.

"I'm glad many saw it. I don't think we should accept it because we aim to do better in this competition than we have the past two times. But there's nothing we can do about it now. If we get through this round it means we have already improved from last season, where we couldn't make it past this stage."

In between the two legs, Pirates played two league fixtures, winning one and losing one to remain second in the table, but they were beaten 4-1 by the third-division side Maluti FET in the Nedbank Cup.

**2 March 2013, Stade Said Mohamed Cheikh, Mitsamouli, Comoros
Djabal Club 0 Orlando Pirates 4**

Without the strikers Myeni and Collins Mbesuma, the midfielders Daine Klate

and Oupa Manyisá and a number of other key players, Pirates chartered a flight to the tropical paradise without their assistant coach Tebogo Moloi. He stayed behind in the belief there was "no way Djabal will bounce back" and worked with those who were recovering from niggles. He also went to Swaziland to watch the match between Mbabane Swallows and Zanaco of Zambia, the winners of which would play Pirates in the first round proper. The absences made little difference: Pirates went two goals up in the first eight minutes and doubled that advantage by full-time. Chinyama was among the goalscorers again.

Aggregate result: Orlando Pirates 9 Djabal Club 0

**First qualifying round
16 March 2013, Nkoloma Stadium, Lusaka
Zanaco 0 Orlando Pirates 1**

Davies Mwape was a teenager when he found himself on Pirates' books in 2005. He never made it into the team, as he was loaned out and eventually let go. As leader of the Zanaco attack, he wanted to use the match to show Pirates what they missed out on and they were well aware of the threat he posed. "I played with Davies," Lekgwati said. "He is a very aggressive striker, who can shoot from any angle. We just need to keep a close eye on him so that he does not embarrass us."

Pirates' supporters club travelled by bus from Johannesburg to Lusaka, a journey which takes 27 hours and passes through neighbouring Zimbabwe.

The team was without defender Siyabonga Sangweni and there were concerns over their defence but they had little to worry about. On a pitch which was later criticised for being sub-standard, they were rarely troubled by the home side and Ndumiso Mabena gave them a precious away goal. Their functional style was what De Sá wanted to see more of as the competition went on. "The Champions League is won by heart and not by being flashy," he said. "If we carry on this way, we can definitely go far."

The last two weeks of March saw Pirates extend a lean run in the league to six matches without a win. There were calls for De Sa's head and the team went into the return leg against the Zambian champions under enormous pressure to produce.

6 April 2013, FNB Stadium, Johannesburg
Orlando Pirates 2-1 Zanaco

The match had to be moved from Pirates' usual home ground in Orlando to Soccer City, where the 2010 World Cup final was held, because of a church service. Pirates didn't seem too unsettled by the surroundings, though, taking an 18th-minute lead through Khetokwakhe Masuku. There was a minor tremor when Musona Mwape was left unmarked to equalise four minutes after the break but Pirates were back on safe ground after Mpho Makola's free-kick curled into the top right corner of the net with 13 minutes remaining.

De Sá admitted the side got a "bit of a scare," when the Zambians got back on level terms but he was happy with the way Pirates controlled the match after that. "We still have a lot of work to do," he said, "but we're getting there."

A second-round tie against the DR Congo giants TP Mazembe, though, would be a much stiffer test.

Aggregate result: Orlando Pirates 3 Zanaco 1

Second qualifying round
20 April 2013, Orlando Stadium, Johannesburg
Orlando Pirates 3 TP Mazembe 1

All reason said this should have been the end of the road for Pirates. They were hit by a spate of injuries that left them without Sangweni, ManyiSá and Andile Jali for the home leg. With only 17 of their squad fully fit, it seemed they'd be taking on the DRC heavyweights with one hand tied behind their back.

But Pirates went ahead within the first two minutes. Mbesuma provided the cross and Onyekachi Onkonkwo fired home. TP Mazembe equalised but Mbesuma, the Zambian forward who was such a disappointment at Portsmouth, put them back into the lead. He then doubled it from the penalty spot.

The decision to award the penalty had far wider ramifications than anybody would have thought at the time. A journalist working for the national broadcaster, SABC, Velile Mbuli, tweeted that after the game the referee,

Swaziland's Smanga Nhleko, had been "floored by a vicious punch from a TP Mazembe official." Later, he spotted police waiting for the official to get onto the team bus so they could question him. He was hiding in the dressing-room.

None of the officials present knew the identity of the man, Kabila Kanga, and Mazembe denied any association with him. In a letter to CAF, Mazembe claimed Kanga was a Congolese expatriate living in South Africa and was not involved with them at all. They also blamed Pirates' security for allowing Kanga to have access to the tunnel where he punched Nhleko.

Given that Kanga was in a restricted area, Mazembe were held responsible for the assault and fined US$5,000 while Kanga was banned from attending football matches a year.

De Sá remained worried that Mazembe were still in the tie because of their away goal. "It gives them an opportunity," he said. "If they score two unanswered goals at home, they go through." But he saw one thing which gave him hope. "I don't think they are as solid at the back as they are good going forward," he noted.

Mazembe received a massive confidence boost between the two legs, beating their arch-rivals V Club from Kinshasa. They also cut the price of tickets for the game by 60% in the hope of drawing a full crowd to intimidate the opposition. Having appeared in the group stage in four of the five previous seasons, they were determined not to miss out. Pirates' indifferent domestic form went on as they lost to the minnows Chippa United.

5 May 2013, Stade TP Mazembe, Lubumbashi
TP Mazembe 0 Orlando Pirates 1

Pirates were full of fighting talk, buoyed by the return of many of their injured stars. "This is going to be war," Moloi said, the term insensitive given the conflict in the DRC. There was animosity, much of it from Pirates' hosts and the officials. De Sá had prepared the team for a hostile reception, showing them videos of previous matches played in Lubumbashi. He encouraged them to walk around the stadium when they first got there and take in the crowd's vibe. He said that before kick-off they "felt no fear."

The same could not be said for some of their countrymen. South African cameramen were kicked out of the stadium and some arrested without explanation. The feed to South Africa was cut off minutes after the game started so South Africans were unable to see how their team was doing.

What they missed was Lekgwati being shown a red card after 35 minutes after kick-off for, as the Pirates head of administration, Senzo Mazingisa, put it "no apparent reason". Two penalties were awarded against Pirates in the second half but Meyiwa saved both, first from Eric Bokanga and then from Mazembe's talisman, Trésor Mputu. He could not, though, keep Jean Kasusula out in open play.

One goal, though, was not enough and Pirates progressed to the group stage with the bruises to show for it. Lekgwati said the way the match was handled was "killing African soccer" while acknowledging that Pirates "came here expecting these things, including poor refereeing." Meyiwa said the match would stay with him for life: "I will never forget this game, it was tough and tense."

But Mazingisá was far more critical of the way his men were received by Mazembe. "The treatment was bad," he said. "Our technical staff were harassed. Our dressing-room was left wide open. Prior to the start of the game, people here were able to speak English. When the game started, they started communicating with us in French, clearly to frustrate us."

Pirates left the country as soon as they could. On his return home, De Sá admitted to Neal Collins, a local journalist, that he was close to quitting football altogether. "I feel a bit like Rambo," he said. "We expected trouble but nothing like that. I couldn't sleep last night thinking about it. To be honest, I feel like walking away from the game. If somebody called me and offered me a job outside football I'd take it. But then you calm down and you realise the national pride in our result. Look, what these people did is bad for the game, it's bad for Africa. Still, we're through. There must have been a stronger force at work for that to happen."

15 May 2013: The Draw

Pirates were unseeded for the draw and were handed what was considered the tougher of the two groups with both Egyptian heavyweights, the defending champions Al Ahly and Zamalek, and one newcomer in AC Leopards of Congo. The South Africans chose to see the positives. Trips to Cairo meant direct flights, while there was something invigorating about the challenge of facing two former champions. "It will help in developing the mental toughness of our players," said Irvin Khoza, the Pirates chairman.

"We are also African giants in our own right," said Meyiwa. "We respect Al Ahly and Zamalek but we are not scared of them. We are going to conquer Africa."

Having won just two of their last twelve league games, Pirates finished a disappointing third in the league. [The South African league runs from August to May, and the Champions League from February to November]. There was less of a break for them than usual as they brought forward pre-season training to prepare for their opening Champions League game, against Leopards.

**Group stage
Match 1. 20 July 2013, Orlando Stadium, Johannesburg
Orlando Pirates 0 AC Leopards 0**

Like Djabal Club, AC Leopards were a largely unknown quantity. Having risen through the ranks quickly in their home country, following a cash injection in 2011, the acquisition of many top players and a stunning run in the 2012 Confederations Cup, which they won, they had a reputation for being gutsy and physical but doing research on them was tricky.

De Sá gave himself a week to study video footage and determined they were a side that was easily shaken. "We will have to look for a goal early to unsettle them," he said. "If we allow them to settle, they can cause problems."

Being the first match of the season, the contest was surrounded by hype. Pirates were talked up in local media as being the most talented of the eight sides in the competition and near certain to finish in the top two. Orlando Stadium was kitted out in black and white for the group stage opener, save for a corner set aside for the small group of Congolese fans. Those few away fans ended up with more to cheer than the home crowd which watched its team fire blanks despite controlling significant periods of the match.

Pirates had made a late change to their starting XI. The midfielder Tlou Segolela, who had trained as a first-teamer through pre-season was pulled from the squad because he was yet to sign a new contract. De Sá was informed a few hours before kick-off that Segolela was "not a Pirates player" and that there was a "boardroom issue and they couldn't come to an agreement." De Sá selected Daine Klate in Segolela's place and, at first, it seemed an inspired move. Klate had three chances in the first half, while Myeni was denied only by a goal-line clearance. As the goal failed to arrive, Pirates became increasingly desperate and when Manyisa's late effort was saved, it became clear that the expected emphatic victory was actually going to be a drab stalemate.

De Sá gave his men a pass mark, but only just. "If it was a boxing match I think we would have won it on points but it wasn't, so you have to put the ball in the back of the net," he said. "The guys are a bit rusty but they were still competitive out there and will get better. For our first performance, and at this level, I wasn't entirely unhappy but we have to do better and take our chances."

Before the second group game, Pirates signed the promising striker Kermit Erasmus, finalised Segolela's contract and played their domestic season opener, a friendly, against their arch-rivals Kaizer Chiefs. The fixture is given a twist by the fact that fans select the starting XIs. Pirates lost 1-0.

Match 2. 4 August 2013, El Gouna Stadium, El Gouna
Al Ahly 0 Orlando Pirates 3

With the political situation in Egypt tense, Pirates were uneasy about the prospect of playing in Cairo. "With the political issues, obviously we have concerns," De Sá said. "What we see on television is a worrying factor."

As the game drew closer, the situation worsened. Violence escalated and there were deaths among demonstrators the weekend beforehand. The Egyptian military told Al Ahly they could not host the match at the Air Force Stadium because security could not be guaranteed leading the hosts to seek a postponement. Al Ahly argued that they could not find a stadium with adequate lighting facilities because all the suitable venues were in major cities, where the army had banned matches. And they could not play during the day because it was Ramadan. CAF rejected that request as well as Pirates' call for the match to be moved to a neutral venue.

For a few days, it was unclear where the game would be held but Pirates tried to put that uncertainty of their minds. "We must forget about other things," Lekgwathi said. "We're not sure about the venue but we must focus on what we will do on the field. The senior players will sit down with the youngsters, motivate them and make sure they are not scared."

Pirates were wary both of the crowd and their opponents. They watched Al Ahly's derby against Zamalek the weekend before their tie and realised just how tough the task would be. Three days' before kick-off it became a little easier. The Red Sea resort of El Gouna, more than 400km from Cairo, was chose to host the game, with no fans to be permitted.

De Sá wasn't sure how his players would react to the silence. "An empty stadium could take the pressure off Al Ahly and help them play better," he said. "It could motivate their players or demotivate them. Even us. We are used to playing in front of big crowds. It could feel like a training match. I don't know what it will be like, but I hope it goes our way and it gives us a bit of an edge."

It ended up being so much of an edge that Pirates recorded one of their greatest ever victories. They seemed to surprise even themselves when they took the lead after 12 minutes following a nifty one-two between Thandani

Ntshumayelo and Mbesuma. Meyiwa saved a penalty and, after Ahmed Abdul Zahar had been sent off for a second yellow in first-half stoppage time, they completed a comfortable win as Andile Jali converted a penalty and Myeni added another three minutes later. It was the first time a South African club had beaten Egyptian opposition away in any CAF competition, while Myeni's goal was the 100th Pirates had scored in continental competition.

Pirates promptly lost their first game of the league season, against Amazulu. They eliminated former the title-holders SuperSport United from the MTN8, a knockout competition featuring the top eight teams in the country. De Sá admitted the packed schedule was causing him concern.

Match 3. 17 August 2013, Orlando Stadium, Johannesburg
Pirates 4 Zamalek 1

Zamalek were bottom of the group and seemed to be struggling as Egypt's political crisis went on. "We expect Zamalek to fight like wounded tigers as they are still chasing their first win in this tournament. But we will push them deeper into the mud," Lennox Bacela said before the game. "Now the other clubs will respect Pirates after what we did to Al Ahly."

The striker had netted his maiden goal for Pirates in the win over SuperSport and was brimming with confidence. "I feel good because the pressure of scoring my first goal for Pirates is over," he said. And when it rained, it poured. Bacela scored the first goal of the match, after being set up by Klate but Shikabala equalised within two minutes. After half-time, though, Pirates ran away with it with goals from Tlou Segolela , Myeni and Klate.

For Zamelek, it was a record-breaking defeat in the group stages and reports emerged of infighting within their camp, with some players reluctant to take the field.

Al-Ahly won in Congo to ensure the group was still open. "Yes we have won," De Sá said. "But we haven't won anything. We still might not qualify for the next round despite two massive victories over the Egyptian sides. We still made mistakes and so we still have a lot of areas to work on. We conceded a silly goal after we went 1-0 up and maybe on a different day we wouldn't have been able to bounce back. We can't afford to make such mistakes at this level. We also know that going to their home ground in a couple of weeks' time is going to be difficult."

With another trip to the north of the continent looming, Pirates had to play in yet another Soweto derby, this time for the MTN8 semi-finals. They beat Kaizer Chiefs 1-0, with De Sá joking he had told his team to treat their rivals as "just another Egyptian side". They were given some breathing space with the second leg scheduled for a month later and their league match against Ajax Cape Town postponed as South Africa's administration tried to offer them as much assistance as possible.

Match 4. 1 September 2013, El Gouna Stadium, El Gouna
Zamalek 2 Pirates 1

Pirates went into the game knowing that victory would guarantee them a semi-final spot. The fixture was played behind closed doors in El Gouna, a "home away from home" as De Sá dubbed it. For Zamalek it was a last chance to stay in the competition and Lekgwati perhaps sensed a change of mood saying Pirates were expecting "a totally different team to the one we beat in Johannesburg".

The first game, though, inevitably was at the forefronts of Pirates' minds. "The good thing is that we are going to this match with a broad understanding of the team we will be up against," Lekgwati said. "They are not a closed book to us. I've earmarked this tournament as a benchmark for myself. Having won all trophies in our domestic league, with the prospect of qualifying for the semi-final, has given me motivation to inspire the rest of the guys and continue fighting."

Pirates gave away an early penalty that Ahmed Malek converted. Bacela, continuing his rich streak of form, equalised but Salah Soliman restored their lead in their second half. De Sá was unimpressed. "We shot ourselves in the foot today and we were punished," he said, suggesting the searing heat may have been to blame. His assistant, Teboho Moloi, claimed the team had learnt the value of scrapping. "You don't always have to play the best of games to win," he said. We have to apply that strategy in the remaining games because the clubs we play against tend to park the bus at the back, which frustrates our players."

Match 5. 14 September 2013, Stade Denis Sassou Nguesso, Dolisie
Leopards 1 Pirates 0

Dolisie is only two-thirds the distance from Johannesburg as Cairo but the journey is much more arduous. For a start, there are no direct flights. Until last September, there wasn't even a route between South Africa and Congo but South African Airways has since introduced flights on Wednesdays and Saturdays to the capital Brazzaville, a city 300km away from Dolisie. With Pirates due to play Leopards on a Saturday and in a league fixture scheduled the preceding Wednesday, they had to charter a flight to their destination, planning to fly in a mere 36 hours before kick-off.

The day before the match, De Sá celebrated a year in charge of Pirates. His tenure had not brought the league success that had been expected — after two successive titles, Pirates had finished only third — but his run in the continent was keeping him at the helm. De Sá called the job "a way of life" and felt he had adjusted to the challenges of coaching a giant. "You haven't coached in South Africa until you coached one of the big clubs," he said. "It has been an unbelievable ride and I have enjoyed every minute of it, even the hard times. This is why I do the job, this is why I coach, for these kinds of opportunities.

"The level of passion from fans, which I can tell you also stretches all the way up into Africa — that was one of the biggest surprises for me — is something I maybe didn't expect. The brand is just unbelievable. Obviously there is pressure to win, but that doesn't come from the club's board or from the fans. It is pressure I put on myself."

The weight of that expectation was increased when the group was thrown wide open by the Congolese club's win. Klate and Bacela missed good chances and Dimitri Bissiki scored from a corner to ensure that Leopards moved level with Pirates and Al-Ahly at the top of the group.

De Sá had described the trip to Congo as the toughest in the group because of the difficult conditions. Pirates had no complaints, though, about how they'd been treated and knew their defeat was down to missed chances. They had gone from potentially being able to ensure a semi-final spot at the halfway stage of the group to needing a win in their final fixture. Lekgwati was embarrassment by the turn around but remained optimistic. "We apologise to the South African nation for the defeat, but we still promise them that the second star is coming," he said. "All that we have to do is beat Al Ahly in the last game to qualify for the semi-finals. There is no way we will lose to them. We want to win this tournament. Our aim is to feature for the Club World Cup in Morocco in December. We just have to beat Al Ahly at home."

Moloi was sure Pirates could still go all the way. "The dream of the second star lives on despite the defeat," he said.

Al Ahly beat Zamalek 4-2 to knock the White Knights out of contention. For Pirates, victory over Al Ahly at home would see them top the group and play the runners-up in the opposing group in the semis. That would allow them to avoid Tunisia's Ésperance. If they drew, they would need Zamalek to beat Leopards but if Leopards also drew or won, Pirates would be out. And if they lost, they would definitely be out.

They had one league match before the final group stage game and struggled to a 1-0 win over Polokwane City, a game that hinted fatigue was becoming an issue.

Match 6. 22 September 2013, Orlando Stadium, Johannesburg
Orlando Pirates 0 Al Ahly 0

Since the teams had met in El Gouna, Pirates had beaten Zamalek at home but lost two matches away while Al Ahly had managed wins in all three games. The Egyptians seemed back to their best and ready to secure their place as group winners. The match was billed as the most important one for a South African club in seven years, since Pirates had last qualified for the Champions League semis. But for all the expectation, little happened on the field.

Pirates dominated but could not find a way through the Al Ahly defence. They had two chances in the first half — Myeni shot wide and Klate hit the crossbar — and went into the break to be greeted with the news that Zamalek had come from behind to lead Leopards 2-1 which, if it stayed that way, meant a draw would be enough.

More chances came in the second half but Pirates lacked a finish. Then the news came through from Egypt: Zamalek had won 4-1 and all Pirates had to do was ensure they did not

concede. Bacella and Klate both wasted opportunities that would have guaranteed top spot, but a goalless draw meant both side progressed, Al Ahly to face Coto Sport of Cameroon and Pirates to face Ésperance, who had lost to Al Ahly in the previous season's final. The Al Ahly coach Mohammed Youssef said he thought that his side would meet Pirates again in the final and that there was no opposition they would rather come up against. His words would be remembered.

Semi-final

Champions in their own country four years running, finalists in the Champions League in two of the three previous seasons and winners in 2011, Ésperance were not a club to be taken lightly. In their ranks was the highly rated striker Oussama Darragi while they also had four Tunisia and two Algeria internationals.

Pirates had a much lower profile and, worse, there were murmurings of discontent in the camp. Lekgwathi, the captain, had been left out of the last two matches and went public with his frustration, claiming a personality clash with the management — De Sá excepted — had led him to be sidelined. He was called to a disciplinary hearing but did not attend a scheduled meeting with Khoza, saying his father was ill. He did, however, apologise for the comments.

With the captain a doubt and the team having just been booted out of the MTN8 by Platinum Stars in a penalty shoot-out, Pirates did not go into the first leg with the best morale. "It's a supreme test for Pirates against the most consistent team in Africa and we are looking forward to the challenge," De Sá said. "There is so much at stake for not only the club but for South African soccer as a whole."

First leg. 5 October 2013, Orlando Stadium, Johannesburg
Pirates 0 Ésperance 0

Myeni, who had been nursing an injury, was passed fit. He could have given Pirates the lead with a header, but it flashed across goal. Bacela also missed a decent opportunity and it was Thabo Matlaba who went closest to scoring, his long-range shot saved by Moez Ben Cherifia, the experienced Tunisian keeper.

With their focus on attack, Pirates opened themselves up to being caught unawares and found Ésperance were strong on the counter. "Ésperance were going to get chances because we were trying to press the game. They played on that counter-attack," De Sá said. "But Senzo Meyiwa made a save in the first 10 minutes and after that he didn't really have to again. We were happy with that. I just think at this level the half-chances we get we have to put away."

De Sá stressed the importance of not conceding at home, which he thought would give them an advantage going to Radès, where Ésperance would "open up".

Maher Kanzari, the Ésperance boss, was disappointed his men had not played in a more attacking fashion. "Pirates are a strong side but 0-0 is a bad result to us," he said. "I would have preferred to lose 2-1; at least we could have scored an away goal. Both teams played a tactical

game but now I must prepare for a tough game at home."

A busy program followed for Pirates. They played Mpumalanga Black Aces in the Telkom Knockout, yet another South African club competition, and won 3-1. The defender Siyabonga Sangweni, who was captaining in place of Legkwathi, was stretchered off amid reports he had ruptured his Achilles tendon. The club soon backtracked, saying he would undergo an MRI scan, but confirmed he would not be able to travel to Tunisia.

The statistics favoured Ésperance. They had only been defeated three times in sixty matches at the Stade Olympique de Radès, a run stretching back to 2001. The last time they had lost there was to Al Ahly in the previous season's final. In the 13 games since, they conceded just five goals and kept a clean sheet 10 times. They had scored in each of their 28 previous home Champions League matches. They were not going to roll out a red carpet for Pirates and neither was their travel agent.

Travel to Tunisia is not simple. Pirates had to travel via Dubai. They planned to train in Johannesburg on the Tuesday and Wednesday before the match and then fly to the Emirates on Wednesday afternoon. They would only reach Tunis on the Thursday but scheduled another training session there. That would be followed by one practice at the stadium where the match would be played.

Lekgwathi was not part of the travelling party. The mystery of his exclusion had deepened when he wrote in his column for a local newspaper that "sinister forces at the club" did not want him to succeed. But on the eve of the team's departure, Lekgwathi assumed the usual captain's duties of introducing the members of the squad to dignitaries, including the country's minister of sport, Fikile Mbalula, at their departure function

De Sá tried to play down any talk of a spat, saying Lekgwathi knew why he was left out and had not protested against the decision. "We've got to play those guys we think are ready for the next match," he said. "Lucky has missed four matches and to go and throw him in against Ésperance is a bit unfair. There are no issues around him being left out and I don't think it affects the team morale at all. There are no problems at all because Lucky is a good professional and we have spoken about it"

Second leg. 19 October 2013, Stade Olympique de Radès, Radès
Ésperance 1 Pirates 1

Having faced hostile crowds in Lumbasbashi and Dolisie, Pirates believed they were tough enough to handle whatever awaited them in Radès. "For this match, we really have to be well prepared psychologically, because the home fans won't make it easy for us," De Sá said. "We have had it worse in this tournament and I don't think whatever happens in that match or during our stay in Tunisia will shock the guys."

In the end, it was Pirates who stunned the crowd into silence. After Klate threatened to open the scoring in the fourth minute with a free header, it was Rooi Mahamutsa who put the visitors ahead, heading in from a corner after 52 minutes. Iheb Msakni restored parity three minutes later but Mahamutsa's strike counted for far more. Meyiwa parried a free-kick and was fortunate there was no-one to follow in, but Pirates held on for an away-goals victory.

A delighted De Sá said afterwards that Pirates simply "love" playing North African opposition because they are usually guaranteed good stadiums and pitches. Had the mood not been so light, his comments could easily have been taken as disparaging to the rest of the continent, as he painted the central countries as unconquerable jungles. "The trip to Congo to play Leopards was always going to be the most challenging. We don't like those conditions," he said. "But Ésperance, they a true football side, like Al Ahly and Zamalek."

They would again meet Al Ahly, who had won their semi on penalties, the side they said provided them with the best hospitality and the team who wanted to play them in the final.

History beckoned. The second star shone in the distance. On to Soweto and on to Cairo.

Before the final, Pirates beat Golden Arrows 4-0 in a Telkom Cup match and drew 1-1 in the league against Kaizer Chiefs. They had only played three PSL games since the season started but the

Champions League and the cups meant many were beginning to feel weary.

De Sá promised a few days' rest before the first leg of the final, focusing on video sessions and tactical training. "I can't say whether we'll play well or badly, but the one thing that we know is that we'll try our best," he said. "We're going to give everything we have. These guys will run for 90 minutes plus and give it their best shot. I think we have a 50-50 chance, without a doubt, but when you look at where they've been and what they've done in this competition, we have to be at our best. Al Ahly are a special side but we've got our strengths and we have a couple of things up our sleeves."

Support was pouring in from everywhere, including from members of the Chiefs side. "We just have to walk the streets and we get messages of support," De Sá said. "From the beginning of the competition, we said it was not only about Pirates, but carrying the flag of the nation. This is probably for some of us the closest we're going to come to representing the nation."

For someone like Meyiwa those words had particular significance. Playing second fiddle to Ithumeleng Khune at national level, he saw this as a chance to show what he was capable of. "I told myself that even if I don't get time to play in the national side, it's the one chance for me to make my name in African football," he said. "I want to be one of the best goalkeepers in Africa."

Moloi called it the "the most important game in the history of South African football after Bafana Bafana won the 1996 Afcon finals on home soil," and

said they team would not give "Al Ahly space to breathe." Jele, the new captain, assured all South Africans there was no way his team would lose. "We are playing at home and have no business to defend: our plan is to go for a win with goals," he said. "We want to score goals so that there is no pressure when we go to Egypt the following weekend. We promised the South Africans the second star when we started with the campaign in February, we want to deliver on the promise as early as this weekend."

First leg. 2 November 2013, Orlando Stadium, Johannesburg
Orlando Pirates 1 Al Ahly 1

Rows of cars snaked their way to Orlando Stadium throughout the afternoon. Kick-off was at 2030 but traffic was already backed up by around 1700. The atmosphere was part-celebration, part-anticipation, with the familiar vuvuzelas providing the soundtrack, while a number of Egyptian fans had come dressed as Pharaohs. What was once a competition South Africans regarded with indifference had become an event they were desperate to win.

Their hopes were dented severely in the first quarter of an hour as Mohammed Aboutrika, who had announced he would retire after the final, curled in a free-kick to give Al Ahly the lead. Pirates pushed forward but they were found defensively wanting and Walid Soliman had what would have been a second away goal incorrectly ruled out for offside.

Again and again Pirates created opportunities, but as in so many previous rounds, they struggled to find the final touch. The home crowd grew restless, sensing hope was fading. And then, in injury time, Thabo Matlaba struck from long range. Pirates had had a number of shots from outside the box, but this one caught Sherif Ekramy unaware and snuck into the bottom right corner. The celebrations made it seem as though there would be no second leg.

The equaliser meant Pirates had made their job slightly less difficult in Cairo and shown their fighting spirit. Many had given up after Aboutrika's goal but Pirates kept going. Although the missed chances remained a source of regret, De Sá said he "could not have asked for more" from his men. "We kept on trying, kept our patience, we didn't just play long balls and kick and pray," he said. "We controlled the game. We showed character and kept fighting to the last minute. We're in with a fighting chance. I know it's going to be very difficult - there's no doubt about it. But we'll certainly have a go, and the team I've got certainly have the character to try and turn it around."

He promised Pirates were ready for the final push. "So the way we've got to go to Cairo is to play the way we normally do," he said. "We've done it before. The mountain keeps getting higher and higher. But I really don't know what the limit is of this lot - they keep going. So let's see how far we can go."

Aggregate result: Orlando Pirates 1 Ésperance 1 (Pirates win on away goals)

Al Ahly's Mohammad Youssef was similarly pleased with the result in

Johannesburg. "They pile on pressure up front but leave gaps at the back, which we tried to expose through counter-attacks," he said. "I want to salute my players for doing exactly what they were asked to."

He also warned Pirates that Al Ahly were a far better side than the one they had beaten in the group stage. "The last game was played in our fasting month of Ramadan, and we played at 2.30pm in 45°C heat. And it was not our home ground," he said.

Permission had been granted for the return leg to be played in Cairo, rather than at El Gouna, and Al Ahly had been assured their fans would be allowed into the match. The 30,000-capacity Arab Contractors Stadium was chosen as the venue, but Al Ahly wanted the game moved to the much bigger Cairo International Stadium, where they could fit 70,000. The pitch at the International Stadium was deemed in better condition but the military were still concerned about large gatherings so the teams had to settle for the poorer pitch.

The surface was a concern for Pirates but even more troubling was the absence of Jele and Jali through suspension. That reopened the door for Lekgwathi, who had been out of action for six weeks. De Sá confirmed the Pirates veteran would travel with the team, would be part of the starting XI and, to end things off as they had started, would captain them. Having Lekgwathi back added to the emotion of the event. De Sá maintained he had never had any problems with Lekgwathi and it was clear he was pleased to be able to bring him back.

The sentiment grew. De Sá remembered his father, who died of a heart attack during the coach's playing days, and told the media he would have loved him to be at his side now. "I've learnt to live with him not being here but there are just times when I miss him," he said. "It was his birthday last Saturday, and there I was going into one of my biggest matches as a coach. You can imagine just how great it would have been for us to share those special moments."

South Africa's sports ministry held a departure function for the team on the Wednesday before their flight, wishing them well and instructing them to come home with the cup. The winners of the CAF Champions League take home US$1.5 million, while victory means participation in the Club World Cup which has a participation fee of $500,000. The African champions were drawn against the Asian winners: win that and reach the semi-final and that figure rises to US$2 million.

**Second leg. 2 November 2013, Arab Contractors Stadium, Cairo
Al Ahly 2 Orlando Pirates 0**

Two hours before kick-off, the stadium was overflowing. Journalists had to fight their way through the crowds, terrified they would not make it through the chaos in time for kick-off. Once inside, they found supporters climbing over the walls trying to get in and others sitting anywhere they could find space, including on top of the scoreboard.

As more people streamed through, the media had to be evacuated from

the press box and the South African journalists found themselves seated in the players' dug out. It was the only space for them although they were assured they would be moved to a special area half an hour before kick-off.

When Pirates came on to the field to warm up, they were stunned by the noise. They walked around the ground and then stood in a huddle. Was it fear? Was it solidarity? Were they completely overwhelmed?

Perhaps it was a combination of all three. They kicked off with green lasers providing the lighting as supporters shone them on the opposition players throughout. Their own fans, who numbered three, were given a private section in the main stand, sealed off by the military. The chanting was constant, sometimes low and droning, at other times much louder and more aggressive.

Pirates had a clear chance in the first half as Klate crossed for Segolela, who headed wide. Pirates had shown attacking intent but at the break it was goalless and tensions were running high with players having to be separated.

Al Ahly began the second half more positively and when Abdullah Said's deflected shot fell into Aboutrika's path, the veteran poked home. He ran through the military barricade and towards the fans, allowing them to share in his success. Bacela could have equalised when he rounded the keeper but blasted his shot across the face of goal and, with 12 minutes remaining, Abdel-Zaher finished matters off with a second.

Sherif Abdel Fadil received a straight red card for a foul on Klate with six minutes to go but by then Pirates' race was run. They'd gone toe to toe with the best on the continent since February, and their lungs were at bursting point. When the final whistle blew, Al Ahly's joy bubbled over and they carried the trophy as close to the fans as they could. A few of them hung back to shake hands with their South African counterparts. The two teams had formed friendships and those were worth preserving.

Aggregate result: Al Ahly 3 Orlando Plrates 1

After 10 months, 70,000 kilometres of travel, 91 hours in airplanes and 16 matches across the continent, Pirates had nothing but battle scars to show. The best team had emerged as champions. And the second best? They had learned lessons that will probably last a lifetime. B

Football's Only Part of It

To prosper in the African Champions League you have to play the game off the pitch as well as on it

By Colin Udoh

Here is a brave statement: the African Champions League is the most difficult club competition to win across all continents.

Is that the sound of a snigger? Well, save it until you read the stories of what clubs have to go through to climb that podium.

While it takes a great squad of players to win the African Champions League, just like its European equivalent, there are also a huge number of hurdles, both spiritual and temporal, that teams have to negotiate which have little bearing on the actual football.

While clubs from Europe and elsewhere usually only have to worry about matters on the pitch, and maybe pockets of fan violence and abuse every now and then, their counterparts competing in the African Champions League deal with matters ranging from officially-sanctioned discomfort to some very primordial dark arts.

To start with, here's a story from 1994 involving the South African club Kaizer Chiefs as told by veteran journalist Thomas 'TK' Kwenaite. "I travelled with Kaizer Chiefs for a Champions League game in Burundi," he said. "There was a tribal war going on, so the situation was quite tense when we arrived. About 60,000 people had packed into the stadium and there were quite a lot of soldiers.

"Chiefs raced into a 3-0 lead in the first half and were looking good to run up a big score. Then one of the Chiefs defenders brought down a local guy in the centre-circle. Before we knew what was happening, some of soldiers had run onto the field and were chasing the Chiefs players around the centre-circle. The referee then picked up the ball from the centre line and awarded the home side a penalty.

"Seeing the situation on the ground, the coach issued instructions to [the captain] Lucas Radebe to tell [the goalkeeper] Brian Baloyi to make sure he dived the other way and not to save the penalty. Then he instructed him to tell the rest of the team not to score again if they wanted us all to leave in one piece."

Willy Opara, who played for another South African club, Orlando Pirates, when they won the competition in 1995, has many tales of their adventures, but perhaps none that he tells more often than what they faced in his home country Nigeria when they played BCC Lions.

At half-time, the players were heading into the dressing room when Opara says he called the team back. An official of the club went in first and was hit by an odour so pungent he almost passed out The squad ended up having to do their half-time team talk on the pitch. Pirates won that game and went on to be crowned champions.

Fast forward to 2003, when the Nigerian club Enyimba were in Senegal for a group match against Jeanne d'Arc. One of the team officials had a gallon of crude oil packed in his luggage on the flight from Nigeria. His amused response when he was asked why he was carrying it was, "Wait. When we get there, you'll see."

On match-day, before the team left the hotel, he headed to the stadium to check out the dressing room. What he met inside was what looked like fresh blood sprinkled underneath the seats. He calmly scrubbed off the blood, washed everything with detergent then proceeded to pour the oil all over the dressing room before locking it with a big padlock he had brought from Nigeria.

Only then did he call for the team, while he stood guard in front of the door. Enyimba drew that game 0-0.

Back at the hotel, he explained what he'd done with the oil. "Crude oil neutralises any kind of juju," he said. "It's a natural oil and it comes from what is already dead, so it takes everything down."

Enyimba went on to win the African Champions League that year, but not before a major hiccup in the next fixture. Drawn against Egyptian club Ismaily in the first game of the group phase, Enyimba travelled with high expectations of a good result. In the dressing room, the players were told about the Egyptian club's 'spiritual forces' and warned not to shake hands during the pre-match formalities.

Instead, they were asked to make fists and bump knuckles. The goalkeeper Vincent Enyeama, a deeply religious Christian, was having none of that. He was the only player who shook hands.

Enyimba were absolutely torn apart by a 6-1 score, with Enyeama conceding the first four before he was hauled off for Dele Aiyenugba.

In the inquisition that followed, team officials heaped the blame on Enyeama's refusal to heed the spiritual advice.

A player from Cameroon, who does not want to be named, speaks of how his club would bribe hotel staff to spike food and drinks of visiting teams during their stay to weaken them on match-day. Corroboration comes from Victor Ezeji, a striker who played for two Nigerian clubs, Enyimba and Dolphins, in the Champions League. "We never ate food from the hotels," he said. "What the officials used to do would be to have someone look for a Nigerian living in that country who ran a restaurant, and they would bring us Nigerian food. Our water was usually purchased from stores far from the hotel."

Ezeji then adds two stories of his own. "When I was with Dolphins, we went for a match in Togo against Maranatha. As we approached the dressing-room, we saw that they had sprinkled something that looked like palm oil mixed with some sort of creamy stuff. We avoided the dressing room after that. But going into the pitch for warm up, some fans poured smelly water on us from above. The stink kept us uncomfortable throughout the game. It was hard to go near your teammates because we all smelled so badly. But we won 1-0.

"And then when Enyimba went to play ASEC in Côte d'Ivoire, we met broken eggs in front of our dressing room while there was something like a red rag over the door. We just prayed outside, then went to play. We also won that game 1-0."

As if these dark arts were not enough, administrators regularly conjure up more conventional methods of discomforting opponents. CAF rules make home teams responsible for local transportation and accommodation of the away sides. In reality, visiting clubs who choose to depend on the home team's hospitality have already lost half the battle.

On arrival, teams are sometimes met with rickety buses, complete with make-shift wooden seats, no air-conditioning and the odd roach or resident rodent for good measure. As for the hotel, a point is made to book hotels located well within the city's most cacophonous areas, proximity to the red-light district constituting an additional benefit.

"What we would do, is to send an advance party who would check out the hotel, then go and book a more upscale hotel in consultation with our embassy,"

says Felix Anyansi-Agwu, who has been chairman of Enyimba since 1999. "Our travelling fans and media would then be put in the hotel booked by our hosts."

One area home teams are not responsible for, but which provides a more troubling hurdle is travel times. The Congolese club TP Mazembe were forced to acquire their own aircraft as a result. "You want to play a game in Cameroon, which is one and half hours from Congo and we have to fly first to Europe, then back to Cameroon, a journey of more than 12 hours," lamented the club president Moise Katumbi at the presentation of the second of two aircraft. "Four years ago, we were eliminated from a competition because we couldn't make the trip down due to lack of flights. Now, that will be history. Our team can now travel more easily, more safely and more rapidly."

Not many African clubs can splash out in that manner. But if they want to win, they have to find if not the means, then the strength of character to overcome hurdles that would, in all probability, traumatise a European player for life.

And so we return to our initial premise: the African Champions League is the most difficult club competition to win across all continents.

No snigger this time?

In Memoriam

Al-Ahly's seventh Champions League triumph was about more than football

By James Montague

Rades, Tunisia. November 2012

72. 74. 22. These are the numbers that Al Ahly football club now live and die by. Football is a numbers game, filled with facts and vintage years to be compared and contrasted, to be argued about and fought over. Attendances, assists, clean sheets. Sometimes even goals. But not in Egypt. In Egypt, football has been deprived of almost all of its statistical fuel as well as its petty controversies and concerns. There are no more league matches to discuss. No goals between local rivals to dissect. No attendances to weigh against the previous years. There are just three numbers that exist above everything else. 72. 74. 22.

72. The number of Al Ahly fans killed at a football match in Port Said on 1 February 2012. Al Ahly, Africa's greatest ever club team, travelled from Cairo to Port Said for what should have been a routine league victory. It was a little over a year since the January revolution and Egypt was still a hopeful if anarchic place. Tahrir Square, the epicentre of the revolution, was still occupied by a coalition of activists and protesters. Almost every shade of political opinion was represented there, be they secular or Islamist, united by the single cause of ousting Hosni Mubarak. Then came the hard bit: building the new Egypt.

A military government by then existed with a splendidly Orwellian acronym: the Supreme Council of the Armed Forces. Scaf. But the protests and the arguments continued. Several thousand Al Ahly fans travelled up to Port Said to see their team play Al Masry. It was always a tough place to come. The last game there had seen Al Ahly's fans run out of town. But they returned. They lost 3-1, a rare thing in Egyptian football for a team that has won the league 36 times. When the final whistle blew, thousands of Al Masry fans rushed onto the pitch like an invading army.

"The fans were coming, sprinting. I knew they hated me and all the players. All the players ran," Ahmed Fathi, Ahly's right-back, would later tell me. In video footage, the players can be seen sprinting back to the dressing-room just as the human wave crashes into the Al Ahly stand. At first Fathi was just relived to have escaped. "I didn't know what was happening outside," he said. "But something was happening outside. After this they killed the boys. Not the men, the boys." The lights in the stadium had been turned off, the gates to the Al Ahly stand locked. 72 young men were crushed, beaten and stabbed to death. Fathi only knew how serious things had become when the bodies and walking wounded started arriving in the dressing-room. "One of the fans came to the room and said: 'You have a problem outside. Someone has been killed.' And then another has been killed, and another," he recalled. The Al Ahly players watched as fans were brought in, some dead, some dying. "After this another comes in and he has a wound." Fathi slowly ran a finger from the left side of his temple to his chin, to illustrate the gash on the young man's face.

74. The dead were all members of the Ahlawy, Al Ahly's ultras group. They had become much more than a group of supporters. They had played an important, some say crucial, part in the January revolution. During the Mubarak years there were no political parties, independent unions or opposition groups allowed. But there were the terraces, and it was there, at Cairo International Stadium's Curva Nord, that the Ahlawy became an anti-authoritarian thorn in the regime's side. They would fight the police on a weekly basis. But then members and leaders would be arrested. Their numbers exploded. Songs began to be sung against the regime demanding greater freedoms. Those songs would later become the soundtrack — and their distinctive red flag, an eagle atop a shield, would become the aesthetic — of the revolution.

They say violence is in our blood
How dare we fight for our rights?
Stupid regime
Hear what we say
Freedom!
Freedom!
Freedom!

But it was more than flags and songs. Come the revolution, the ultras from all of Egypt's clubs were 15,000 strong in Tahrir Square, the only group that had any experience fighting the hated police force. Mubarak was toppled. The ultras had helped to win the freedom they had sung for. And then 72 of their members were dead in suspicious circumstances. Who locked the gates? Why were there no police on the pitch? Why were the floodlights cut? Who had a vested interest in punishing the Ahlawy? Immediately, the season was cancelled and Al Masry thrown out of the league. Protests and vigils for the dead followed. Not for the 72, but for the 74. The Ahlawy considered this number the number of mourning. The 72 that died in Port Said and two members who were killed during the revolution. They were the *shahid*, the martyrs. For the Ahlawy the link between the revolution and Port Said was clear. They would use any means necessary to prevent the league from restarting until they secured justice for the 74.

22. Mohamed Aboutrika is celebrating with his teammates on the pitch of the Stade Olympique de Rades in Tunisia. Al Ahly have just won their record seventh African Champions League titl (a year later, they would win an eighth), beating Esperance 2-1, 3-2 on aggregate. The striker Mohamed 'Gedo' Nagy fired them ahead just before half-time before Walid Soliman scored a brilliant breakaway second with half an hour left. But they would not be here if it wasn't for Aboutrika. He is more than simply one of the greatest players Africa has ever produced. He is the team's soul, the club's moral compass and beloved in Africa and the Middle East. He wears 22 on his shirt. But this is perhaps the greatest victory, the sweetest. Or at least, the most

bittersweet, and certainly the hardest fought. Aboutrika, like almost all of the players celebrating on the pitch, had been there in Port Said. He had held a mortally injured supporter on that day. "You know the story?" Bob Bradley, the Egyptian national team's American coach would later recount. "The fan says to Aboutrika: 'Captain, I always wanted to meet you...'." The fan died in Aboutrika's arms.

With the league cancelled, the African Champions League was all that was left for the club. Its players had been deeply traumatised by what they had seen. Several, including Aboutrika, had quit in the immediate aftermath before returning. The players, the club and the fans vowed to win the title to honour the dead. They had survived Port Said, but that wasn't the only setback they had to overcome. Their coach quit. They survived a coup in Mali. Protests had seen two matches come within minutes of being cancelled. They had fought back on the pitch when seemingly dead and buried. All of this while a revolution was taking place in the background and while they played their home games behind closed doors. And now they celebrate. Aboutrika's iconic number 22 cannot be seen any more. The team is wearing T-shirts with the names of the 72 on the front. The players dedicate their victory to the men who died at Port Said. In the stands a few thousand Al Ahly fans have made the trip to Tunisia. Flags with the number 74 are flown.

Alexandria, Egypt. March 2012.

It is a few weeks since the tragedy of Port Said. A march has begun on Port Said Street, behind Alexandria's famous library. Tens of thousands of men and women fill the streets as far as the eye can see. Those with the loudest voices sit on their friends' shoulders to face the crowd and lead them in revolutionary song. They are here to commemorate the death of Mahmoud Ghandour. He was the leader of the Alexandria chapter of the Ultras Ahlawy but died in Port Said. Walking with the thousands of others is Shady Mohamed, Al Ahly's most decorated captain, having won four African Champions Leagues and six league titles. He doesn't play for Al Ahly any more, but that doesn't matter. "I played for Ahly for 11 years and I must fight for these people," he says as the crowd chants around him. "72 people died. This is difficult. More young people, 14 and 16 years old. But I am coming to support all the fans."

There is no such thing as a former Al Ahly player. The bond between player and fan has always been closer at Al Ahly than at any other club of its size in world football. The fans have always expected victory, true. But the players have always expected their support too. There is an affinity between the two that has always existed. Their love is given, and their love is returned. Shady didn't think twice about coming to the march. "Ahly win everything, understand? The problem isn't just now or one month ago. It is for years," he says when asked to explain why he believes the Port Said tragedy took place. "Port Said don't like Ahly. But if the police are strong, good. If they are not strong than they go to the other side and kill the fans. My friend, the Ultras Ahlawy, they have a good mentality. They support the fans every way they can. The police must protect them. This is not football."

It takes three hours for the march to snake through the streets. All the while they are cheered by the watching crowds on the balconies. An old lady holds up a handmade placard denouncing the army. The march eventually stops at the gates of the headquarters for Egypt's army in the north of the country. Troops stare back atop armed APCs. There is a tank and a dozen foot soldiers. All their guns are trained on the crowd. The troops don't move. The gate stayed locked. The protesters kneel down and pray before peacefully dispersing.

Military Academy Stadium. Cairo. May 2012.

Thoughts switched to the African Champions League. Initially it was thought that Al Ahly would pull out of the tournament, given how traumatised their players were. But the Ahlawy urged the players to win it for the martyrs of Port Said. Aboutrika and the club's legendary midfielder Mohamed Barakat agreed to rescind their initial decision to retire. Al Ahly were drawn in the first round against Ethiopia Coffee from Addis Ababa. The first match ended 0-0 but security concerns meant the second leg almost wasn't played. It was only a few hours before kick-off that permission was granted for the match to take place at Cairo's Military Academy Stadium. No fans were allowed in. In deathly quiet Al Ahly won 3-0. Mohamed Aboutrika scored twice. When he scored he fell to his knees and kissed the grass. But arguably Al Ahly's greatest match came next.

Hossam al Badry had always been a faithful servant to Al Ahly. He had risen

through the youth ranks in the 1970s and played for eight years in the first team before injury finally cut his career short. He had played for the club at various levels for 17 years. He returned in a coaching role as assistant to Manuel José, the Portuguese manager who would led Al Ahly through the greatest and most successful period in the club's history. He had briefly taken charge of the team when José had left, but both returned to prepare for the second-round match against Stade Malien. No sooner had the team landed in the Malian capital of Bamako than a coup began. The players were stuck in their hotel for a week after their 1-0 loss as vicious street-to-street fighting played out around them. "We remember when we were waiting for the flight to take us back. Every minute, every hour, waiting for the plane to Mali," El Badry recalled with a shake of the head. "Actually Al Ahly had a very bad time for almost one and a half years. We tried to change the problems to motivations."

It looks as though Al Ahly's Champions League campaign is over. They quickly go 1-0 down in the first half of the second leg, again in the empty Military Stadium in Cairo. They need three goals in the second half to progress. Mohamed Aboutrika is brought on at half-time. This is his time. His first goal, after 54 minutes, is a stunning 30-yard free-kick into the top left-hand corner. His second, in the 82nd minute, is a penalty that he skewers into the bottom left-hand corner. The third, six minutes later, is perhaps the finest. Aboutrika starts the move and feeds the ball out to left. The cross isn't dealt with by the Stade Malien centre-back. Aboutrika is near the penalty spot. He swivels and volleys the ball just inside the left-hand post. He runs in a zig-zag, unable to decide which direction is best to celebrate in before he is engulfed by bodies. They qualify for the group stage 3-2 on aggregate. The Stade Malien tie is enough for Manuel José. He resigns and is replaced by El Badry, largely because, with no league, no one else will take the job. El Badry is now in charge of the team for the group stages. Al Ahly are drawn in a tough group alongside TP Mazembe from DR Congo, Ghana's Berekum Chelsea and their perpetual Cairean rivals Zamalek. They will lose only one game, against TP Mazembe in Lubumbashi, and top the group. But the team were without their 22 for the final group game against Zamalek.

Alexandria. September 2012

It is September now, seven months since the tragedy of Port Said and still the league has not resumed. As the Ahlawy had promised they successfully boycotted the league until a verdict in the Port Said case had been delivered. 73 people had been arrested and were awaiting trial, mainly Al Masry fans but also key security figures. In some cases, the Ahlawy would picket stadiums where matches were about to take place. The Egyptian FA, so tainted by their close association to the Mubarak regime, crumbled in front of the Ahlawy's opposition. As the trials are delayed, so is the league. But in September the FA arranges for the season opener, the Super Cup, to take place anyway in the vast Borg al Arab stadium outside Alexandria. The Ahlawy vow to storm the stadium if the match goes ahead. Mohamed Aboutrika refuses to play. "[I

am] not participating in the game for fears that another massacre will happen in Borg al Arab Stadium in Alexandria," he says in a statement. "For the sake of avoiding bloodshed, the game should not have been played so that the Port Said massacre doesn't happen again." Al Ahly ban Aboutrika for two months for his refusal to play. He will miss the semi-final against Sunshine Stars of Nigeria.

Cairo. November 2012.

It is now an hour and a half before Al Ahly are due to play Sunshine Stars in the second leg of the African Champions League semi-final. The first match, in Ijebu Ode in south-west Nigeria, had ended 3-3. Gedo had scored twice but Al Ahly had twice thrown away a lead. This match in Cairo is again to be played behind closed doors but the Sunshine Stars players are nowhere to be seen. They are trapped in their team hotel. Outside it is inundated by Egyptian protesters. They aren't the usual protesters you would see at Tahrir Square, nor are they the Ahlawy, but a gathering of professional footballers, angry that their livelihood has been taken away from them. They are angry that Al Ahly were still allowed to play in the Champions League, tapping into a resentment that had existed long before the revolution that the club received special treatment. The players had hoped that if they barricaded the Nigerian team in the hotel, the match would be cancelled, Ahly would be kicked out of the competition and their cause would finally be understood. Instead the Ahlawy sprung into action. "We only found out during rush hour that the players were having a march," says Mohamed, a founding member of the Ahlawy when we talk about the protest. "We embarked on a mission to 'free' the Sunshine Stars players. We contacted each other by BBM and SMS and congregated. There were fights with the players. I think one of the players had a gun. They prevented the Sunshine players from going to the game. We had to let the game go on. We cleared the way for the bus."

The Ahlawy led the Nigerian players to the bus and arranged an escort to the stadium. The Nigerian journalist Colin Udoh, who was embedded with the Sunshine Stars, saw the whole thing. "When the players were coming down the fans were applauding them," he recalls. "On the drive to the stadium 2,000 fans were lining the road applauding us. Inside the bus they didn't understand it. They thought they were angry with them ... It is a unique position, to see fans with that much power." The final obstacle to the final had been overcome. Al Ahly beat Sunshine Stars 1-0. "That is how we want to honour the people who died at Port Said," Mohammed explains. "We honour them by winning this trophy."

And honour them they did.

Postscript

Port Said, Egypt. February 2013.

Somebody still cuts and waters the grass at the Port Said Stadium. It is almost exactly a year since the 72 fans of Al Ahly were killed here. It is midday and I can see the fresh green grass through the locked gates. The lines have been painted on the pitch and the sprinklers are pffting. No football has taken place for a year but someone still loves this stadium, still loves this grass. The green pitch feels like the only splash of colour in the city.

The Port Said Stadium had been refurbished for the 2009 Under-20 World Cup, but it resembles any other crumbling 1950s relic found in any other dying town in the Middle East. And Port Said is dying. It sits at the mouth of the vital Suez Canal. But it is isolated and down on its luck. Unemployment was high here even before the revolution and Egypt's subsequent economic collapse. Near the stadium burned out cars and barricades litter the street. The previous night I had arrived in Port Said an hour before an army curfew had come into force. 30 people had been killed in the city after the initial verdict in the Port Said trial had been delivered. 21 Al Masry fans were sentenced to death. The families of the accused and the guilty stormed the prison, killing two policemen. The police fired back. Port Said had burned every night since and more deaths had followed, a cycle of funeral, protests and killing, funeral, protests and killing. The Port Saidis I had spoken to talked of a conspiracy, of how Al Masry was being sacrificed to prevent Cairo from descending in to chaos. That night another protest snaked thorough Port Said's streets, this time in defiance of the curfew. One protester was shot dead.

It is late morning now and the gates of the Port Said stadium are locked. I circle its grey walls looking for a way in, past graffiti from the Al Masry ultras, the Green Eagles, denouncing the verdict.

Another says, "NO TV. GO TO THE STADIUM." Each door is firmly shut with brand new padlocks. But one gate has been carelessly left unlocked. I push it open. It is next to the gate where the crush took place, where the majority of the Ahlawy perished on 1 February 2012. The stairwell where they were crushed looks horrifically tiny. The gates that had eventually sheered away from their concrete pillars still lay discarded on the floor 12 months on. It looked as if it had happened yesterday. I take some pictures but I'm chased out of the stadium by a security guard shouting that I am an Israeli spy.

That weekend the football league finally returns to Egypt. The Ahlawy had successfully prevented the league from restarting three times over the past six months until justice for the 74 had been served. They believed it had. A few months later there were more convictions too, including for the head of security for Port Said. The prosecutors' report alleged some form of collusion: a meeting had taken place before the match between the police and some of the 21 Al Masry fans sentenced to death. But many questions remain unanswered over what happened on that night in Port Said.

Africa's new champions begin their first league match in a year in an empty stadium on the outskirts of Cairo. They win 1-0 but one number is missing. 22. Al Ahly, even with the Champions League success, still have a financial black hole to fill. Gedo, the goalscoring hero from the final, and Ahmed Fathi are sent out on loan to Hull City in the English Championship. Mohamed Aboutrika is loaned out to Bani Yas in the UAE league, where he thrives. He wears the number 72 on his shirt. He will also later announce his retirement. The Egyptian league won't last long. It will finish without a conclusion thanks to further instability. Mohamed Morsi will be deposed in an army-led coup. Hundreds more will die protesting on Egypt's streets.

But, for now, this is still the future. Back in Port Said I run from the stadium for fear of being lynched as an alleged Israeli spy, back to the burned out cars. Hundreds of people are here now, gathered outside a mosque. As in the preceding days, it is the funeral of a young man killed in clashes with the police. The body is carried through the crowd on a stretcher, wrapped tightly in linen, back towards the barricades. Ⓑ

March of the People's Elephant

How Enyimba became only the second team to retain the African Champions League

By Oluwashina Okeleji

In December 2003 Enyimba, with victory over the Egyptian side Ismaily, became the first Nigerian side to win the Champions League. The 'People's Elephant', as they are known, broke a 39-year drought with a 2-1 aggregate win at the end of a game that had featured two major on-field brawls, rioting in the stands and a delay before the post-match presentation ceremony: the tempestuousness seemed entirely appropriate given Nigeria's frustrations in the competition.

Under the coach Kadiri Ikhana, who had begun his playing career with the army and had been part of Nigeria's 1980 Cup of Nations winning squad, Enyimba romped through the preliminary rounds and, despite suffering a 6-1 defeat away to Ismaily in their second group game, beat them 4-2 back in Aba in their final game to edge out Simba SC of Tanzania and qualify for the semi-final.

They trailed in the away leg of the semi-final against USM Alger before the youngster Michael Ochei snatched an equaliser. "I was a strong fighter and very religious," he said in an interview with *MJ* magazine. "I remember that everything I did then turned out perfect. Even the senior players would come to my room after a game and say, 'Boy, how did you do that trick?' I couldn't tell them

because I honestly didn't know. I think God's grace was strongly upon me." A last-minute winner from Ekene Ezenwa in the second leg sealed their progress.

Enyimba won the home leg of the final 2-0 with goals from Emeka Nwanna and Ndidi Anumunu, but in Egypt Hosni Abd Rabbou pulled one back for Ismaily with a 27th-minute penalty. Enyimba dug in and as the game became increasingly frantic, punches and kicks were exchanged on both sides, culminating in two brawls, the second of which led to the game being held up for six minutes before it could be restarted. The violence spread to the stands, with the game ending amid a riot, missiles raining onto the pitch as Enyimba celebrated.

With hardly any away fans having made the trip, home fans attacked anybody who wasn't identifiably one of them, including the police and journalists. One shirtless fan screamed obscenities at the BBC's Farayi Mungazi, a Zimbabwean, assuming he was Nigerian. "An officer in riot gear whisked me away to the safety of the dressing-rooms," he said. "I was to stay there for the next five hours as we waited for the orgy of violence, which had shifted away from the terraces into the streets of Ismailia, to end. When things eventually calmed down, I saw a scene outside the ground that resembled the aftermath of a bomb blast — cars with smashed-out windows and all kinds of debris strewn everywhere."

That wasn't the end of it, though. Ismaily protested that Enyimba had fielded Ahmed 'Yaro Yaro' Garba, noting that he had been registered with Kano Pillars in the Nigerian league that season, playing at least 15 matches, rendering him ineligible. Their evidence included footage of the third-place play-off in the Nigerian Cup between Kano Pillars and Sunshine Stars played on 25 October 2003 in which Garba scored. The Confederation of African Football eventually rejected their appeal on 7 June 2004 after being informed by the Nigerian football federation that the game had taken place in October 2002; it hadn't.

Nonetheless, the success established Enyimba as a major power, giving them a prestige beyond that of the traditional giants of Enugu Rangers, Shooting Stars of Ibadan and Insurance of Benin, and gave a boost to the whole of Nigerian football, offering a template for others to follow.

Formed in November 1976, Enyimba were crowned Nigerian champions three times in a row before that memorable night in Egypt. They were well-conceived, well-financed, visible and consistently progressive and had risen in a decade from obscure provincial outfit to continental champion. The election of Orji Uzor Kalu as governor of Abia State in 1999 proved a turning point for the team. A passionate Enyimba fan, Kalu had risen to a position in which he was able to ensure a whole new level of funding for the team. With better player incentives,

the once intractable problem of the mass exodus of players to foreign leagues came to an end. But Kalu was not content with one Champions League. The ambitious governor wanted more.

No team had ever retained the African Champions League, although TP Mazembe of DR Congo had defended it in its guise as the Champions Cup, lifting the trophy in 1967 and 1968. Ikhana left — in circumstances that have still not been adequately explained — and was replaced, to general surprise, by the comparatively inexperienced Okey Emordi.

Enyimba's progress was far from serene. Although three goals in nine minutes seemed to have given them a convincing lead in their last-32 tie against ASC Diaraf, they conceded twice in the second leg in Senegal and were clinging on by the end. It took a late David Tyankale goal in Angola to see off Petro Atlético and get them into the group stage. They limped through it, losing their penultimate game to Africa Sport and then hanging on at 1-1 in Blantyre against Bakili Bullets when a goal would have eliminated them.

They were behind in both legs against Espérance but drew both 1-1 and won the tie on penalties — having brought on the reserve goalkeeper Dele Aiyenugba to replace Vincent Enyeama specifically for the shoot-out — to set up a final against anther Tunisian side, Étoile du Sahel. Emeka Nwanna gave Enyimba the lead in the away leg, but Étoile came back to win 2-1. The second leg was switched to Abuja because of security concerns. The goalkeeper Enyeama put Enyimba ahead with a penalty just before half-time and Mouri Ogunbiyi made it 3-2 on aggregate eight minutes after the break. But Kais Zouaghi levelled 10 minutes later and the final went to penalties. Again Aiyenugba came on for Enyeama, and again the tactic paid off as he saved Saber Ben Frej's kick to give Enyimba the advantage. In the end it came down to Enyimba's captain Obinna Nwaneri to convert the decisive kick and Enyimba had done what hadn't been done in 36 years.

Fans poured on to the Abuja pitch and ripped up advertising hoardings as officials and players ran to the dressing-rooms. As the unruly celebrations continued and the police struggled to restore order, the presentation of the trophy had to be delayed by an hour.

"It was very easy for Enyimba because of the funding from governor Orji Uzor Kalu," the lawyer and sports businessman Dudu Orumen said. "They recruited very good players who were well motivated with huge incentives. It was unprecedented in the history of Nigerian club football. But more significantly, the club chairman Felix-Anyansi Agwu discovered how to play politics of African football outside the pitch. Match day came with fewer problems because someone could stand up to other clubs on and off the field."

Enyimba's quest for a third straight title ended in the group stage the following year, with a defeat to Al-Ahly in Cairo. The club's chairman, Felix Anyansi-Agwu, insisted Enyimba had been cheated. "There was definitely a conspiracy against us," he said. "All the Arab teams didn't want Enyimba in the next round because they're scared of us. I think the system was manipulated to make sure that we don't get to the next round."

There was never any evidence, though, to back up his claim. Although they reached the semi-finals in 2008 and 2011, Enyimba have failed to reach such heights again. 10 years on, though, there remains great pride in having been the first Nigerian side to lift the title. Ⓑ

The Flight of the Ravens

The rivalry between TP Mazembe and Asante Kotoko dominated African football in the late sixties

By Ian Hawkey

A fairly compelling case can made that international club football in Africa, or at least in black Africa, started in Katanga. The men who organised it may not have been from very likeable institutions, but even bad regimes occasionally come up with good ideas.

This one came into the heads of a pair of civil servants, not long after the Second World War. One was a representative of what was then called the Non-European Affairs Department in Johannesburg, the other a military commandant based in Élisabethville, then the second city of Belgian Congo, who had a special interest in sport. "How about we arrange a series of matches?" suggested the South African, a privileged white employee of a government putting into legislature a ghastly new policy called apartheid. "How about," added the Belgian, "we call it a decider for the International Football Championship of South of the Sahara?" They concluded it was a grand notion and might well be helpful in keeping the oppressed mineworkers from both their regions distracted for a while.

After some difficulties in getting the divided football community of Johannesburg to commit — many would not — a team from the city duly set off north in 1950, players travelling second-class, white administrators in the more comfortable section of the train. The journey had been arduous. The match would be even more so: Katanga 8 Johannesburg 0. So much for the grandiose "Football Championship South of the Sahara". You'll have to come up with something better than that, thought the footballers of Élisabethville.

By the time 14 years had passed, the Confederation of African Football (CAF) had done so. Its Champions Cup would quickly find a rather wider reach than simply the great mining centres of the central and southern regions. The continent had transformed, of course, since the mid-1950s. Belgian Congo had become Zaire, Élisabethville was Lubumbashi, or just 'L'shi' to its cooler citizens. Katanga had been through some secessionist efforts and failures before being corralled into line by Mobutu Sese Seko, a cunning and increasingly authoritarian Zairois head of state. He soon began to appreciate the high quality of footballer produced in Katanga and how far their successes might resound across independent Africa.

Eighteen clubs initially entered the third Champions Cup, in 1967, though there would be five withdrawals before the quarter-final stage. Lubumbashi's Tout-Puissant Englebert, who took the last part of their name from a tyre manufacturer, had actually been quite fortunate to reach the last eight. Though the away-goals rule, had it existed, would have squeezed them past Abeilles of neighbouring Congo-Brazzaville after a 3-3 aggregate score in the first round, they progressed by the drawing of lots. The withdrawal of Al Ittihad then spared them a long trip to Libya for the quarters, so it was really not until the semi-finals, and a 4-3 aggregate win over Saint George of Ethiopia, that Tout-Puissant, 'All Powerful', got to show off what they had.

What they had was the spine of what would become a dominant Zaire national team. In goal, Mawamba Kazadi, celebrated for his suppleness and serenity; in defence, Pierre Katumba, provoker of wild whooping from the crowd for his athletic volleyed clearances; up front, Martin 'Brinch' Tshinabu, a showy but effective dribbler and, above all, the striker Mukendi Kalala, alias 'Bombadier'. By late 1967, this group were embarking on a run that would sweep through all major international trophies available in Africa and in some cases would take them all the way to a World Cup finals.

What Tout-Puissant also acquired during their glory years was an intimidating aura. The club's logo, with the distinctive crocodile, open mouthed as its jaws clench around a football, suggests a little of that. The welcome they granted visitors, from the late 1960s into the early 1970s, gained notoriety. For their big Champions Cup matches, they would relocate to the capital Kinshasa, and the big 20 May Stadium, there to represent not just Katanga but all Zaire and to inflict the full martial entourage on visitors.

Mastering that fervour would become a long-term project for Ghana's Asante Kotoko, whose duel with Tout-Puissant was to define African club football and significantly shape the upper hierarchy of the Africa Cup of Nations over the period. TP Englebert contested two of their four successive finals, 1967 to 1970, against Asante Kotoko, and Zaire followed up the first with victory over Ghana in the final of the 1968 Nations Cup. The rivalry would be stimulating, but very edgy. It could hardly help being so, after the deeply frustrating way in which the first summit meeting was resolved.

Like Lubumbashi, Kumasi, home of Asante Kotoko, is its country's second city. Independence, post-colonialism, had also nourished in the Asante kingdom some ideas of regional autonomy. As with Katanga's separatist urges, they were resisted from the capital. Kwame Nkrumah, first president of sovereign Ghana, had a firm One-Nation philosophy and at one stage specifically looked to rearrange the hierarchies of club football to galvanise it. He encouraged the setting-up of a superclub, Real Republicans, with a view to fostering national unity and eliminating the traditional Hearts of Oak — the main Accra club — versus Asante Kotoko rivalry. Nkrumah would see the Real Republicans project fail to capture supporters' imaginations, though it would not turn him away from the sport. The African Champions Cup, after all, was a competition whose prize was a piece of silverware known as the Kwame Nkrumah trophy, although by the first time a Ghanaian club, Kotoko, were in its final, he had been deposed and would be listening out for the result from his exile in Guinea.

Logically, Asante Kotoko began the 1967 finals as favourites. Ghana had won both preceding Nations Cups, in 1963 and 1965, and the Kotoko players involved with the Black Stars had acquired a level of worldliness. They had been quarter-finalists, knocked out by the eventual winners Stade Abidjan, in the Champions Cup of 1966 and, although they had lost the mercurial winger Baba Yara to Real Republicans, they had plenty more in the way of attacking trickery from Osei Kofi and the young Ibrahim Sunday. Robert Mensah, six foot-and-something tall with his lucky cap on, was on his way to being celebrated as the best goalkeeper in Africa; 'Yashin' Mensah — nicknamed after the great Russian goalkeeper — also had a precise, powerful throw, a useful weapon for Kotoko's quick breaks. Wilberforce Mfum could, reputedly, strike a ball as hard any man on the continent and when he and Ben Acheampong were in the same line-up there would usually be goals. Kotoko had put eight past Stade Abidjan over two legs in the 1967 semi-final to earn their first crack at the Nkrumah trophy.

The first leg, in Kumasi, finished 1-1. For the return, Kinshasa heaved. For a young outsider in the Asante Kotoko party, the atmosphere felt genuinely frightening. "The stadium had been packed with what seemed liked 90,000 or 100,000 people for hours before the start," recalled Carlos Alberto Parreira, later a World Cup winning coach with Brazil, but at that stage working as an assistant coach with Kotoko and with Ghana's Black Stars, on a placement through the Brazilian Ministry of Sport. "Then armoured cars would roll in and circle around the athletics track outside the pitch, with president Mobutu in the central one, waving to the crowd, with the guards pointing guns. It was scary, especially when they seemed to all start shouting 'Mercenary! Mercenary!' at me, who stood out as a foreigner."

Once the second leg was under way, Parreira's respect for the group of Ghanaian players he had been sharing digs with for several months grew by the minute, for their poise, their courage. Kotoko had scored twice, Tout-Puissant once as the match entered its last moments. A Tout-Puissant ball into the Kotoko penalty area then hit a Ghanaian chest, or at least that was how it looked from the visiting bench. "The referee was under huge pressure," Parreira said, "with the soldiers there, from the noise of the crowd. So the referee says 'Handball' and he gives a penalty." Tout-Puissant scored. On away goals, they would have lost; under the rules as they then stood, there was extra-time.

But a problem emerged. What to do once the supplementary 30 minutes had not produced any further score? "At the end of extra-time," Parreira said, "the referee told us the winner would be decided on the toss of a coin. But people were invading the pitch. Things were out of control."

Either unbeknown to the referee, or as result of an *ad hoc* decision from the VIP seats, the Confederation announced there would be a play-off, a replay. They designated a neutral venue, Cameroon, and from here the story descends into farce. Somewhere between Kinshasa, Accra and Kumasi, the message that Asante Kotoko should ready themselves for a third meeting with Tout-Puissant, two days after Christmas, got lost. "No one told us," insists Parreira. So the Zairois club won the Cup by walkover.

If that felt like a rip-off on top of what the Ghanaians already regarded as refereeing robbery in the second leg, they were still obliged to acknowledge that, poor officiating or not, hostile ambience apart, Tout-Puissant were a formidable side. A month after the third Champions Cup had gone the way of the lads from L'shi, Zaire won the Cup of Nations in Ethiopia, deposing Ghana's Black Stars as African champions. Kalala, spearheading a Leopards side that included his club colleagues Kazadi and Katumba, scored the only goal of the final in Addis Ababa. The defeated XI included the Kumasi crew of Ibrahim Sunday, Mfum and Osei Kofi.

By the end of that year, 1968, Tout-Puissant had retained their Champions Cup title, emerging on top after a final that had little of the taut balance of their clash with Kotoko. Togo's Étoile Filante were the opposition this time and they wilted in the Kinshasa kiln, 5-0. Remarkably, the Togolese scored four goals in the Lomé return. TP Englebert still won 6-4 overall.

In 1969, another Ghana-Zaire duel seemed likely in the Champions Cup final. But Kotoko lost their semi-final to Ismaily of Egypt, who then escaped Kinshasa in the first leg of the final with a 2-2 draw. Tout-Puissant, missing the injured Kalala, lost the Cairo leg, 3-1. Their reign as African champions, the only team to retain that prize in the 20th century, had come to an end.

Come the next final, Tout-Puissant's fourth on the trot, the Ghanaian grudge

would at last be settled. Kotoko actually looked a little depleted that season, Mfum and Acheampong having left for careers in the USA. For Zairois footballers, by contrast, that sort of option was becoming harder, because president Mobutu decreed the country's best players should stay in Zaire.

But Kotoko still had Ibrahim Sunday. And they had Mensah between the posts. In Kumasi and Kinshasa over the 180 minutes of the final, the long, pent-up rivalry between the two clubs, between Ghana and Zaire, seemed for periods to distil into a simple face-off between Kalala and Mensah. The Bombardier against Yashin. The more the striker peppered him, the sharper Mensah's reflexes became. As in 1967, the teams drew 1-1 in Ghana. As in 1967, Kotoko would lead 2-1 in Kinshasa. Unlike three years earlier, they held on, Robert Mensah lionised for his efforts.

Tragically, only 10 months later — the 1970 final was actually played in January 1971 — Mensah was dead, the consequence of stab wounds apparently sustained during a fight outside a bar. He was only 32. Several of the tributes, of which there were many, focused on his role in delivering to Ghana, and Asante Kotoko, a first Champions Cup. "He handled a football with same contemptuous ease that Joe Louis treated the gloves," wrote the Ghanaian newspaper *The Daily Graphic*.

An era had ended. Ibrahim Sunday was now being scouted by European clubs — he would move to the Bundesliga with Werder Bremen — and although Asante Kotoko reached two more finals in the three years that followed, they would have to wait until 1983 for their next Champions Cup triumph.

Zairois football's pendulum was swinging, meanwhile, towards the capital, Kinshasa's Vita Club the winners of the continent's major club prize in 1973. Zaire won the Nations Cup a year later, and, as sub-Saharan Africa's first ever representatives at a World Cup, travelled to West Germany that summer. Their squad, including seven Tout-Puissant players, would return with no points from expedition and to a fearful ticking-off from president Mobutu himself. For the goalkeeper, Kazadi, there had been one especially stinging humiliation at the World Cup. Despite an alert performance in Zaire's opening match against Scotland, he found himself substituted after 21 minutes of the second, with the Leopards 3-0 behind against Yugoslavia. The change was tactical, but not fruitful. Zaire ended up losing 9-0.

Zaire declined both as a national team and in terms of its club football. Zaire, indeed, disappeared, the country renamed the Democratic Republic of Congo in 1997. TP Englebert had also reverted to their more traditional title, TP Mazembe. Neither they, nor DR Congo's Leopards, registered very often at the business end of major international competitions through the 1980s or 1990s.

For Tout-Puissant, however, that would change dramatically after the turn of the millennium. Under the chairmanship

of the wealthy governor of Katanga, Moise Katumbi Chapwe, they have become one of the continent's best resourced clubs and in 2010 achieved a significant milestone for African club football's principal tournament. As the representatives of the CAF Champions League in Fifa's Club World Cup, they reached the final, where they lost to Internazionale. No African club had ever contested a Club World Cup final before.

TP Mazembe had retained the African Champions League that year. They are the only club to have twice won the trophy two years on the trot. They intend to their record books and seem to have the means to do so. Mazembe now pay the sort of salaries that, unusually in Africa, allow them to keep good players, even when clubs from European leagues bid for them. They have also made Lubumbashi something of an El Dorado for footballers from elsewhere in Africa, recruiting heavily in Zambia, and, lately, in Ghana.

Asante Kotoko, as it happens, have sold two players — Daniel Nii Adjei and Yaw Frimpong — to TP Mazembe in the last year. The Kumasi club would hesitate to say they now occupy a place so far down the food chain relative from their fierce rivals the late 1960s that they are at risk of becoming a feeder club to a voracious TP Mazembe, but Kotoko would certainly start as second favourites in a tie against the modern Tout-Puissant. The Katanga crocodile has some of the sharpest teeth in Africa, once again.

Unity and Faith

Images of the passion stirred in Nigeria by this season's African Champions League

By Segun Ogunfeytimi

Fans at the entrance of the Enyimba Stadium in Aba

Sunshine Stars fans

Enyimba Fans at the Enyimba Stadium, Aba

Enyimba Fans at the match with Jeanne d'Arc of Senegal

Sunshine Stars fan

Enyimba v Jeanne d'Arc of Senegal

Sunshine Stars fans

Enyimba Fans at the Enyimba Stadium, Aba

Enyimba Fans at the Enyimba Stadium, Aba

Enyimba Fans at the Enyimba Stadium, Aba

SPIEL POSTER SHOP

This selection of posters is a collaboration between SPIEL, Well Made Studio and th
contributing artists to Field. Each print is available in a limited edition of 100 copies
and is printed on high quality fine art paper.

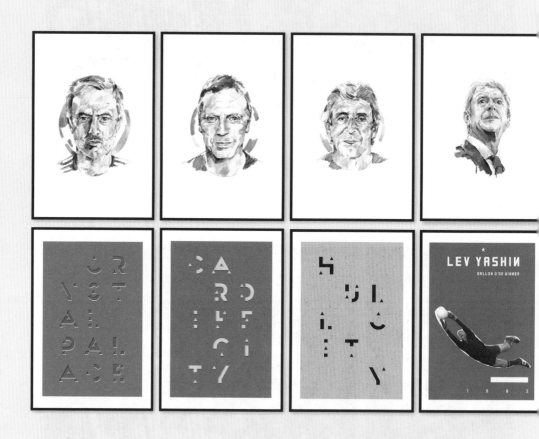

£25+p&p. Prints are available at:
www.spielmagazine.co.uk/shop

www.spielmagazine.co.uk
www.wellmadestudio.com

SPIEL

WELL
MADE

51
Interview

"I don't coach stars, I coach people."

Oscar Washington Tabárez

El Maestro on how he keeps Uruguay living up to the standards of the past

By Martín Mazur

There are two things that Oscar Washington Tabárez doesn't like: controversy and short answers. Once he agrees to an interview, he takes time to think and tries to give detailed, elaborate answers. He is in Montevideo, at the new headquarters of *La Celeste*, which he helped to design and build from scratch. There, members of the Under-15, Under-17 and Under-20 squads share facilities with the senior players. It's nothing revolutionary, but for Uruguay, it is.

For Tabárez, developing the young national teams and reshaping the Uruguayan style of player was more important than the astonishing results he achieved in his second spell as Uruguay manager, including the fourth place in the World Cup in 2010 and victory in the Copa América in Argentina 2011. As he prepares for the 2014 World Cup, his new project is to improve the network of talent scouts in the rest of the country, as most of the clubs are based in Montevideo. Tabárez, now 66, thinks of the present day but is also fixated on the future. Before being appointed by the Uruguayan federation, he'd been unemployed for four years and many people thought he had retired after a long and illustrious career that took in spells at Peñarol, Boca Juniors, AC Milan, Cagliari, Real Oviedo and Vélez Sarsfield,

as well as leading Uruguay at the 1990 World Cup.

His idea was to act not just as an emergency pilot in the turbulence of the qualifiers; he instead asked for a role that took in all aspects of the playing side of the game. An admirer of the youth set-up that José Pekerman had implemented in Argentina from 1995, when he took over he started working on an integrated project based on youth development. While other national managers admit that it can be frustrating, or boring, to wait until they can finally train with the team for three or four days, Tabárez works full-time supervising the work of the youth teams, each of which has its own coach. His presence is papal. He is revered and admired for his humility and polite manners, but also respected for the professionalism he exudes. Tabárez is the man you just can't let down.

⊕ *Is this your best moment since you became a manager? It seems that everybody in Uruguay is happy with you at the helm.*

In the past years I've felt a recognition, something like a positive feedback, that is unprecedented in my country. The only thing that could compare to this is what I experienced with Boca fans after winning the Apertura in 1992, the first domestic title in 11 years. But what I consider more important, from what I hear and from what I sense, is that this recognition is beyond winning a football game. There is an image that this group of footballers that work with us has been showing in these years and that has had repercussions in all the population, the young people, the women, in sectors where football was not that important.

⊕ *Is it different for you to go on the streets? Did you have to learn again what it was like to belong to the people?*

It's probably the only thing that you must adapt to, the affection they show to you. When you go out on the streets, you must be ready to cope with that and understand that perhaps things will take longer than you'd planned before leaving. But it's something really nice that is happening to all of us and therefore it's easy to get used to it. I wouldn't say I'm proud, but there's definitely an inner satisfaction in having done something we believed in, something that we were convinced of.

⊕ *How important was winning, to them, and how important was winning to you?*

Let's be clear: the stories that are told through generations are usually, with a very limited number of exceptions, of those who have won something. The other stories, even if they are told, years later they are played down, making us think that they were not that important after all, because they didn't end by achieving their main objective. Therefore, I don't feel any different, because we've been working for a while in the same

way. And even in times when we didn't win, or when we couldn't achieve a stabilisation in our performances, we kept pushing and insisting on the same concepts and guidelines. That meant that we didn't change in order to win and, more importantly, we didn't change our way of thinking because we were not winning. If you're convinced of something, you must go for it.

⊕ *So you hardly apply the "what if?" in your philosophy.*

Actually, I do. I go through the exercise of thinking what might have happened. And I think that we could have lost a game that we won, or, as happened in the World Cup, we could have won the game we lost. This exercise is important to keep your feet on the ground and at the same time to understand that there are certain things that are not impossible, if certain conditions are in place.

⊕ *You've always been described as down-to-earth: what's the secret to keeping quiet when others would scream in ecstasy or agony?*

You have to be subject to what reality dictates. Looking at it, interpreting it, is fundamental. If we force reality to look like something else, out of an act of vanity, or thinking that our mission goes beyond the circumstances, we'd be making our first big mistake, at least to my way of seeing and analysing the football scenario. And not just for football, but for any other activity, too. The difference is that football is full of unexpected things, so you can't just judge the final result to understand what happened. There are lots of things that don't depend on effort, planning or even performance. They are fortuitous and they can provoke confusion. So the only solution is to stick to reality. A strategist must do this, planning and analysis cannot start from a result: they must start from reality.

◆ *When you mention reality, the first thing you must face is numbers: Uruguay is a nation of fewer than 3.5 million people.*

Exactly. The first thing that had to be done was to understand the real chances of Uruguay in the world football scenario of the present day, which is very different from the time when we enjoyed a domination of football in the first half of the 20th century, when Uruguay was never beaten in Fifa competitions. Half a century unbeaten is not for anyone, but Uruguay was another country and the relation with the rest of the countries was also different. We enjoyed supremacy not only in football but also in the democratic system, in public education, in welfare, in the sense of poverty, because being poor in those days was to eat homemade *puchero* [stew] every day, as opposed to certain ways of being poor today that make me feel embarrassed. So the question we asked was clear: How can we pull this off?

◆ *And what was the answer to that question?*

The analysis was also clear: in a third-world country, a land that exports footballers, we had to determine a team profile. We couldn't just live based on the glory of the past. It was enough for us to look at the best teams of the moment to see how they played and what they did. It's as simple as that. Not just look

at them, but understand them, and after that, define a footballer profile that fits in that style.

◆ *Is that why youngsters are so important in your project? Because they can be moulded into the profile that you want?*

When we took over, several players from the Under-17 team were playing abroad or had just been sold to European clubs. We didn't like it. Footballers cannot grow up alone and we believe it's important not to interrupt the learning process. The U-15, U-17 and U-20 teams are vital in order to maintain the process. The key is to stimulate the feeling of being part of it and also to get them to know the history of our football, of *La Celeste*. It's not a feeling based in an irrational faith, but in knowledge. They have to realise that there is an illustrious history and that they might be part of it, in the future, if they try hard enough and establish themselves.

◆ *Do you motivate your players by using famous quotes or phrases?*

I'm an enemy of the set phrases. Sometimes I dictate to myself some guidelines and then I repeat them, as a sort of memory aid. I believe the most important things are concepts; words can differ. During training sessions, we try to apply the same football concepts in different exercises and ways of working, in order to keep variety and not make it a monotonous routine. In language, we must use the same philosophy: if you start repeating phrases, after some time they might start to lose the real meaning, and instead of having a positive impact you'd be risking creating hollow talk.

I don't like sticking notes on the walls or repeating motivational speeches. I respect those who do it, but I try to avoid being seen as a slave of fixed expressions.

● *Those guidelines you mentioned, can you be more specific?*

Every time we meet before World Cup qualifiers, I sum up the objective of these kind of matches with three concepts: "Performance, result and behaviour". It's a way of summing up the image that we want to give. Performance, referring to the style and the way we want to play. Result, because it implies the work we did to achieve it and is also a guarantee we'll act professionally towards the national team that plays against us and to all the fans that watch us. And behaviour, because it's the way we've chosen and we are convinced of it.

● *Uruguay is known for "la garra" [literally "claw", the supposedly characteristic combination of toughness and streetwiseness], the stamina of the Maracanazo [the victory over Brazil in the Maracanã that won the World Cup in 1950], but in the last decades, it had prompted more red cards and bust- ups than results. How did you change behaviour that seemed to be already established as normal?*

It was important to understand that history is a huge asset but we have to understand it well. It's true that we've made mistakes in the past, when a result didn't arrive and, out of impotence, we reacted. That notoriety, which I believe was also exaggerated, was only good for the opposition, because they tried to make us react. In the last few years, I believe we have changed the

tendency. In South Africa in 2010, we were the team with the fewest cards, even though we were the ones that ran most without the ball and had the best defence, according to the Fifa stats. And all this in an atmosphere of respect, to ourselves, to the rival players, to the referee and the public. Of course, football is a game and there's always the chance of making mistakes.

● *How did you decide to become a football manager?*

During my last years as a footballer, many friends suggested it because I was also a school teacher. I would take it just as a simple remark. But at that time, I also noticed that many young footballers tried to talk to me, to ask me for an opinion or explain some problem. And that also helped me realise that it could be a possibility. But I only decided to take the manager's course when my football days were over, when I had no money and I needed a new source of income. After many years of playing football, I had only managed to buy a modest house. I was married and had become the father of three daughters. But I have to be honest: at the time it never crossed my mind that everything that has happened to me could have happened.

● *When did you realise that you actually had a future as coach?*

As with most things in life, everything happened in a very casual way. I managed to be put in charge of the Bella Vista academy and from there I started doing work that slowly helped me to achieve other levels of expertise. With the help of some good results, I achieved some goals. It's the same story for every single manager who enters in the professional world. Perhaps, those who had an illustrious career as footballers visualise the future more clearly but it wasn't my case. I was never expecting it.

⊕ *How would you describe yourself as a footballer?*

The best way to put it is that I couldn't have played in the present era. I didn't have the physical quality or the profile needed to become a decent player, let alone a high-level player.

⊕ *Your nickname is 'Maestro' [teacher]. Do you consider yourself a football teacher rather than just a simple manager?*

I think I'm still learning. Every day, I learn something, especially when it comes to football. It's not that I sit and give lessons to my footballers. That said, in football I believe that being a coach is also being an educator, because first and foremost you're dealing with a group of people. Watching them face new challenges and by witnessing how some of them are way beyond the expectations you originally had set on them, I think a lot. I think of why such things happen and what special qualities they have in order to produce such an effect. In that thinking process, I learn. Some would say that's becoming more experienced.

⊕ *What is experience to you, if it's not that?*

Experience is not just waiting as time passes, if you ask me. Sometimes you associate experience with age, but there's not an unambiguous relationship between the two. There can be young people who quickly capitalise on lots of events that are happening in their lives

and there can also be old people who do not take a little time to reflect on things that are going on and, no matter their age, will never be experienced. Everything is very relative. But there is always a chance to learn, that's for sure.

⊕ *What's the most important attribute for a coach, do you think?*

One of the gifts I believe I have is to be professional. When someone offers you a contract, they expect you to coach a team and perform well. The path I take is the group philosophy: I share information, instil an atmosphere of respect and try to get the same professionalism from the people who work with me, footballers and assistants. I want that to be a distinctive feature of my squad, not just something else. The rest, football-wise, is watch, read and be informed about what's going on and trying to be more prepared, learn a lot, to be part of the constantly changing picture that football is.

⊕ *Do you follow any particular teams or league to see how football is changing?*

Look, when the moment comes and I must make decisions in order to start a new project, I take into account the great teams. At the moment, other than following the clubs where Uruguayan footballers play, I also follow Barcelona, Real Madrid, Manchester City and United, the national team of Germany, of Holland, among others. I'm always trying to discover some details to enrich myself and sometimes, because it's neither a felony nor anything illicit, use those concepts to the benefit of my own team.

⊕ *Was Guardiola's Barcelona the best team ever?*

The wonderful thing about Barcelona is that the more developed football is, the more difficulties you find. So when you bump into a team that is able to maintain a total domination like they did, I have to admit that it's the best Barcelona version I've ever seen. Nowadays the level of competition is superior to the past ages, when teams weren't that good and supremacies happened more often. There are lots of examples of teams that made history: the Holland of the 70s, the stages of evolution of Barcelona, in which the Dutchmen, with Cruyff, were very influential. It's hard to compare different ages. Every brilliant performance of a team is brilliant in its respective historical context. You can't remove it from its context. Milan's 4-0 win over Steaua in the European Cup final in 1989 was a great display so I've made my players watch the video. Such footage is key to summarising what happened during a certain period. It's not that they arrived and suddenly they said, "OK, let's do this." That was the result of a long planning process that took place with the arrival of [Silvio] Berlusconi, the emergence of [Arrigo] Sacchi and a proposal that was different to what was being done. In that process of change, they dared to enter the books of football history, at least of tactical history. One of the good things about evolution is that today we can see lots of historical games, anyone can do it.

Do you think that tactics definitely took over and that strategy is no longer mentioned in football?

Books can say lots of things, but a manager must have his own concepts, and to me, that's called strategy, or game-strategy. I say that game-strategy is the ideal way of playing, how you really want your team to play. Tactics enter the argument when there is an opposition side, but many times, as a manager, you train without knowing when the tournament starts or who you'd be playing against. At those times, you're working on the game-strategy, which is something ideal, unalterable, that has certain physical, technical, tactical and psychological grounds. The tactical plan before a certain game will always be based on the game strategy you've been preaching for a long time, which is the cornerstone of everything that you later work on on the pitch.

For some managers, opposition sides are not that important. They don't change tactics, which they think is a sign of weakness.

There are teams, take the example of Barcelona, to name just one, that don't change too much no matter the opposition, because they are, or feel, capable of imposing their strategy in every situation. In our case, we act differently. There are many reasons. We are few and we don't have a huge quantity of elite players; and national teams only meet from time to time and there is no permanent training or possibility of emphasising concepts every day, so in the end, I assume that Uruguay must play depending on the opposition. We feel good doing this. Actually, we feel strong in limiting their opportunities in order to create problems for them, as we also acknowledge the top level of some of our attacking players.

How obsessive are you as a manager?

I try not to be obsessive. I respect and sometimes even admire people who are obsessive in their jobs, but I believe more in being demanding then resting, and that I try to inculcate this in my players. As long as they comply with the general obligations we've previously agreed, I like to give them freedom on and off the pitch, because in the end, it's them who must make decisions. When things don't depend exclusively on what you do, being obsessive can become a mistake.

⊕ *Do you treat stars differently?*

I don't coach stars, I coach people. I understand that some of the performances they have and the attention they get in the world media mean that there are footballers more prone to being idolised and being seen on a pedestal of idealisation, but that doesn't change the fact that I coach people, with feelings and common duties and obligations, and that football is a collective game, not an individual one. When I want to see stars, I look at the sky. If you're willing to form a solid group, you have to start by giving the same respect to the one who is famous as the one who isn't. Luckily, in the Uruguay national team we've proven that it's possible. But when those famous players have that group-sense and positive leadership that they show, things get easier.

⊕ *What's your message to the players? How do you convince them?*

How you treat players can have a huge impact. Sometimes we ask them for an extra effort, to play for them, for their teammates and their families, but also for their country and their manager. And even if they'd given all, you still expect something else. Only those who feel

fully committed are able to try to give that extra bit, the tiny bit that at the same time is so difficult to find. But the way to find it is when you point to the person, not to the footballer package.

⊕ *How do you point to the person and leave the footballer aside?*

When you treat him with respect, when you put things in perspective, when you use common sense, when you criticise him for a mistake but always with the positive tone that implies a way of making him become better in the future. I want to go back to the previous question. You asked me about how to treat important, well-known and established players. The proper answer is in the U-15 team. As you don't know which one will be transferred to Europe and which one will end up being a simple football fan; you must bet equally on all of them. And by doing that, you understand that nothing has to change in the future. Sometimes, and I can guarantee this, predictions vanish. At that age, the one who seems to be a 'crack' has nothing guaranteed and some other, the fat boy who was in goal, can end up surprising the entire world. That's what people do. They surprise you.

⊕ *Did you surprise yourself as a manager, then?*

There's nothing written, you know. I don't see fate as something that is already established over your personal effort and making your own way. I don't believe in such things. They might exist, there could be people that believe in them, but to me, it's not real. I, like [the poet] Antonio Machado, believe that you make your way while you walk: "Walker, there is no road, the road is made by walking." Oh, what a great poet he was, summing up, as only the greatest writers do, such a huge concept in a few words.

Who were the people who inspired you as you walked?

Oh, so many. You never develop yourself on your own. Never. You are a product, a product of a long career full of people that influenced you in one way or another. I've had many teachers, managers, teammates, assistant coaches and they were all my teachers, still are. I've never had only one, one defining person that makes you change your way of seeing things. I've learned from all of them, sometimes things that it was not possible to apply in my teams and sometimes very important things. But there's also room for the unknown. The unknown people who surround you, my friends, who would never allow me to say their names publicly, because friendship, when it is true, doesn't need to be brought to the public. Friends walk with you in a private way, as does your family.

What can you say about your family?

Family is fundamental when you become a public person because of your profession. The more important your task in football is, the more it absorbs more and more time and the more it leaves you as a potential target of critics. The ones who really suffer this are your relatives. I consider myself a common person, someone who's been through the stages that most people experience: falling in love, getting married, having children, creating a family, looking for a job, working. I got married in 1969 and I am still with the same person. We've had four girls and two grandchildren, Santiago and Sofia. The problem is that when your daughters or your grandchildren grow, they start to understand what's being said about you. And that can make them suffer. A couple of years ago, Santiago refused to go to the stadium because he couldn't put up with the fact that someone had dared to insult his grandfather. It had happened during the qualifiers. That's why, when you manage good results, you instantly think of them, because they really suffer. They just can't conceive what people say about someone who, for them, is not a public person, but a member of the family.

What's next for you?

Keep walking, trying to avoid things that can be negative and trying to favour those other things that can be positive, but always starting from reality, because if we have built this project, it was based on reality. But it's not good enough just to have it, we have to be aware, update it, modify it. We're working on it. **B**

WORKSOFARTICLES

THE BLIZZARD
GOALS ARE OVERRATED...
THE BEAUTY IS IN THE STRUGGLE

BLZZRD03
COMPARING APPLE WITH ORANJE
SIMON KUPER AND DAVID WINNER

BLZZRD08
THE BICYCLE THIEF
LARS SIVERTSEN

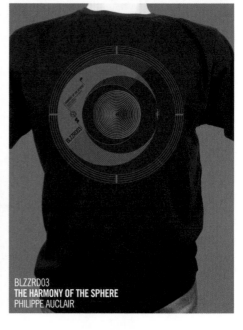

BLZZRD03
THE HARMONY OF THE SPHERE
PHILIPPE AUCLAIR

THE BLIZZARD BY GOALSOUL
A PARTNERSHIP BORN OF FOOTBALL

The Blizzard by goalsoul partnership is a commitment to style and substance in equal measure. Our stunning and original story-inspired, graphic tees look and feel great. Lovingly hand screen-printed on 100% combed-cotton and shrink-resistant fabric — you can be sure of the highest possible quality, durability and wearability.

Exclusively available online from www.theblizzard.co.uk, www.goalsoul.net and instore at goalsoul's flagship store in Sheffield. Only £25 each, plus shipping.

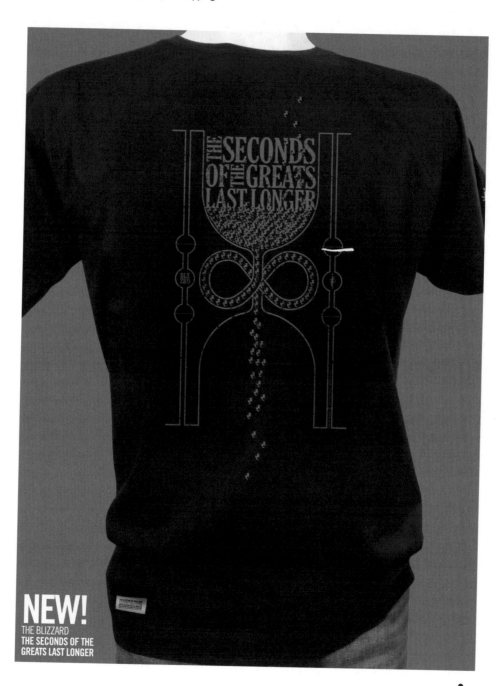

62

Theory

"A colleague is selling platitudes on
television in a manner as if the Bundesliga
coaches were a bunch of dimwits."

Roy's Swedish Revolution

How Roy Hodgson transformed the face of the Swedish game

By Gunnar Persson

Roy Hodgson — young, unknown and unproven — got his first experience of front-line coaching in November 1975 when he was appointed by the Swedish no-hopers Halmstads Bollklubb. A year later he could light a cigar and enjoy the sweet smell of success as Halmstad had won their first ever league championship. Hodgson was still only 29. He stayed on at Halmstad for five seasons, winning the league again in 1979. That period caused an ideological civil war within Swedish football, the repercussions of which are still felt today.

The story begins two years before Hodgson's arrival. Åtvidabergs FF, a club residing in the smallest of towns, had broken the dominance of mighty Malmö FF and won the league in 1972 and 1973. They had achieved this by using sheer talent, combined with stamina and self-confidence, playing in a style not dissimilar to Ajax. With a solid defence and strikers like Ralf Edström and Roland Sandberg they were able to unsettle (almost) any opponent. Their players could run as well as think and made a habit of enjoying the game as well as winning. For a short period they were the dashing cavaliers of Swedish football.

They even made international headlines, until then a rarity for Swedish clubs.

The first bomb went off in 1971, when they eliminated the reigning champions Chelsea from the Cup-Winners' Cup. But just two years later they were already on the wane. The club depended heavily on the local (and international) company Facit for support. Facit, manufacturers of mechanical calculators, had made good business in the 1950s and 1960s, often selling more goods than they were able to produce. But their business collapsed when the Japanese company Sharp developed the electronic pocket calculator.

The club had no choice but to sell its biggest stars to survive. Hanging on to them for a long time was never an option, as Allsvenskan was (at best) part-time, but for Åtvidaberg it became a matter of urgency to raise cash. Edström (PSV Eindhoven) and Sandberg (Kaiserslautern) both left in the summer of 1973. Still, the remaining players were good enough to keep the team ahead for the remainder of the year and secure yet another championship. But it was a triumph won under dark skies. Some of the players had already lost their jobs and were looking for new clubs. The club barely held together, but the team was definitely breaking up.

But there was to be one last hurrah before the goodbye, an episode still cherished. In contrast to their sponsors, the club usually had a sound approach against international opposition. The European Cup of 1973-74 was no exception, not even after being drawn against Bayern Munich in the first round. The odds were so overwhelmingly against the Swedes that the pressure was all on the Germans. Åtvidaberg enjoyed the situation immensely — and put up a hell of a fight.

Just before kick off in the Olympiastadion in Munich, Jan Olsson, the little weasel at right-back, asked for a direct long ball towards the corner flag. He got it and made a dash. But the libero Franz Beckenbauer saw the ball coming, rushed to the flank and toed it out of touch. Good start. Three minutes later Gerd Müller, surrounded by three defenders, scored. But no more goals fell for over an hour. Åtvidaberg defended heroically. Midway through the second half something odd happened. The midfielder Reine Almqvist broke into the penalty area from the right. His teammates expected the usual attempted thunderbolt, but then — as he drew close to Beckenbauer —perhaps recalled what Almqvist had said in the bus heading for the stadium. "I had a dream last night," he had said "about me nutmegging the Kaiser." And then he did, before shooting. Bernd Dürnberger chased the ball into the net and was credited with an own goal. Shame. The Bavarians then got their act together and won 3–1.

As the scene shifted from the Olympiastadion to picturesque Kopparvallen the Swedes grew in confidence. They had coped reasonably well in Munich and wondered if maybe they would be able to surprise Bayern at home. They did. After 15 minutes Åtvidaberg led 2-0; Conny Torstensson had hit the first, via the crossbar, after a one-two with the veteran Veine Wallinder, who added the second heading a cross from the right. The aggregate score was 3–3, with an away goal giving Åtvidaberg the edge. Bayern Munich, ousted by Ajax in the quarter-finals the previous March, were once again heading for the exit. Again, nothing happened for almost an hour. Not before Torstensson came running from behind. Served by the right-winger Benno Magnusson he added a third with a crisp left-footed shot that went just inside the post. But one minute later Uli Hoeness scored the goal that took the game into a scoreless extra time. The outcome was decided on penalties. The central defender Kent Karlsson and the substitute Leif Franzén missed and Bayern won the shoot-out 5–3. Weeks later they came back for Torstensson, who starred in the final against Atlético Madrid next spring, while Magnusson joined Sandberg at Kaiserslautern. By then it was all over. The cavaliers were not so dashing anymore and the tune of Swedish football was about to change. Åtvidaberg was a poor club, but they had earned the love and admiration of the people. They still thrive on it.

Meanwhile Eric Persson, about to step down as the chairman of Malmö FF after serving on the board since 1929, was making plans. Malmö were the big guns at the time. The Spanish coach Antonio Durán had led them to four league wins in eight seasons between 1964 and 1971, the last two on the trot, before leaving. They replaced him with the inexperienced Kalle Hult, who tried to modify the tactical approach along West German lines, but that had only led to failure — 6th in 1972, 4th in 1973 — creating the power vacuum Åtvidaberg took advantage of.

Persson, born in 1898, had always been a visionary. Whether on the board of the Swedish football federation (SvFF), acting as national team selector or just doing his job for Malmö FF, he untiringly tried to expand and make others aware of new possibilities. Since the early 1940s the youth department at MFF had been the best in the country (and it still is, by the way), every year lining up one or two youngsters ready for the first team. He had also seen many of his youngsters develop into players of international calibre. He never denied any of them the chance to leave amateur football in Sweden to secure their future with a professional contract abroad.

Persson was acting on three fronts late in 1973. His plan was to replace his omnipotent self with three people — a chairman, an administrative boss and a team manager/coach, who in turn would become the first in the history of the club responsible for selecting the team. Persson found the chairman, a well-known banker and the office boss. But when it came to football matters he turned to Börje Lantz, an agent-cum-impresario, who knew lots of people. This little round man had a reputation for succeeding in doing impossible things. At one time during the Cold War era he held the commercial rights for Moscow airport. Finding a new coach for Malmö FF was, perhaps, an easier task.

Lantz turned to Allen Wade in England, who at the time knew all about young

coaches on the way up. Wade, technical director of the FA between 1963 and 1983, was educating them. His general approach to the game had been presented in the book *The FA Guide to Training and Coaching*, published in 1967 and clearly taking a step further the achievements of Alf Ramsey and his wingless wonders the year before. Could Wade recommend someone? He could, and the name was Bob Houghton.

Houghton had realised early on that he would never become a top-notch player. His active career had many stops: Stevenage Town, the reserve teams of Fulham and Brighton, a lengthy spell in the Southern League with Tonbridge, Crawley Town, Hastings United and as player-manager at Maidstone United. He also had worked as youth coach at Ipswich Town as well as enjoying summer football in South Africa with Berea Park and Arcadia Shepherds. He had all the coaching badges. Lantz made a thorough check and got recommendations from people like Bobby Robson and Gordon Jago, the latter about to offer Houghton the coaching job at QPR. Lantz located Houghton in South Africa and promised to pay the ticket back to England, provided he stopped by at Malmö.

Persson, aged 75, was the first to take to Houghton, aged 26. Others, notably the board members and coaches at the club, were horrified. The snag was his age, younger than the leading players at the club, and that suede coat. Houghton took a look at the set up. He also watched the team play. Afterwards he gave a full and impressive analysis about what could be done. Then he headed for London. A few weeks later the deal was done. He took charge immediately, giving each player a stern look as he shook their hand and greeted them by their full name. That flattered the players. When he went on to say that all training should be done on the football field they almost kissed him. Love at first sight, as they all had come to loathe thecustomary wintry running sessions in nearby Pildammsparken.

Malmö had lost their way when they changed from the strict disciplinarian Durán (No alcohol at any time! No sex before games!) to the more happy-go-lucky Kalle Hult. Durán had given the players an admirable stamina and then trusted them to solve the more practical problems by themselves. That was the general approach at the time in Sweden, with all teams more or less doing it the same way. Tactics as such had not been invented, apart from occasionally providing "overcoats" for feared opponents. The outcome of games depended on individual strengths, such as 'is our right-winger capable of going past their left-back?' Most Swedish teams were also uncomfortable in the air. The goalkeeper Ronnie Hellström knew next to nothing about cutting out crosses before he left Hammarby for Kaiserslautern. Swedish football was played mostly on the ground, along the same unreflective lines that had governed the outlook for decades. Åtvidaberg were clearly 'old school', even if they had picked up on what teams like Ajax were up to.

Houghton used pre-season in 1974 to teach his players new ways. He taught them how a team could grow and collectively add up to a sum greater than its parts. There were a lot of do's

and don'ts, such as "don't mark your opponent, cover your space instead." Zonal marking was hitherto unknown. They should also help each other while defending — "press and support" — instead of fighting individually. The stopper Krister Kristensson, the oldest in the team, was back to his favourite assignment. Physically impressive, and a former wrestler, Kristensson loved to 'eat' opposing strikers. Kalle Hult had tried to convert him into a Beckenbauer-esque sweeper, behind a man-marking line of four. Kristensson appreciated that as much as wearing a skirt. Now, at 32, he was looking forward to his best and most purposeful years as a player.

Kristensson, like all other team members, received specific orders. Every move suddenly had meaning. The line-up was a strict 4–4–2, with the offside trap a significant part of the defence. Even the attacks had their distinctive patterns. Either a long ball aimed at the striker Thomas Sjöberg (who mostly played with his back to the goal) or a search for set pieces. The right-back Roland Andersson and the right-sided midfielder Staffan Tapper both hit specially conceived crosses with a banana-curve by which the ball seemed to be headed for the goalkeeper, but turned away at the last second. One or two Malmö players would patiently be waiting at the far side of the penalty area, and with the keeper out of position it was usually a fairly easy job to score. The attackers were also told to start defending as soon as they had lost the ball. They started chasing opposing defenders, who were used to starting play in a calm way. These wolf-packs would later prove especially irritating for Italian teams. This whole package was alien to the old school.

What angered experts the most was the offside trap, with its endless interruptions to the game.

"At first you got irritated by that trap," said Thomas Nordahl, a striker with Örebro SK. "And then you gradually learned how to deal with it. I dropped back and instead fed a speedy winger with passes aimed behind the back four. The problem was that the Malmö defenders always looked for offsides and had an arm in the air for most of the time. That got to referees and linesmen, who were pressed to stop play and it was especially difficult at the Malmö Stadion."

A debate arose. Everyone outside the province of Skåne was against Houghton's approach, while Malmö FF (and their supporters among the scribes) were ready to duel after every verbal attack. Eventually it boiled down to, "If this is so simplified and so boring, then come and beat us." Right. Malmö won the league in both 1974 and 1975 (Houghton had promised the first win and took the second in his stride). Houghton also introduced new tactics in dealing with journalists. He systematically praised the players who needed it most, the ones who had failed during the game. It took a while, but after a few months the journalists saw through this. Some even started to mock Houghton for it. Dear Bob wanted to win, all the time and at all costs, and there was an air of extreme tension around him. He couldn't deal with that kind of opposition and once, after a game, he picked out one particular reporter: "It's not your writing I dislike, it's YOU!"

"Two league wins in two seasons. This guy must be on to something." Stig

Nilsson, chairman of the hopeless on-the-edge survivors Halmstads Bollklubb, couldn't ignore the success of Malmö. His own club had never won anything. Coming second behind Djurgården in 1955 was still the closest they had come to a trophy, and the 20 years that had passed since had sometimes been an awful ordeal, with numerous coaching changes and a drop down to the third tier.

Nilsson was a man of contradictions. One of his favourite sayings, and one he often returned to in football matters, was, "Oh, these Malmö people. They cannot be trusted." That went for anybody, from the ball boys at the Malmö Stadion to the occasional referee or linesman. Nilsson knew what he was talking about, having been born and raised in the city. While growing up on the fringes of the circles around future film director Bo Widerberg and the one and only Anita Ekberg he was himself raised and nurtured through the Malmö FF youth system. Eric Persson gave him three outings on the wing when Malmö won the league in 1950-51. Later Nilsson moved to Halmstad, where he played 11 first division games in 1959, scoring six goals.

After establishing himself locally in the oil business, he came back to football as a board member at HBK, "the ball club", and after the umpteenth crisis in the late sixties he took on greater responsibilities. Nilsson had a strong will and developed into a mini version of Eric Persson, an omnipotent leader of men who preferred action to getting stuck in endless discussions.

Halmstad had made a short visit to Allsvenskan in 1972 and after relegation bounced back immediately, finishing 11th and 12th in the 14-team league in 1974 and 1975. Towards the end of 1975, the coach Sven-Agne Larsson (who had won the league with Åtvidaberg in 1972) was on his way out. "I have nothing more to give this lot," he said. Nilsson looked for a replacement. Not being shy he simply called Bob Houghton and said, "We need a coach. Do you have any suggestions?"

"Yes, I do," Houghton said. "His name is Roy Hodgson, an old friend of mine. We both grew up in Croydon, in south London, and we took our coaching badges at the same time. We also played and worked together, at Maidstone as well as in South Africa." Nilsson thanked him and went to work. At the same time Houghton thought, "Beautiful, now I don't have to fight this war alone."

After establishing contact with Hodgson it was agreed they should meet in Bristol. Halmstad were going there post-season to play Bristol City, a reward for the amateur players who had secured survival in Allsvenskan for one more year. The team didn't impress Hodgson, losing 4-0. But he still jumped at the chance to coach a first team, in a top league with the opportunity to play in European competitions (even if that seemed a long shot at the time). At that point Hodgson's career had taken him from Crystal Palace youths and reserves to Tonbridge, Gravesend & Northfleet, Maidstone United and Ashford Town via Berea Park to Carshalton Athletic. Instead of continuing to bounce between clubs in the Southern League, he was given the chance to start a whole new chapter.

Stig Nilsson had a team in need of rescue. He would soon understand that he had found a saviour. And Roy Hodgson

nowadays, accordingly, describes this first year with Halmstad as his "water into wine experience". Roy tried to learn Swedish from the start, and by the end of that first season he had mastered the language well enough to be able to celebrate his success in the same tongue as his players. Just like Bob, he also found a rapport with his players. The veterans liked him most, the ones who had been around and knew how miserable things could be. Every training session brought something new and the squad accepted the whole package of innovations. Soon Halmstad were acting like a carbon copy of Malmö. And it worked. But Roy downplayed their chances, even after beating Hannover 96 4-0 in a pre-season bout: "Well, you know these Germans," he said, "they always stop fighting after conceding a goal."

Early on he talked to Bob on the phone almost daily. But these conversations dried up when both understood what was happening. Halmstad topped the table for the first time after six rounds. It soon turned out it would be a three-horse race, with Malmö, Halmstad and Öster side-by-side. In the end the gold medals were secured in the 25th and penultimate round, when Halmstad won in Norrköping and Malmö drew 1-1 in Örebro, with Nordahl scoring for the home team.

Houghton and Hodgson had obviously studied the same material, the book by Allen Wade, and shared the same basic beliefs about the game. But where Houghton was (and still is) a 4–4–2-devotee, using his own map in all situations, Hodgson was always more balanced, more open to new ideas and more willing to develop his insights into the possibilities of the game.

The squad at Halmstad was very different to the one Houghton had at Malmö, where the players were used to being on top. They were also used to playing international opponents (Houghton actually preferred this in friendlies, so as not to give away too much to domestic teams) and most of their players were either regulars or candidates to play for Sweden.

Hodgson had none of this at Halmstad. His first task was to rebuild the defence. The solid keeper Lennart Ljung was still there but three of the four defenders who had made a mess of things in Bristol had left soon after. His solution was simply to use what was left from the previous year. Claes Carlsson, until then a fringe player without any claim to a specific position, was converted to right-back. The right-sided midfielder Jan Ryding covered the left flank. The left-back Bertil Andersson shared duties in the centre with the physically impressive stopper Alf Peterson, who was back after a year spoilt by injury. These four employed the offside trap, just like Malmö.

The attacking game of Halmstad was very different to what Malmö could offer. There were basic similarities, but at the same time a vast difference in character. The veteran Hans Selander, who had been ready to quit after the disappointing 1975 season, was re-ignited as anchor man in midfield. Selander had been a revelation as an overlapping right-back for Helsingborg in the 1960s. Since then he had been a striker for Sirius while he studied at Uppsala to become a farmer. Now he would soon gain a few more caps in his newly found position in midfield.

On Selander's right Hodgson used the only new addition to the side, Lennart 'Lie' Larsson — his nickname means 'scythe' in Swedish. That was a bit confusing, as the tall and elegant Larsson was an offensively very capable player, able to go past his man as well as shoot or deliver the odd decisive pass. Larsson would make the World Cup squad in 1978, as well as the Bundesliga with Schalke 04. On the left Bengt-Göran 'Divan' Svensson blocked the path for anyone trying to get past him. Again, the nickname — the Diva — was somewhat at odds with a player who did almost anything for the good of his team.

In front of these three Hodgson put the former striker Lars-Erik 'Svängsta' Larsson (named after his birthplace), as a somewhat withdrawn No. 10. Up front, the tall and lanky striker Rutger Backe, top scorer of the league with 21 goals, possessed an admirable work rate as well as positional sense and poise in the box. But the key figure in the attack was the winger Sigge Johansson. Not a regular in 1975 but still there when the two other regular wingers abandoned ship after that season, he had the advantage of being able to play on both flanks. Johansson got a few chances for Sweden, but was generally considered too slow and lacking in aggression. Still, he teamed up perfectly with Backe and was also very adept at taking corners and free-kicks. Apart from these 11 players, Ingvar Flink, a former international defender, held a key role as substitute and handyman. The four other players totalled 15 appearances between them.

This was clearly a motley crew, the unlikeliest of champions. And winning the league created problems for

Hodgson. His training sessions became less efficient in 1977, when a few of the players were called up to play for Sweden, and in both 1977 and 1978 the team failed to win a single league game away from home. Consequently they fell back to eighth place in both years. Then, in 1979, Halmstad secured a gem in the midfielder Stefan Larsson. At the same time a few of the youngsters recruited earlier had grown into first-team players. Halmstad were ready for more success and that year they won the league, a point ahead of IFK Gothenburg.

At the same time, Malmö and Bob Houghton reached the European Cup final, facing Nottingham Forest. But the team was depleted by injuries and the only thing that really worked for them in that game was the by now mechanical offside trap, which caught Forest 21 times. Keir Radnedge's report in *World Soccer* ran under the headline "Is the European Cup finished?"

A year later Houghton left Malmö for Ethnikos. But as soon as the job as manager of Bristol City became available, he deserted the Greeks after only four league games and immediately called Hodgson to join him as assistant.

By then the tune of Swedish football had been changed forever. The domestic debate would continue as Roy and Bob discovered the world. The Swedish national team manager from 1980 to 1985, Lars Arnesson, declared war on 4-4-2 and even persuaded the board of the SvFF to issue a declaration on "how football should be played" (ie the West German way). They gave up the fight in 1983, when IFK Gothenburg under Sven-Göran Eriksson achieved international success with a new concoction of 4–4–2. Eriksson didn't rely as much on the offside trap as Houghton and Hodgson and had more individually gifted players. Arnesson used the formation for the first time against Holland in 1983 (3–0, away), and after that there was no way back for Swedish football. The copycat coaches soon took over, at all levels, and excluded any other view, creating ideological rifts within the domestic game. As Tomislav Ivić was quoted as saying in *The Blizzard* Issue 10, "It's much easier to learn how to defend than how to attack. It also takes less time." The result is a kind of football that seems institutionalised, stale in its limitations and forever unable to solve its real problem — what to do with the empty space in front of the twin stoppers.

Meanwhile Houghton and Hodgson have gone places. The ever adaptable Hodgson got the England job. Houghton, forever true to his principles, reached the end of the line in India.

And Åtvidaberg returned to Allsvenskan in 2010, after an absence of almost 30 years.

The Waiting Game

The strange world of the back-up goalkeeper, in which nothing is something

By Andi Thomas

Sometimes, football is a game of heroes. The striker who scores the title-winning goal, or the defender who clears the ball off the line. The maverick manager who revolutionises the way people think about the game, or, modern football being a modern thing, the suit-strutting visionary who finds a novel approach to maximising revenue and leveraging the brand across disparate and multiple territories, going forward. These are the men (and rarely women, modern football being not all that modern) with the big stories. The important stories. Doubtless there are fine articles on such people throughout the rest of this magazine.

But life, and football, isn't all about such obvious heroes. Somebody has to carry the water. Somebody else has to be on hand if the water-carrier does his ligaments. Utility players, second-choice full-backs: football has a wide and varied supporting cast. And somebody has to take perhaps the least glamorous role of them all and be the one player that nobody wants to see entering the field. Someone has to be the Back-Up Goalkeeper.

Brendan Rodgers once compared managing a football team to building a plane, mid-flight. If that's the case — and when did Brendan Rodgers ever say anything silly? — then the Back-Up Keeper is the parachute. You don't really want to find yourself in a position to have to use one, but when you do, well, you sure as hell need to have one to hand.

Indeed, the very first substitution in the Football League, on 21 August 1965, followed an injury to Mick Rose of Charlton Athletic. In those days the bench was a chair, so on came midfielder Keith Peacock. Back into nets went the centre-half John Howie, who actually had experience of keeping for Charlton: a run of four games in April 1962, back before emergency loans, when clubs had to improvise their way through any injury crisis. He'd managed not to lose any of those games, but wasn't so lucky on this occasion. Bolton Wanderers won 4-2.

An outfield player going in goal is always entertaining — Roy Race once scored a hat-trick and saved a penalty in the same cup final, the big show-off — but can ultimately make the game feel a bit silly. This so concerned football's administrators that when the bench was expanded to three players, in 1994, the rules mandated that one substitute had to be a nominated goalkeeping replacement and couldn't come on for any other player. This was relaxed the following season, and just as well, otherwise the nation would never have been given the chance to see Stuart Pearce bring Nicky Weaver off the bench and fling David James up front for Manchester City, in the optimistic hope that his hair might distract somebody. It didn't work.

But for all that they're a fixture, the life of the Back-Up is a strange and under-scrutinised one. They don't get much in the way of media attention and when they do, it tends to run along the lines of "Well, Lev's in great form, but I just have to keep working at my own game and hope I can impress the manager in training. Friends? No, I wouldn't say friends. We have a professional relationship. Of course I hope to be picked for the final." By way of illustration, a quick search for "Mike Pollitt interview" — 52 games for Wigan Athletic since 2005 — turns up a quite interesting but not ever-so relevant chat with a Mr Michael Pollitt, Operations Director to the Sky Trust, the man responsible for Britain's last flying Vulcan bomber. The highlight of his 2009 was getting through the season safely, so at least they have that in common.

Such a life can yield great rewards. If the currency of footballing success is silverware, then Back-Ups get the best exchange rates. Raimond van der Gouw picked up two Premier League titles, an FA Cup and a Champions League from the Manchester United bench, while former Liverpool sub-custodian Pegguy Arphexad achieved a 100% record in cup finals — six from six — without ever needing to remove his bib. Perhaps even more impressive is the achievement of Sevilla's Spanish goalkeeper Andres Palop, who has one major international tournament winner's medal, from Euro 2008, despite not having any international caps. (The internet also informs us that a post-

retirement Arphexad has established himself as one of Guadeloupe's premier character actors, with particular praise being reserved for this performance as the folk hero Inspektor Gummy, though perhaps the lesson here is that if there's one thing that a liminal relationship with high-profile sport can guarantee, it's Wikipedia vandalism.)

There is also the opportunity, implicit in the very role, for moments of heroism. Plenty of Back-Ups find themselves thrust into action just after a red card and just before a penalty, and there's always the possibility that the right call will see the commentator shouting "and *what* an introduction to the game!" The reluctant saviour, thrown into action by capricious circumstance, rescuing his despondent colleagues: this is the stuff montages are made of.

But heroics like this run somewhat counter to the nature of the true Back-Up Keeper, whose existence is less about seizing the chance for glory and more about an apparent devotion to not playing any football at all. Like all true enigmas, the Back-Up Goalkeeper is beset on all sides by misconceptions, by slander and calumny. Perhaps the most pernicious is the suggestion that shouldering such a burden is evidence of laziness. Of cowardice. Of insufficient devotion to the glory of the self, of the team and of the game itself.

Ross Turnbull is a convenient example. In 2009 he left Middlesbrough on a free transfer for a role alongside Petr Cech and Henrique Hilario at Chelsea. Although he said all the right things on making the move—"I see it as a fight between all three of us"; "The opportunities are here for me"; "Yes, I love celery" — he must have known that dislodging one of the best goalkeepers in the world (not Hilario) was an unlikely proposition. So unlikely, indeed, that he was widely perceived to have prioritised picking up a wage over pursuing a career. And maybe he was: 19 appearances over four seasons later, he's moved on to Doncaster. Still, the nature of the derision bears attention.

It would be indelicate to dwell on the likely response of even the most staunchly Stakhanovite contributor to the non-footballing economy were they to be offered, as Turnbull allegedly was, the chance to earn more for doing less. But *laziness* isn't quite right. True, the Back-Up Keeper spends most matches sitting and watching rather than diving and pointing, but this presumably doesn't extend to the training pitch. Cowardice isn't quite right either: in the place of the regular pressure to perform is the more diffuse but arguably more terrifying prospect of having to come on, at a moment's notice, with the certain knowledge that your teammates, your manager and your fans are all thinking, "Oh, no."

After all, preparation is crucial: think of David James's disastrous substitute appearance for England against Denmark in 2005. Introduced at half-time with the game goalless, James later admitted that he'd skimped on his usual pre-game ritual because he'd known he wouldn't start, which perhaps goes some way to explaining why he charged from his box at the first opportunity and made a considerable mess of things. Always visualise your catches, kids. Always make sure your shoelaces aren't tied together.

Perhaps some footballers are lazy cowards, but the true Back-Up knows that he can afford to be neither. England lost 4-1.

Such a well-read audience as yourselves will doubtless have noticed that it is almost compulsory for any serious piece of writing about goalkeepers to mention Peter Handke's novel *The Goalkeeper's Fear of the Penalty*, later adapted into a film by Wim Wenders. Back-Ups too have had their moment of arty glory. *Perseverare Humanum Est*, a one-hander by the Italian playwright Matteo Belli, addresses such fundamental questions as the complaints of the mothers of Noah and Moses and "the eternal battle between an electric shaver and a hair". But it also spends time dwelling on Massimo Piloni, formerly of Juventus, and understudy to the great Dino Zoff.

Piloni's career — he took advantage of an injury to play and excel in the semi-finals of the 1971 Fairs Cup; he injured his wrist in the first leg of the final against Leeds; Zoff arrived — is taken to symbolise an entire generation of Italians that were born in the mid-sixties and grew up through the economic and social tribulations of the seventies. His Piloni, according to *La Repubblica*, is, "No longer a footballer but a metaphor, perhaps a victim, but more likely a hero of the resistance, trusting, blindly, that tomorrow will be better. It is almost never is."

This is the Back-Up as frustrated dreamer, as an optimistic victim, crushed by implacable externalities yet foolishly and romantically refusing to give up hope. But where the children of sixties Italy were the victims of economic circumstances beyond their control and where Piloni, in those pre-Bosman and pre-player power days, had to grow a large beard in order to escape to Pescara, the Back-Ups of today have more control over their own destinies. As such, they are perhaps less sympathetic figures, but may also be more intriguing. Where the lack of football is borne with an enigmatic silence, there is a constantly unanswered question. If the actual game is both the purpose and the reward of all that training, all that ambition, all that being the best that you can be, then what does it mean to know that you almost certainly won't be enjoying it? Why are you staying, if you're not playing?

Stuart Taylor, who has successfully avoided football matches for the majority of his top-flight career, once told the *Manchester Evening News*, "The moment you switch off is the moment you come unstuck. I could come in and do nothing in training, just take it easy. But then you will gradually start to slip away and you can bet that would be the weekend something happens, and you have to be ready. That is the way you end up making yourself look stupid."

There's a curious implication hidden in that statement, in that belief that fate will take any opportunity to grease one's gloves. If Taylor knows that shirking will end with him making a fool of himself, then by training hard he's not just insuring against the possibility of trying to come on, he's actively working against the likelihood.

For if fate has no reason to look your way, then nor does your manager.

Here, perhaps, is the key to the oddity of the true and dedicated Back-Up. A player that removes himself from the possibility of regular first-team football runs entirely counter to the traditional conceptions of what it is to be a footballer and why anybody would bother. It feels like a peculiar bargain, from the outside, as though they've chosen a quasi-tantric existence of constant almostness and persistent notquiteness. Perpetual readiness; self-denial on a scale that would make Sting reassess the virtues of a quick knee-trembler behind the bins.

It's quite an unsettling idea, the thought that somebody with the requisite talent might not actually want to do what perhaps half the world spends half their lives dreaming they could. That just isn't how things are meant to work. It is strange enough that anybody could think that football — the central 90-minute kerfuffle — isn't necessarily something worth doing in itself, as often as possible. It is beyond comprehension that an actual footballer could … and yet, there they are, game after game, sitting and watching as an entire stadium prays they don't have to stand up.

Happy to play if called upon, happy not to otherwise. If goalkeepers are different, then Back-Ups are entirely other. Theirs is a more reluctant life. The niggling thought occurs that it might also be an eminently more sensible one. **Ⓑ**

Why is the World Cup Boring?

How the nature of international football leads inevitably to sluggish football

By Jonathan Wilson

At the moment, we exist in a realm of perfect possibility. We see the 32 teams that will be at the World Cup and we imagine how it could be if every team is somewhere near its peak and the best players are fit. We imagine Neymar dazzling for Brazil, Lionel Messi thriving in a system built for him with Argentina, Spain wrestling with the weariness of success, Germany with their phalanx of gifted young attacking midfielders. We think of Côte d'Ivoire's ageing golden generation at last doing it on the world stage, of Emmanuel Emenike lifting Nigeria to the heights they reached in the nineties, of Chile's high press and Bosnia-Herzegovina's flair, of the emergence at last of Japan and of Mexico taunting everybody by prospering despite a laughable qualification campaign. We think of Cristiano Ronaldo and Luis Suárez, of Mario Balotelli and Falcão, and think how good it could all be. And at the back of our minds there exists the lurking certainty that it'll all be a huge let-down, that this will be a tournament that drags, as it was in 2002, as it was in 2006, as it was in 2010.

That international football is no longer the pinnacle of the game has been obvious for years. You watch the Champions League and — however much you may regret the financial structures that have led us to this point — see the best football that has ever been played, players of great physical attributes and technical skills, playing at extraordinary pace in sophisticated systems.

Moreover, the football is generally attacking football. It's not an entirely perfect measure, but this season, there were 2.94 goals per game in the Champions League last season. In the best leagues across Europe, goals per game nudge towards 3: 2.93 in the Bundesliga last season, 2.87 in la Liga, 2.80 in the Premier League, 2.63 in Serie A. At the last World Cup there were 2.27 goals per game and in 2006 there were 2.30. I'd be the last person to claim that a game needs goals to be of interest, but where there's half a goal less per game being scored in the premier national competition to the premier club competitions, something is clearly amiss.

Some would argue that the structure of the World Cup is to blame, that playing just three group games makes sides cautious, that there is a perception that a draw will do. But if that were the case, why doesn't that apply to such an extent in the Euros? At Euro 2012, there were 2.45 goals per game, at Euro 2008, 2.48.

The problem, rather, surely lies in the number of sides at a World Cup. At the Euros, there are only 16 teams, of whom probably two thirds believe they have a decent chance of winning (the example of Greece in 2004, in fact, probably convinces every side that they have a chance). The World Cup, by contrast, has roughly the same number of potential winners but twice as many entrants. For many sides, the main objective is simply to avoid humiliation. There is a form of heroism in a draw against Brazil or Germany. The result is the majority of teams at a World Cup are primarily defensive.

That compounds an existing problem in international football, one that has been growing in significance since the game became tactically systematised in the sixties. Once the likes of Viktor Maslov, Gipo Viani, Nereo Rocco, Helenio Herrera, Osvaldo Zubeldía and Alf Ramsey had shown that the coalitions between players were at least as important as the players themselves, football lost its innocence. It developed a second-order complexity so that at the highest level it was played always with a knowledge of how it should be played. That's why the 1970 World Cup stands as a romantic ideal; the heat and altitude of Mexico made a game based on pressing and hard-running impossible and so it stands as the last tournament of the individual.

"The level of detail that goes into games still, to this day, amazes me," the Secret Footballer wrote in his column in the *Guardian*. "Every player has his own script, what to do, when to do it, information on the player he's up against... We memorise every single set piece, where we have to stand, run and end up. We even memorise this for the other players so we know where everyone else will be at any given time. You know that pass when you say to yourself: 'How did he spot that?' Often he didn't need to; he knew the player would be there because, the night before in the hotel, he read about the runs he would be making. It's exactly the same pass after which sometimes you might find yourself saying: 'Who was that to?' The receiving player either forgot to be there or was taken out of the game by a tactical manoeuvre by his opposite number. Football at this level is very chess-like, maybe not to those outside of football but certainly to those inside."

In the club game, in which players train together every day for 40 weeks a year and play perhaps 50 matches a season, it's possible to generate a highly detailed level of mutual understanding. At international level, in which coaches have players for perhaps a week at a time six times a year, it's impossible.

Most coaches, given the limited time frame, choose to focus on the defence. Present a solid unit and hope to nick something at the other end. And, as Tomislav Ivić noted, outlining a truth so profound that the line is quoted elsewhere in this section. "It's much easier to learn how to defend than how to attack. It also takes less time." Pack men behind the ball, get the structure right, and it's difficult for an opponent to break you down. At club level, well-oiled attacking structures can get beyond that; at national level it's much harder. A player receiving the ball at club level will already have an idea where his teammates are likely to be; the playing of a pass becomes semi-automated. At national level, it takes an extra fraction of a second to size up the situation, which makes attacking moves slightly slower and thus easier to defend against. That is also why it helps a national team if a lot of its players play for the same one or two clubs, as is the case with Spain and Germany.

So at a World Cup, what we get is a series of teams intent on defending playing against opponents who, even if they are minded to attack, lack the slickness of a top club side. The result is stodgy football. The 1998 World Cup didn't feel that special at the time — it was no better than 1994 and no match for 1982 or 1986 — but it stands now as a beacon, as the last good World Cup. Perhaps the institution of the World Cup is too great to disappear, at least in the short term, but sooner or later the poverty of the product is going to become an issue.

Brazil, for all the issues of infrastructure and the near-certainty of demonstrations, still has a cachet as a cradle of the game, but will fans still flock to Russia and Qatar for drab football? Perhaps that doesn't matter unduly when television rights are sold years ahead, but eventually if the football is poor people will stop watching. For all the talk of the distasteful politics around Fifa and the World Cup, it may be that the greatest threat to international football comes from the game itself. Ⓑ

Learning to Press

The tactical revolution that led to the transformation of the German game

By Uli Hesse

The rise of German football began on television, shortly before Christmas 1998. Late in the evening, a young, curly-haired presenter welcomed a few million viewers to the latest edition of a popular German sports show. His name was Michael Steinbrecher. He had once been a fairly talented footballer and had been schooled for almost seven years in Borussia Dortmund's youth system. Later he played in the third division until he came to the realisation that a career as a journalist was more promising than trying to break into the professional game.

On this cool but not chilly Saturday night, Steinbrecher stood in front of a tactics board when he introduced his main guest on the show, a 40-year-old man dressed in a dark suit and wearing the type of rimless glasses John Lennon made popular. After the polite applause from the studio audience had died down, Steinbrecher said, "For years, we've been talking about flat back fours and zonal marking. One has the feeling there is almost something like awe when this system is discussed. There are still very many people watching this show who say, 'I don't really understand what this is all about.'" Steinbrecher then gestured towards the tactics board and asked his guest, "Could you briefly explain it to us?"

The man with the Lennon glasses hesitated for a moment, glancing over to the side as if he was wondering where to start. Then he said that the flat back four was merely a means to an end for his own team, which was trying to play "extreme pressing". He spoke with a Swabian accent, but it was not as thick as Jürgen Klinsmann's, so you could easily follow him. Even when he warmed to his subject and rapidly moved the magnets on the tactics board around, animatedly speaking about new positions such as holding midfielder — "our vacuum cleaner", he joked — and explaining how the entire team moved as a unit into the general direction of the ball.

It was a critical moment in German football history, but of course nobody knew it at the time. Only in retrospect does this December evening symbolise an atmosphere of change that was about to engulf the whole culture of the game and would eventually lead to a new German football. Back in late 1998, all that the man with the rimless glasses got for his effort was ridicule and criticism. On the very next day, Germany's recently appointed national coach Erich Ribbeck was asked about the biggest disappointment during his first 100 days on the job. "I'm disappointed by this exaggerated debate about tactical systems," the 61 year old replied with astonishing venom. "For instance when, as happened on Saturday, a colleague is selling platitudes on television in a manner as if the Bundesliga coaches were a bunch of dimwits."

Many other members of the football establishment — and large parts of the press — were equally critical of the tactics-board demonstration. After all, "the colleague" had never been a well-known professional and had never played higher than the third division. And when he made his television appearance, he wasn't even coaching a Bundesliga team, just a small, unfashionable club in the second division. Add to this the dark suit and the glasses and it comes as no surprise that the tabloids made fun of him by spreading the sarcastic nickname "The Professor".

And there was another reason why nobody suspected that this late-night sports show had been a pivotal event: "The Professor" seemed to represent renewal where it wasn't needed. After all, German football was in robust health and as successful as always. Granted, the national team had disappointed at the World Cup in France during the summer. But it was still the reigning champion of Europe, while German club sides — Borussia Dortmund and Schalke, respectively — had won the Champions League and the Uefa Cup the year before. And while the man who resembled a short-haired version of John Lennon was explaining the flat back four, Bayern Munich were on their way to reaching the 1999 Champions League final. Led by a sweeper called Lothar Matthäus who was closing in on his 38th birthday.

Most people thought everything was fine. There was no reason to listen to

the man in the suit whom the national coach simply referred to as "a colleague". Almost as if he didn't know that his name was Ralf Rangnick.

"Sometimes you have to be cruel to be kind," says Frank Wormuth. He is in his early 50s, but looks much younger, perhaps because he often flashes you a boyish smile. In late 1998, when Rangnick was laughed at for explaining modern football on television, Wormuth was Joachim Löw's assistant coach at Fenerbahce. Today, 15 years later, he coaches Germany's Under-20 side and, more importantly, instructs coaches at the German Football Federation's (DFB) sports academy in Cologne. It means that if you want to acquire the top-level coaching badge, the one you need to coach a professional team in Germany, you have to sit and listen to this man talk about football.

Which is an enjoyable experience, as Frank Wormuth is smart, eloquent and very likeable. Even when he says things such as that you have to be cruel to be kind. It's one of the (many) answers he gives when asked to explain the dramatic rise of German football over recent years. "What happened was that — to a certain degree — the German clubs were forced to do things they didn't really want to do," he says. "In the late 90s, the DFB realised that there had to be major changes to how talent was found and schooled. They said, we're going to invest a lot of money, but we can only achieve our goal if we work together with the clubs."

This is, in a nutshell, the story that has been making the rounds outside of

Germany during the last few years, ever since people have noticed that German football has undergone a major transformation: from overaged, lumbering and dour sides to teams that play fluent, technically accomplished attacking football. Or simply: from sides nobody fancied to an all-German Champions League final this year and a national team that is second favourite to win the World Cup next year.

But all the countries and football associations that are currently looking at Germany, trying to learn more about the model and perhaps copy it, should be warned. Because the story is not quite as simple as that. Even if you have the money, even if you are as rich as the Germans and can afford to pump roughly €70 million into the youth set-up every single year, as the DFB and the 36 professional clubs have done over the last 10 years, it doesn't mean that a Mesut Özil and a Champions League-winning team will inevitably come out at the other end. In fact, a knowledgable man you will soon meet claims that the DFB's role in the revolution of German football has been exaggerated. And even Wormuth, who works for the DFB, says that the massive "Extended Talent Promotion Programme" (which was launched in 2002 but had, as we shall see, a predecessor) was not the most important reason for the German football revolution. "The decisive factor," Wormuth says, "was social change."

Wow. That sounds as if a simple article in a football magazine about Germany's rise to the top could turn into an academic master's thesis. Wormuth chuckles. "Well, it's indeed a subject you could talk about all day long, there are so many aspects

to it," he says. "But by and large, you can explain the boom pretty well if you have a close look at what happened to Borussia Dortmund over the last fifteen years or so."

Only it's not easy these days even to get to Borussia Dortmund. The club's sprawling, state-of-the-art training area is situated some seven miles north-east of Borussia's famous ground, in a somewhat remote part of the city. The nearest station is more than a mile away, so you're better off taking the bus or travelling by car. And if you do that, you'll meet the lions.

A pair of stone lions — one male, one female, both slightly larger than real lions — are perched in the middle of a roundabout a few hundred yards from the entrance to Dortmund's training complex. They are a strange sight, because Borussia don't have any lions in their crest and the club's mascot is a harmless, innocent bumble bee. There is no sign that explains the presence of the lions, so you have to ask the middle-aged steward with the Borussia baseball cap who guards the entrance. "Oh, these are the British lions," he says. "They are here to remind people that this whole area was once used by the British Forces. It was called Napier Barracks and the two lions stood by the Officers' Mess." If he's in a talkative mood, the man will then tell you about the days before this training complex was built, the days when Dortmund's first team was among the best in Europe and yet had to train on a small pitch close to the stadium that was frozen in the winter, water-logged in the spring, hard as stone in the summer and slippery in autumn. Then he will shake his head. "This has all changed beyond recognition," he says. "It's crazy, really. We were in the Champions League final, then we were broke, and now, in May, we were in the Champions League final again. It's crazy." The steward points towards the two stone lions. "Whenever I see them, I have to think of all that's changed."

The area he is guarding measures 185,000m². There are six regulation pitches and two smaller ones dotted around the complex. There is one low, simple but elegant building reserved entirely for the first team and another one for the club's other sides, from the reserves to the various youth teams, because everybody trains here — from the Under-9s to the Champions League finalists. Behind this second structure is a smaller, cube-like building. It contains a futuristic training device known as the Footbonaut. It was built a year ago and cost roughly €1m. Imagine standing in a giant cage made up of 72 different panels. Now imagine being surrounded by eight ball machines. What happens next is that one of these machines shoots a ball at you that you have to control and then place against one of those many panels. The problem, of course, is that you don't know which machine will shoot the ball and it's only at the last moment that a coloured light tells you where to put the ball. The Footbonaut is supposed to hone ball skills and improve reaction time. It seems to be used mainly by the junior teams, because when I happen to run into Ilkay Gündogan, the German-born son of Turkish parents who orchestrates Borussia Dortmund's play from deep midfield, and ask him about the Footbonaut, he says he's never been inside.

To the Footbonaut's left, there are diggers and cement-mixers. They are here because Borussia are currently constructing yet another building. It's a boarding house for youth-team players who don't live at home, usually because they come from far-away places. At the moment, 10 of them live in a small villa in central Dortmund and travel to the training complex every afternoon, when school is over. As soon as this building is completed, these young talents won't have to be shuttled from one place to another anymore but can spend most of their time here.

It's all very impressive. But the reason Frank Wormuth has sent us to this place is not that the whole complex is so professional and sleek and modern. It's that Borussia Dortmund didn't want it.

You may find it hard to believe that Borussia — the club which now effectively personifies high-speed football and the new German youth movement — once had very little interest in improving their training facilities and talent development. But back in the late nineties and the early part of the last decade, this was a different club. Back then, Borussia had an excellent, star-studded team and earned lots of money, but most of it was spent on astronomical players' wages and huge transfer sums. That's why Borussia weren't exactly enthusiastic when the DFB and the German Football League (DFL) suddenly imposed obligations on the clubs that would not come cheap.

The first one was that all Bundesliga teams had to have a training complex with at least three grass pitches, two of which had to have floodlights. (It has a touch of the absurd, but at the time, Borussia Dortmund — the 1997 Champions League winners and soon-to-be Uefa Cup finalists — were training on a pitch that was smaller than the regulation size. In fact, it was so small that then-coach Matthias Sammer had to admit his team couldn't properly practise corners.) Then, in 2002, the DFB and DFL went a step further and also demanded that every professional club in the country had to run a youth academy, or Centre of Excellence, to nurture talent. This new rule was very thorough. It even specified how many players eligible for a German national youth team had to be in the squads, how many coaches and physios the club had to employ, how the clubs had to interact with local schools and so on and on.

Yet more than three years later, in 2005, Borussia Dortmund were the only Bundesliga club which still had neither the training complex nor the youth academy. At first the club had been merely unwilling to spend money on these things and came up with numerous excuses for the delay — for instance unexploded aircraft bombs from the war that had been detected under the former Napier Barracks and now had to be defused and removed before building could begin. Later, the club was simply unable to spend money on these things. All the expensive transfers and wages had put Borussia deeply in debt. In March 2005, the club barely avoided bankruptcy. Then, six months later, Dortmund at long last began construction on the training complex. One reason was that the club's new management was hoping it would one day pay dividends. The bigger reason, though, was that there was an ultimatum.

And right here is a German peculiarity that immensely boosted the boom but will be difficult to duplicate elsewhere. "The great advantage of the German system," said Wormuth, "is that the DFB has a large network and wields a certain amount of power, for instance through the licensing process." In Germany, every professional club has to apply for a licence ahead of a new season. This procedure has become famous outside of Germany during recent years, because it's considered to be the reason why German clubs are financially healthy. While Dortmund's near-bankruptcy in 2005 indicates that this aspect of the process is overrated, the custom does give the DFB and the DFL considerable power, because it's not only about finances. Basically, the DFB can withhold or revoke a club's licence — and thus bar it from playing professional football — if it doesn't meet a list of requirements. Around the turn of the millennium, having a training complex and running a youth academy was made part of those licensing requirements and that is why the clubs had no choice and why even Dortmund were finally forced to play by the rules. "Sometimes you have to be cruel to be kind," as Wormuth says.

Then he adds, "In England, the FA has no influence over the clubs. And that is why they will always have problems with their youth development." Another man who knows a thing or two about this complex subject couldn't agree more. "They do everything wrong in England," says Edwin Boekamp. "They have all that money — from their television deals, their big sponsors, their owners — and just buy players. Even in youth football! They do spend money on nurturing talent, but not on their own talent. They sign a lot of youngsters from European clubs instead of developing their own English talents. They will never make progress if they don't break up the old structures, the way we have done."

Edwin Boekamp is 54 years old. He was made Borussia Dortmund's youth-football coordinator a few months ago, but he has already spent more than two decades at this club in various capacities, often in the youth set-up. He is still very proud of the fact that Borussia's Under-19 team won a record five national championships in a row between 1994 and 1998, partly under his tutelage.

"Back when we won those titles with the juniors," he says, "we trained at various city-owned grounds all across Dortmund, often on a cinder pitch. Sometimes the shower stalls were infested with mould. And in the winter, the city would close the pitches and we, the coaches, had to improvise. We'd do running exercises or even rent a pitch in an indoor arena!" He shakes his head and lets out a short laugh, as if he can't believe it was just 15 years ago. "It was a totally different era," Boekamp says. "Now everything has become really professional."

As you sit there, listening to this jovial man dressed in a simple checked shirt and blue jeans, you can't help but think back to the steward who guards the entrance to the training complex and his assertion that everything "has changed beyond recognition". Didn't he tell almost the same story — players having to train on a shoddy pitch under unprofessional conditions — about the first team? A strange picture of German football in the nineties begins to emerge here. Could it be that the country everyone always thought of as efficient, organised, thorough and methodical was actually more like a hopelessly amateurish footballing backwater until the DFB woke up and felt that drastic measures were needed to turn things around?

"I think too much is made of the DFB's role in all this," Boekamp slowly says. "Sure, it's true that everything happened a bit faster because the DFB was pushing things and introduced this law. But I'm convinced most of it would have happened anyway, that the clubs would have sooner or later built centres of excellence and all the rest. For the very simple reason that they could no longer afford the transfer sums. It was just a question of time until the clubs had to become a lot more professional on every level, right down to the scouting."

There is probably a lot of truth to Boekamp's theory. In 2002, five years after the glory days of Dortmund's Champions League success, two German clubs were in the finals of the Champions League and the Uefa Cup again (Bayer Leverkusen and Dortmund). But this time, both were defeated. Of course this may have been just a coincidence, but it was a highly symbolic one. After the turn of the millennium, German clubs found it increasingly hard to compete with teams from the other big footballing countries, especially England and Spain, in the transfer market. There are many reasons why the Bundesliga clubs couldn't raise as much money as their counterparts from the Premier League or the Primera División. The almost proverbial German fan-friendliness played a role, because modest ticket prices and plenty of football on free, terrestrial television narrowed some of the classic revenue streams for the teams. Then there's the now equally famous German club structure, which prohibits private ownership and all but discourages outside investors, which means there was never the sudden influx of foreign money that would soon turn the Premiership into the footballing equivalent of Las Vegas, a place where American billionaires, Russian entrepreneurs or Arab oil barons gamble away their spare money. Finally, truth be told, the Bundesliga lacked the glamour surrounding the leagues in Italy, Spain and England, which is why German clubs still make only €70m per year from selling foreign rights to lucrative overseas markets like Asia or the Americas, not even an eleventh of what English clubs earn from abroad.

So, yes, it's likely that at one point the clubs themselves would have decided that a new approach was needed, that it ultimately made a lot more economic sense to produce your own talent than to buy it from others at ever increasing costs. Then again, most people resist change until the pressure becomes almost suffocating, so there's no telling how long the Bundesliga teams would have waited until they changed their ways. After all, Boekamp's own club refused to turn around and do things differently until it was on the brink of the abyss.

And so it was left to the DFB to decide that something had to change. The first "Talent Promotion Programme" was based on the models of youth development that were up and running in France and Holland. The DFB hired 400 additional youth-football coaches, then it gave each of its 21 regional associations DM2m

(about €1m) to improve scouting and schooling at Under-13 level. Finally, the DFB spent an additional DM3.2m on 120 youth-football bases across the country where boys and girls between the ages of 13 and 17, specifically those not already playing for a professional club, could work with qualified, salaried coaches. In other words, it was not so much an elite programme but aimed at the grassroots level. Egidius Braun, then the president of the DFB, said, "We want to make sure that talents don't have to drive hundreds of miles to receive proper schooling but will be nurtured around the corner."

The most interesting things about this initial programme were not the numbers, though, but the timing and the creator. The programme was launched in August 1998, four months before Ralf Rangnick appeared on television to explain the flat back four and about six years before the general public realised that there was something seriously wrong in German football. In later publications, the DFB would sometimes state that this first programme was started "not least in response to the harsh public criticism following the national team's early exit from the 1998 Fifa World Cup in France". But it was not so much the national team's disappointing performance or the public outcry that worried the DFB (after all, neither of that was without precedent), it was the demographics.

The average age of the squad Germany sent to the tournament in France was 30.3. Many of the 1990 World Cup winners were still there: Stefan Reuter, Jürgen Kohler, Thomas Häßler, Andreas Möller and the inevitable Lothar Matthäus. All you needed to know, really, was that another one of them, Rudi

Völler, was dyeing his hair because it was greying. This alarming state of affairs was not the fault of the national manager — Berti Vogts had spent the first 11 years of his coaching career in youth football and he would have liked to call up some younger players to the national team. But they just weren't there. Which is why this initial "Talent Promotion Programme" was drawn up and eagerly lobbied for by none other than Vogts himself. Shortly after it was started, however, Vogts resigned from the post of national coach and was replaced by Erich Ribbeck, who wouldn't even last two years on the job. After an embarrassing showing at Euro 2000, Ribbeck was forced to step down.

In a way, the question why German football had sunk so low in the late nineties is as interesting as how it managed the turnaround a decade later. Lots of it has to do with the sort of complacency that is one of the trappings of a long history of success — "Everything seemed to be fine, the trophies came almost automatically," said Wormuth — and also with the fact that, by definition, you tend to recognise social changes only once they have happened. For many decades, almost every athletically gifted German boy took up football, his country's sole national game. But then, in the eighties, a wholly unexpected tennis craze gripped the country thanks to Boris Becker and Steffi Graf. Suddenly football had to vie for young people's time and enthusiasm with other pastimes, a development that caught the DFB unaware and that would become much more dramatic in the 90s. "It took the DFB a while," said Wormuth, "but it finally realised that it had to make an effort to get young boys and girls on board by offering them something that was modern, hip and fun."

That was another problem. Those boys who did choose football in the eighties and nineties learned a game that was not modern and not hip. Almost without exception, kids played in teams built around two strong, muscular man-marking centre-backs and a sweeper at the back. And at the lowest, local level, where all boys started out, football practices were rarely fun. I know what I'm talking about. I coached youth teams in the late nineties and would regularly watch in amazement as my colleagues told nine-year-old boys to run endless laps or even sprint up and down the long flight of concrete stairs that led from the stands to our bumpy cinder pitch. If kids stuck with it despite such conditions, you were lucky. If they blossomed, it was a miracle.

When you ask Edwin Boekamp why hardly any of Borussia Dortmund's Under-19s who won those five national championships in a row in the nineties managed to break into the first team, he doesn't hesitate for a second before replying, "You have to say that they just didn't have the quality to play Bundesliga football. Our scouting was better than the other clubs' scouting, that's why we won all those titles. But when you look back at it realistically, the players we produced weren't good enough." In contrast to the clubs, the DFB couldn't react to this development by simply buying players from abroad, so it had to improve the schooling of German talents dramatically.

Two days after my conversation with Boekamp, Borussia Dortmund played their second home game of the new season, under Friday night floodlights against Werder Bremen. It's a special game, because almost exactly 50 years earlier — on 24 August 1963 — this same match-up produced the first goal in the history of the Bundesliga. It tells you a lot about how stubbornly Germans can resist change that it took the country more than six decades of organised football finally to legalise professionalism and introduce a nationwide league.

And it's a special game for another reason. In 2004 — which, as we shall see, could be called the Year Germany Woke Up — Werder Bremen were the best team in the country, winning the league and cup double. Dortmund, meanwhile, didn't even qualify for Europe and rumours began to circulate that Borussia were almost €100m in the red, forcing the long-time president and CEO to step down under accusations of mismanagement on a monumental scale.

Now, only nine years later, Dortmund are not only back from the good-as-dead, but have won two league titles in the past three years, gave mighty Bayern Munich a good run for their money in an exciting, excellent Champions League final in London and have such a great attacking side that Werder — a proud and tradition-laden team themselves — put every man behind the ball and unashamedly parked the bus. It meant that Dortmund's Nuri Şahin, the most creative man on the pitch and playing in front of the back four as a replacement for the injured Ilkay Gündogan, had to find gaps and passing lanes to set up one of the numerous offensive players. He did so admirably. Dortmund, who would finish the game with an improbable 32 shots on goal, hit the crossbar,

forced a Bremen player into making a goal-line clearance, and then Werder's goalkeeper saved in a one-on-one situation. At half-time, it was 0-0.

It's odd how closely Dortmund's story in the last two decades mirrors the changing fortunes of the national team and also the reputation of the league as a whole. While Bayern Munich are not really representative of German football, inhabiting their own solar system since at least the eighties, Borussia know all about ups and downs. They did very well in the early nineties, losing the Uefa Cup final a year after Germany had surprisingly lost the final of the European Championship to Denmark, then winning the Champions League a year after Germany won Euro 96, before falling into decline. There was one false dawn, an undeserved Bundesliga title in 2002 Borussia were almost gifted (in the same year the national team lucked into the World Cup final), and then the sudden realisation in 2004 that everything was headed for disaster.

As regards the national team, that was the year when Germany crashed out of yet another European Championship and yet another national coach stepped down, the third in six years. (His name was Rudi Völler. He was no longer dyeing his hair.) Abruptly, the country — fans and media — woke up to three undeniable facts. One, the national team was rubbish. Two, there were no young players coming through. Three, a World Cup on home soil was only two years away.

As regards Dortmund, that was the year the long-simmering money problems were finally leaked to the public. It triggered a chain of events that forced the club to rebuild and get rid of anyone who was old and overpaid. Over the ensuing years, Borussia would finally give young players a chance. And, crucially, a young coach. In 2008, shortly before a Germany team still in the process of being rebuilt reached the final of the European Championship in Austria and Switzerland, Dortmund signed a 41-year-old Swabian who'd never played top-flight football himself and had only ever coached one other team, Mainz. His name was Jürgen Klopp and he would soon become not only the face of Borussia Dortmund but one of the men who now represent the new German football — emotional, entertaining, modern.

With 53 minutes of the Bremen game gone, this Jürgen Klopp was pacing the sidelines and the huge crowd — more than 80,000 had come out again to support their team — was getting restless, because Bremen somehow refused to crumble under Dortmund's constant pressure. Then Kevin Grosskreutz played a short pass into the path of Marco Reus. Both players were born in Dortmund, both played for Borussia's youth teams, both left shortly before the training complex was built and the youth acadamey opened, both were brought back after Klopp took over the team.

In the split second before the ball reached him, Reus glanced over to see if the centre-forward Robert Lewandowski was where he should be, then he sent in a low first-time cross. Lewandowski easily put the ball away from five yards out to score what would turn out to be the only goal of the night. The noise was deafening as the crowd erupted.

Klopp punched the air, then he clapped his hands, relieved rather than ecstatic. Lewandowski jogged over to Reus to thank the provider. Nuri Şahin was one of the first players to join them. At the end of the game, he would have been in possession of the ball 94 times — far more than anyone else on either team.

Şahin was born 25 miles south of Dortmund in 1988. He refers to himself as a member of the "third generation". It means that his grandfathers came from Turkey to Germany as so-called guest workers at some point in the sixties. They thought they'd earn some money and then go back home. Once they had settled down, they either started a family in Germany or sent for a family that was still back in Turkey to come and join them. Their children formed the second generation. They typically didn't learn German too well and also thought that, one day, everybody would go back and live in Turkey. But they, too, eventually stayed. Their children are the third generation of ... well, what? Turks? Not really. Germans? Not really, either. Maybe they are Turkish Germans, maybe they are German Turks. It doesn't really matter.

Except in football. Because in football you have to make a choice. Şahin made the choice everybody from the first two generations made almost automatically — he decided to play for Turkey. But it's no longer the typical choice, because many players who share Şahin's background and are in the same age bracket have chosen to represent Germany. Arsenal's Mesut Özil (born in 1988) is currently the most famous one, but there are also former Stuttgart defender Serdar Tasci (born in 1987), who once seemed to have a glowing future in the game and Şahin's Dortmund teammate Ilkay Gündogan (born in 1990).

For many non-Germans, it came as a surprise that all these players — and many others with what is usually referred to as a "migration background", from Gerald Asamoah and David Odonkor to Sami Khedira and Jérôme Boateng — were suddenly playing for Germany after the turn of the century. Perhaps this was the first, or just the most noticeable, sign that German football had undergone some form of change. However, a man who knows all about having to make a choice uses terms we have heard before from others. It was "just a question of time", he says. It was down to "social change", he says.

Yildiray Bastürk was born 15 miles east of Dortmund in 1978. In his heyday, he was one of the best creative midfielders in the Bundesliga and became the first Turkish footballer to play in a Champions League final. That was in 2002, when he was at Bayer Leverkusen. In the same year, Bastürk played at the World Cup. For Turkey, not for Germany. "If you think back 10 or 15 years," he says, "it was almost unthinkable that players with a foreign background played for Germany. Now everything has changed, it's become multi-cultural."

Bastürk, who finished his career two years ago, would like to work in youth football and acquire the top-level coaching badge in Germany. (Which means he could soon be instructed by Frank Wormuth.) He has had an offer from the Turkish football federation, which — unusually, but tellingly — has had a branch office in Cologne since 1998. His job would have been to

scout for players in Europe, mainly in Germany, who are eligible to play for Turkey. Bastürk doesn't want to go into details ("It's all up in the air since the national coach was fired," he said), but if you read between the lines it becomes obvious that he thinks Turkey should follow the German model and improve talent development at home instead of putting pressure on young German-born Turks to choose a country they don't really know.

"There are various reasons, why more and more German-Turkish players decide to represent Germany," Bastürk said. "An important one is that they think they'll get better schooling if they are German junior internationals. They are probably right. Of course the DFB also made more of an effort to enlist such players. But generally you have to say that it just had to happen sooner or later. Many members of the third generation feel more German than Turkish. All my nephews and nieces speak German much better than they speak Turkish. That more and more players with a migration background now choose to represent Germany is normal, really. It had to happen." (Şahin says he wouldn't be surprised if a member of the fourth generation becomes German chancellor one day.)

It's all a far cry from 2002, when Brazil won the World Cup and Germany came second but the most pleasing football was probably played by third-placed Turkey, led by three men who could have played for Germany: Bastürk, Ilhan Mansiz (born in Bavaria) and Ümit Davala (born in Mannheim). It was the same year the DFB took the original "Talent Promotion Programme", devised by Berti Vogts, and kicked it up a notch, launching the "Extended Talent Promotion Programme".

After the disappointing 1998 World Cup, most Germans knew that the 2000 European Championship in the Netherlands and Belgium wouldn't end in glorious triumph. However, few expected the disaster that unfolded. In the opening game, the average age of the German team was 29.9 and Lothar Matthäus, almost exactly 20 years after his first international, was still a starting player — and still the sweeper. Germany scored only one goal and finished last in their group.

The tournament made it painfully obvious that the "Talent Promotion Programme" started just two years earlier wouldn't be enough. A lot more effort (and money) had to be invested — and while the DFB had the power to "be cruel to be kind", it also needed more than just grudging consent from the clubs, it needed support. Just one month after the European Championship, in August 2000, a "DFB Task Force" was set up. It consisted of representatives from seven Bundesliga clubs (Borussia Dortmund were conspicuous by their absence) and was chaired by Bayern Munich's Karl-Heinz Rummenigge, who called Euro 2000 "a major shock moment for us all". Bayer Leverkusen's CEO Wolfgang Holzhäuser was another member. On the day the illustrious work group first met, he said, "We all have to look at the national team as if it were the 19th — and best — team in the Bundesliga." It was a highly symbolic turning point: at least some of the clubs, who traditionally don't have the same interests as the DFB, realised that it would ultimately be beneficial to everyone if they agreed to help the national team. A few months later, the obligation to run a youth academy became part of the licensing procedure for Bundesliga clubs.

The DFB, meanwhile, spent the following two years planning another restructuring of the youth set-up that was far bigger in scope than the 1998 version. It was presented to the public in July 2002 and launched in September. The number of youth football bases was increased to 390, the number of salaried coaches rose to 1,170 and the DFB promised to spend €10m per year on this project for an unlimited period of time. (Add to this the money which the 36 professional clubs annually spend on youth football. In the last few years alone, it has risen from €55m to €77m. It means that German football as a whole has probably spent an average of more than €70 million on talent nurturing every year since 2002.)

When the former Fortuna Düsseldorf goalkeeper Jörg Daniel, the director of the project, presented the "Extended Talent Promotion Programme", he explained that one stated aim was to make sure nobody would slip through the net anymore. "If the talent of a century happens to be born in a tiny village behind the mountains," he said, "we will find him from now on." His determination was probably strengthened by the story of Miroslav Klose, another player with a migration background who had won his first cap for Germany the previous year. Despite his obvious talent, Klose had never played youth football for a big club, let alone for a German junior national team.

In fact, he played amateur football in the fifth division until he was 21, when a Kaiserslautern scout finally spotted him. If Klose had lost interest or self-belief along the way and taken up a regular job after finishing school, Germany would have missed out on the only player in history who has scored at least four goals at three World Cups.

But as massive as it was, the "Extended Talent Promotion Programme" still had to overcome a major problem. Even tons of money and thousands of new coaches and hundreds of new football bases were unlikely to produce players that were up to modern standards as long as the football culture that surrounded them was so unprogressive and deadlocked that a man who explained a flat-back four on television was being ridiculed. You can change the system — but how do you change the minds?

Make no mistake, many minds had to be changed. When Björn Andersson joined Bayern Munich's youth set-up in the summer of 1995, one of his biggest tasks was to convince the Germans that, in his own words, "they are not dumber than other people." He told the Munich-based *Süddeutsche Zeitung*, "Whenever we discuss football, people here tell me: 'Germans cannot play 4-4-2, we cannot cope without a sweeper.' But I don't believe this. All players can play all systems." He wasn't joking — it was indeed the prevalent belief back then that German defenders weren't smart enough for a non-sweeper formation. None other than Franz Beckenbauer had once said that a flat back four was too complicated for Germans. It explains why Andersson never managed to instil a non-sweeper system at Bayern, which was a good thing

for another Swedish player, his namesake Patrik Andersson. The reason Bayern signed him from Mönchengladbach in 1999 was that they needed someone who would replace Matthäus in the sweeper position, because Bayern, the biggest club in the land, stuck with the outdated German system until two years into the new millennium.

However, the whole heated debate over whether German clubs should play with a sweeper or not was just a proxy conflict. It wasn't really about systems, it was about the old guard versus the young generation, about overcoming the stubborn resistance to change that permeated the German game.

"I didn't really learn the finer points of a flat back four until I assisted Joachim Löw at Fenerbahce in 1998," said Wormuth. "But that doesn't mean that there were no young, progressive, modern coaches in Germany in the nineties. Many coaches at the amateur level had really good ideas. And you could also sense the social change I was referring to earlier. In the old days, players just did as they were told. But during the late nineties, they would come up to you and ask why we were doing this or that, why we were playing this way and not another way. They wanted information. They were seeking knowledge."

What was missing were role models. That is why Rangnick's television appearance was so important. Yes, many laughed at him. But for many others it was like seeing the Beatles on television in 1963: you suddenly realised there was a whole new world out there. "Ralf Rangnick was very influential, especially during his time at Ulm," Wormuth said. "And there were two others in the southern part of the country who were ahead of their time. One was Volker Finke at Freiburg. Then there was Wolfgang Frank, who coached Jürgen Klopp at Mainz. I think this explains why the modernisation of the German game began in the south."

However, all three worked at small clubs — Mainz and Ulm were in the second division at the time — and away from the spotlight. The big, popular teams still preferred to sign older, well-known coaches, preferably ones who had been famous players. This is why the public didn't realise that German football had already begun to change. "What was missing," says Wormuth, "was a signal effect. An impulse."

The man who provided this impulse, the spark, has largely been written out of the story of Germany's renaissance, mainly because of an unfortunate stint at Bayern Munich. But it was Jürgen Klinsmann who turned everything on its head. In 2004, after Rudi Völler's resignation, the DFB frantically searched for a new national coach, for someone who was willing to take on what looked like a suicide mission — playing a World Cup on home soil without a competitive team. After Ottmar Hitzfeld, Arsène Wenger, Morten Olsen, Felix Magath, Guus Hiddink, Thomas Schaaf, Otto Rehhagel and Jupp Heynckes had turned down the job, the situation was so desperate — not to say ridiculous — that the magazine *Der Spiegel* published a piece that said, "Have you always wanted to do something for your country? And save German football on the side? Then send us your application for the post of national coach. Time is tight."

"Anxiety is the handmaiden of creativity," TS Eliot wrote, and it was only in the moment of greatest anxiety that the country accepted the fact there had to be a radically new approach to how the most important team in the country was run. The job went to a man who had never coached a team at any level before — the almost notoriously cosmopolitan and open-minded Klinsmann. The man he wanted as his assistant was Ralf Rangnick, but the Professor was unwilling to be someone's deputy and so Joachim Löw was given the post. (Rangnick later joined the village team Hoffenheim and took them from the third division to the Bundesliga.) The rest, as they say, is history. In only his second game in charge, Klinsmann fielded a flat-back four with an average age of 22 — against Brazil, no less. (Germany drew 1-1.) Suddenly extremely young players were routinely called up and played a daring, offensive game. The 2006 World Cup became a marvellous success, both on and off the pitch, and convinced the whole country that change was not just necessary, not only possible, but ... well, fun.

"The way the national team played under Klinsmann and then under his successor Löw was important," said Wormuth, "because it sent out a signal. More and more clubs gave younger coaches a chance and signed someone because of his ability, not his reputation." In the two years under Klinsmann, until he surprisingly declined to sign a new contract after the 2006 World Cup, all the pieces of the jigsaw puzzle — from role models who preached innovation to the effects of social change and the DFB's ambitious programmes — finally came together and formed the basis from which German football would rise.

The role of the two Talent Promotion Programmes may indeed, as Dortmund's youth coordinator Edwin Boekamp has said, have been exaggerated. It was only one piece of the puzzle. However, you can't deny that the programmes were a spectacular success. The most striking example may have come in the second half of the 2010-11 season, when no fewer than four Bundesliga clubs (Mönchengladbach, Kaiserslautern, Freiburg and Hannover) were fighting relegation and yet decided to play largely untried youngsters in the most crucial of positions, namely in goal: Marc-André ter Stegen (19), Kevin Trapp (20), Oliver Baumann (20), Ron-Robert Zieler (22). In each case, the club was rewarded for taking this risk by reaching its goal.

"But it was no risk," Boekamp protested. "These players had quality. It was easy to see that they had received excellent, modern football education. They had all been trained as footballers, not just as goalkeepers and so they were not only comfortable on the ball, they were also able to anticipate situations better, because they knew how outfield players thought and moved. It may have taken a bit of courage to play them, but it was no risk. You cannot argue with quality."

Since the two Talent Promotion Programmes were based on the idea that you shouldn't start at the top but instead improve the schooling of both players and coaches at the lowest, local level, they have produced not just a few outstanding talents but a veritable flood of promising players, in goal and outfield. (In what could turn out to be the great ironic twist of this whole story, though, you have to say that Germany is now producing countless gifted, elegant, almost Brazilian midfielders, but only few classic German defenders.)

This is not just a subjective impression, the statistics bear it out. In the past 10 years, the number of German footballers in the Bundesliga has risen from 46% to 54%. And over the same span, the average age of a Bundesliga player has gone down from 27.6 years to 25 years. It means German clubs have to buy fewer players from abroad because their homegrown talents coming through have as much, if not more, quality.

German football has made enormous strides since the dark ages of the turn of the millennium. The fact that two Bundesliga clubs were in the Champions League final for the first time is not even the most convincing evidence. (That may have been a fluke, considering Dortmund needed two stoppage-time goals, one of which was irregular, to avoid elimination in the quarter-finals.) But, again, the numbers don't lie. Six years ago, Germany was only in fifth place in the Uefa club rankings, far behind France in fourth place and leading Portugal only by a very narrow margin. Since then, the Bundesliga has moved up to third place and is rapidly closing in on England.

As I talk to the steward with the Borussia baseball cap, more and more people walk past us. Today's training session is open to the public. Once that was the norm, now it's less common, which may be another sign of the club's greater professionalism.

By the time the players sauntered onto the perfectly manicured pitch, the crowd was many hundreds strong and fathers carried small kids on their shoulders, because it was the only way they would catch a glimpse of their heroes. All that the players did was jog, but it elicited a round of applause from the crowd and the sound of cameras clicking away filled the air.

The spectacle makes you wonder if perhaps all this indeed had to happen sooner or later. Maybe the game simply had to reinvent itself and rise again in a country that is as large and as football-mad as Germany. If you allow me one

stereotype, once the Germans realised they had to change, it was probably inevitable they would change with their proverbial thoroughness and discipline.

On my way back to the car, I slowly circled the roundabout to take a closer look at the stone lions. Then I notice that the steward was still standing at the gate, watching me. I'm not quite sure, but from this distance it almost looked as if he'd raised both hands to give me the thumbs up.

94

Identity

"You are Irish, stay in Irish. In the
life, your jobs. You not come.
This evening, I am drink."

Size 5

Football, growing up in Leicester and falling out of love with the game

By Nicholas Hogg

Although cricket and rugby would be my lasting, adult affairs, my first love was a size 5 kicked around a Leicester park. For every house on my estate there were two or three kids, and for every house at least one or two City shirts, and at one point even a City goalkeeper, Carl Muggleton. A name that didn't live nearby but was rumoured — a rumour which had as much credence as the bullshit legend that a local hardman had met Reggie Kray at Leicester station and kicked him up the arse back on the train to London — to have played for Syston St Peters, was the crisp thief, TV pundit, and one-time England and Leicester City striker, Gary Lineker.

His goofy smile beamed from his Panini sticker card and that floppy fringe looked like his mum had plonked a bowl on his head to cut his hair. But he was Leicester. Ours. And though a god among men he was grounded by a family who sold fruit and veg on the market while he scored goals at Filbert Street. He also starred in an England team we could watch and cheer, a side that achieved pride and relative success while managed by a general we actually respected in Sir Bobby Robson.

Although the Foxes shirt was ubiquitous, both the blue home kit and the handsome green and gold away strip, my dad was from Nottingham and had moved back after his divorce from my mum — whom I lived with in Leicester, along with my fanatical (and tyrannical) City-supporting stepfather who would brag about once laying out a copper at Filbert Street because he was spoiling his view — and I had a Forest top which he'd given me as a birthday present. The red shirt never left my bedroom. Firstly, for the obvious reason it would've been ripped off and used to hang me from the nearest lamppost. And secondly, it was a special edition celebrating the first million pound player Trevor Francis and garishly badged with a huge, laminated photo of him on the left breast.

But just because I didn't wear my club colours didn't mean my passion for the game was lessened. Before school, at break-time, lunch-time, and after school, I played football. The tennis courts, where I never once saw a racquet swung in anger, were the perfect-sized pitch for the advent of the mini-football. As big as a Florida grapefruit and panelled with leather hexagons just as full-size ball was, our generation should have developed into an era of players with deft feet and a light touch.

Alas, despite the spherical evolutions, we grew up in an age of brutal football. The beautiful game? I'm not sure when the phrase was introduced, but surely not in the 80s, the rampage of the Crazy Gang, Fash the Bash and Vinnie Jones, Brian Clough cuffing fans — then kissing them — and the off field tragedies at Heysel and Hillsborough.

Before all-seater stadiums were compulsory, attending a Leicester-Notts derby was an initiation into manhood. On dark wet nights in the Filbert Street pens, dodging the torrents of rain gushing off the corrugated roofing, I joined in with the chants and insults and became part of something bigger than myself. Part of a tribal beat accompanied by the music of lobbed coins tinkling through the wire fence that separated red and blue fans — I can still recall picking up a fifty-pence piece that thunked off a bloke's head.

Huddling in the middle of the crowd was key to survival and not only as shelter from money shrapnel. Any straggler who wandered within grabbing distance of the Forest pen could be yanked against the mesh and punched and kicked until City supporters could pull their brethren back into the fold.

To be crushed in a mass of half-pissed men was frightening. And a buzz. If City scored and the swaying crowd jumped and leapt, a whole section of fans would go tumbling down the terrace like Domino Rally. From the joy of Lineker banging one away in the top corner to a 20-stone dumpling pinning you to concrete. But fans looked out for young 'uns, and as quick as you hit the deck you'd be hauled up into the brotherhood.

Strutting into school the day after a Forest derby I'd feel 10 feet tall. If I'd

seen someone get a kicking, or been lucky enough to have run in a charge at opposing fans, I'd be courted all day for the story. A kid from the year above arrested and ejected from the ground became an anti-folk hero, gleefully spreading a tale that compounded an already psychopathic personality.

This was the decade of the yob. Picket lines, punks, the Falklands War and football. The 1980s pulsed with the sound of break-dancing and bone-breaking. The fact that Leicester had a nationwide hooligan sect called the Baby Squad became a source of local pride. ITV News ran an item on how to recognise a member, complete with an artist's sketch of a generic white man with gelled hair in a satin bomber jacket — more George the bear than nutty skinhead — brandishing a Stanley knife.

Hooliganism, on and off the pitch, defined my football. On the day I write this, the Manchester United manager David Moyes is calling for retrospective video evidence to be used against diving. Maybe he too harks back to the eighties. A plus from this epoch was that the dive was scorned. Dribbling through a gauntlet of hacking legs was infinitely more manly than a dying swan on the edge of the box and, in my opinion, infinitely more enjoyable to watch and play.

Although not according to my PE teacher. After the National Union of Teachers finally allowed its members again to organise after-curricular activities, such as football, a 'friendly' was arranged against a local comprehensive to gauge whether my reprobate year could be trusted to represent the school.

We were 4-0 up when we blew our chance of reintegration. I saved a penalty before their forward kicked the rebound out of my hands and stabbed it over the line. Before I'd even stood up the remonstrations had turned into right hooks and head butts, and we'd self-destructed from an unassailable lead of four goals into a shameful abandonment.

But the same teacher who decided he had better things to do with his time than cart a mini-bus of feral youth around Leicestershire also understood the restorative qualities of thuggish boys playing football at break-time. Lads too fucked to mess about in double-maths were easier to handle than lads who'd spent an hour skinning up around the back of the sports hall. Better they were inside that sports hall kicking lumps out of each other.

In a draughty gym every Friday dinnertime, a game known as five-a-side football, yet more a hybrid between Rollerball, Tron, and that bit in *Flash Gordon* in which he batters the weird red blokes with a metal watermelon, was some of the most thrilling sport I've ever played.

The classrooms emptied and kids crammed into the spaces behind the goals — two benches stacked upon each other so a score reverberated with furniture crashing onto the tiled floor. The noise of the toppled benches, echoing with the roars and jeers at fouls and fuck-ups was deafening. Think of the Thunderdome in *Mad Max III* or the clatter of spiked chariot wheels and the baying Romans cheering on Ben Hur.

The in-form team were usually the oldest side, as height, size and the doling out of dead legs to younger opposition before matches tended to override any superior footballing skills. By the last year my side was riding high in the table. Named 'Demolition' after the WWF tag team — hardly the worst moniker considering that one side called itself 'Mandela United,' and not in honour of Nelson's crusade against apartheid but because Winnie and her squad were accused of murder — the team consisted of the boys ranked hardest. And, as luck would have it, the fastest sprinter in the school, Kevin Locke. Before half-time we were down to two men, with the Vinnie Jones wannabes red-carded. Still, with Kev up front and me keeping, we were hanging on. I was peppered with shots, and the hordes behind us, many of whom were the suffering kids on the fist-end of the bullies who'd just been sent off, bellowed in hysterics with each screaming shot aimed at toppling the wooden posts. But with Kev's pace and my goalmouth acrobatics, along with my accurate throws picking him out like a quarterback finding a wide receiver, we squeezed an infamous win.

I still have the medal from that year's championship victory. My only football trophy along with various rugby and cricket trinkets. And apart from a season in midfield for a pub team in a Sunday league after I was forced to retire from rugby with a neck injury, the only competitive football I played was that five-a-side inferno.

So why the oval before the round ball?

Why hurl a leather missile at a wooden bat?

In my footballing heyday cricket and rugby were distant sports. I loved Lineker and Barnes, Robson and Waddle. I loved dealing Panini stickers and playing *Football Manager* for hours on a ZX Spectrum. I loved *Match of the Day* and spending school break-times trying to recreate the goals of the weekend.

Yet something happened to the game between the gritty eighties and the meretricious glamour of the modern Premier League. Diving and money. Teams where players are shipped in from across the globe and owned by restaurateurs and oil thieves. Et cetera, et cetera. Blah, blah, blah. The old fan's lament that the olden days were the golden days, when Stanley Matthews played in hobnailed boots and you could have 10 pints of bitter and a bag of chips and still pay your bus fare home.

Nothing stays the same, but some sports change for the worse. Or perhaps they evolve on a tangent opposite to our own shifting characters, values and attitudes.

Cricket, despite IPL wealth, match fixing and bird-brained administration, still has pretensions of grace and sportsmanship. Rugby, I used to contend, was about truth. No player bullshitted about his abilities in the changing room after a game. It was a measure of who you

were, how you'd stand up and fight when the opposition were stamping your head into the mud.

It's truly a shame that I don't follow football with the fervour I used to. The goal glimpsed in a crowded pub, a scan of the headlines to see which team is where and how close the Foxes are to a Premier League return.

Yet despite my cynicism, and regardless of the dollars and roubles pumped into that grossly inflated size 5, football is forever special. A game bigger and better than a global megasport.

As a travelling journalist I've played matches in refugee camps and shanty towns. On the day the Abu Ghraib torture photos hit front pages around the world I faced up against a team of Palestinians, a side of scarred and serious men set on restoring cultural pride by thrashing a team of foreigners. In a Guatemalan slum I played on a pitch made of glass-chipped mud and lethal cans, and here I was dazzled by men dribbling like Messi. On a dust bowl pitch in a Kenyan orphanage, watching a skinny kid streak down the wing and skip over slide tackles before beating the keeper with the most delicate of barefoot lobs, the game is still beautiful. Ⓑ

Booze Boys

Tracing the history of Irish football's sizzled relationship with alcohol

By Dion Fanning

"In the life, in the life, in your jobs, in every jobs, there is the order of the life. In a club, in the team, there is order. The team order the life. Without this, it's impossible to go. No, we are Irish or our habit. But where we go? Where do you want to go?

You are Irish, stay in Irish. In the life, your jobs. You not come. This evening, I am drink." — Giovanni Trapattoni, August 2013.

The story of Irish life and the story of Irish football life are full of those moments when, having considered all available options, a man said, "This evening, I am drink."

Giovanni Trapattoni came from a very different football culture but his time as Ireland manager was marked by his bewilderment at the Irish footballer's relationship with drink. In August 2013, he was asked about rumours that two players had broken a curfew just before Ireland's opening game at the European Championships. He insisted they hadn't but then went on to wonder in his baffling English about the choices Irish footballers made. This was, as he had said before, "the culture, the habit".

Irish football, like English football, Scottish football and Welsh football, always had

a drinking culture which simply reflected the drinking culture in the world around it. This philosophy was encapsulated in a simple phrase. "They did it at the right times," Ron Atkinson said when asked about the group of drinkers he had at Manchester United. Given that one of the group was Paul McGrath it could be argued that no time was the right time.

If one accepts that the five greatest players to come out of the island of Ireland are John Giles, George Best, Liam Brady, McGrath and Roy Keane then three have had what might be described as a complicated relationship with alcohol.

Ireland's relationship with alcohol could be described as complicated too. Norman Mailer believed that the Irish drank so much because they had an over-supply of semen and hormones and if they didn't drink, they would go mad. F Scott Fitzgerald (who described his mother's family as "straight 1850 potato famine Irish") considered the creative mind more prone to the consolations of drink: "As he inflates his imagination, he inflates his capacity for anxiety, and inevitably becomes the victim of crushing phobias that only be allayed by crushing doses of... alcohol."

There were many crushing phobias in the collective imagination of the Irish football, many, many ways to imagine defeat and so few to conceive of victory. For whatever reason, Irish football and drink rubbed along for many years. "Traditionally, this is the way we've been," Niall Quinn wrote in his autobiography as he considered the view that the Irish team was shambolic and disorganised. "We've never pampered ourselves. Under Jack Charlton, when we enjoyed 10 years of good times, we were mostly ramshackle, and part of what made us tick was the disorganisation and the joy we got from pretending to the world that we weren't to be taken seriously. Then we'd go out on the pitch and die for one another."

People in Ireland will bristle if a foreign — and by foreign I mean English — commentator makes a glib comment such as "The Irish know how to party" when reporting on any sporting success. The problem is that the stereotype had some truth. On the finest days in Irish football, there was often an accompanying story of drink and music. When Ireland beat the Soviet Union 3-0 in 1974, the party in the Central Hotel afterwards was full of drink and song as it should have been. Giles recalled in his autobiography that Liam Brady, who had made a memorable debut, gave a rendition of "Ruby Don't Take Your Love to Town".

In 2001, after Ireland had drawn with Portugal at Lansdowne Road, Roy Keane sang Dylan's "Positively 4th Street" in Lillie's Bordello on Grafton Street as he made what was becoming a rare appearance socialising with the Irish squad. The following year, the bar was thrown open at the Irish team hotel outside Tokyo following the draw with Germany at a reported cost of €20,000.

Journalists, officials and anybody who was in the area enjoyed the generosity.

On the night Ireland beat the Soviet Union, the team were joined by Luke Kelly of the Dubliners, a man and a group who knew about music and knew about drink.

The Irish forward Ray Treacy's party piece was "*Whiskey in the Jar*", usually accompanied by himself on banjo. Treacy joked that of the forty-two caps he got for Ireland, the banjo was responsible for thirty of them. Giles wrote in his autobiography of a "day when we were going to the airport and Ray announced he had forgotten his boots. I asked him if he had his banjo. He said he had. 'That's ok, then,' I said. 'Don't worry about the boots.'"

The musical instrument was a perennial in Irish football. Nearly 40 years after Ray Treacy's banjo, it was not unusual to see a guitar case slide along the airport carousel among the Irish squad's kit and equipment. In the early years of the 21st century, the guitar case belonged to Andy Reid but Trapattoni would have strong views on men like Reid and their guitars.

Giles's involvement brought a professionalism to Irish international football that hadn't been seen before but, like Quinn, he saw nothing wrong with a celebration. Giles was always a man apart, somebody who, in his own words, wasn't a "character" but he was able to fit in with those who were.

Irish life has always wanted its characters and when problems arose in later years, another man who couldn't fit the conventional model of the character made things difficult.

In the seventies and eighties, football in the UK and Ireland was governed by the idea that there was this right time to drink and a wrong time to drink. The right time could, of course, turn into the wrong time. As Irish football lurched from one bad night on the field to another, it always seemed like the right time. There were more bad nights than good ones; more nights when Ireland came away from the stadiums of Europe fuelled by an immediate sense of injustice that merged with a deeper-rooted sense of injustice and created that deep restlessness in the soul, the void that couldn't be filled. There were too many nights when there was nothing to do but drink.

When Jack Charlton became Ireland manager, success came. Irish football was slow to recognise any need to change beyond the need to ensure that players were fit and present to appear on the field. In the wonderful documentary *In My Book You Should be Ahead*, two Shelbourne officials discuss the policing of footballers on away trips. This isn't solely about what one describes as "the acting-the-maggot end of it" but involves the best way of unwinding the night before a game. Another official suggests a good book: "I read somewhere or other that the doctors say if you read until the object falls out of your hand, you're completely relaxed."

Traditionally, the Irish player had pursued other methods of relaxation. For many during the Charlton Years, the nights out where they would bond until the dawn were as important as the success. When Ireland qualified for the European Championship in 1988 and the World Cup two years later, the benefits of supporting the Irish football team became clear to many beyond the game's natural constituency.

If Italia 90 provided the party, it also provided the cautionary tale. Paul McGrath was among that squad, possibly still drinking at the right times occasionally but those times were becoming less frequent. The party continued around him. "Italia 90," Declan Lynch wrote in *Days of Heaven*, "was indeed the greatest excuse ever to go drinking in the history of Ireland... it was more than just the greatest excuse to go drinking; it was an excuse to go drinking in ways that we had never gone drinking before... There is hardly a man alive in Ireland who does not have some blissful memory of being terribly, terribly drunk during Italia 90 in the middle of the day, or some strange hour at which he had never been drunk before." And that, it would be tempting to add, was just the squad.

McGrath represented the darkness because in so many magnificent forms he represented the light. He was great in ways we couldn't imagine and vulnerable in ways we could.

In October 1990, I was behind the West Stand at Lansdowne Road when the Ireland team arrived to play Turkey in a European Championship qualifier. We applauded the heroes off the coach but then it became clear that something was wrong: Paul McGrath had stayed on the bus.

Soon Jack was back out and I will always have the memory of the pleading look on McGrath's face as he explained he couldn't leave this relatively safe place, as he was gripped, he would explain in his autobiography, by the fear.

McGrath stayed on the bus which I recall driving away with him in it. In his book, he says he walked through the crowd to be put in a taxi and taken back to the hotel. The official explanation when it became known that he was not available for the game was, as always, 'Paul McGrath's knees', which had already become a euphemism.

We already had plenty of those. McGrath's struggle brought some awareness and twelve years later he would still be struggling and we would still be searching for awareness.

There are those who will still insist that the problems on Saipan, where Ireland went to prepare for the 2002 World Cup, were an administrative issue: that a failure to deliver balls and training gear coupled with a bumpy pitch led to the greatest implosion in Irish football history. The truth may be more complex. The truth may be a story of drink. Training kit, balls, uneven grass and a calamitous team meeting were just Macguffins.

In 1992, after many of the Irish squad had a long day lost in the bars of south Boston, Roy Keane climbed onto the Irish team bus wearing, according to Quinn in his autobiography, a 'Kiss me quick' hat. Ireland were late for a flight. "Look at the fucking state of you," said Mick McCarthy who was one of those not lost in the bars of Boston. "You call yourself a professional footballer."

"And," Keane is supposed to have replied, "you call what you have a first touch."

Keane would claim that version was *l'esprit d'escalier*.

Keane in 1992 fitted well into the traditional model of Irish football but, over the years, he changed as Irish football remained the same.

In 2002, an unforgiving light was shone on Irish football's means of relaxation and whose light is more unforgiving than Roy Keane's?

In his autobiography, ghostwritten by Eamon Dunphy, Keane gives glimpses of the life he once led.

During his rehabilitation following his cruciate ligament injury, Keane states that as he worked hard, "I was also drinking too much." At Christmas, he was banned from the Manchester United Christmas party after he attended the reserves' Christmas night out and argued with a barman. Alex Ferguson promised to fine any player who was seen drinking with him that evening.

At some point, Keane embarked on this change, in truth a revolutionary transformation but one he tried to make light of. "I decided to bury Roy the Playboy," he wrote. "He might get the odd outing but his carousing days were — more or less — over. Appreciation of my family life was one reason for this change. A deep desire to make every day of my football career count was the other."

Ireland headed to Saipan before the 2002 World Cup, a week which was supposed to be about R&R. The night before Ireland played at the Stadium of Light for Quinn's testimonial, Mick McCarthy explained this to the players. One man was not there: Keane. Ireland's captain was managing an injury and stayed away. "Did you want me to sit in the stand and be pestered by people who are drunk?" he said when asked about his absence.

Keane has always expressed a tolerance for other players' drinking — in fact he has been known to encourage it — but the clash wasn't between Keane's non-drinking and his teammates' traditional habits but between Keane and Keane. "I had grown less tolerant of myself," he wrote when explaining the old Keane.

Yet Keane can hardly be seen as a man deeply tolerant of others either and his new way of life added to his separateness. Once Denis Irwin retired, Keane roomed alone and when he stopped drinking, he had to find other ways of relaxing. As he told Paul Kimmage in Saipan, "There's only so much walking you can do... there's only so many books you can read."

The rest of the squad knew how to unwind. A barbecue had been planned in Saipan for the players, the staff and the media. Keane was reluctant to attend and socialise with people from the press he had no time for. But he went for a while, again making the effort, again trying to please people. The rest of the squad had bigger plans as Quinn wrote in his autobiography. "Roy hasn't been drinking for some time now so we keep it low key about what we have planned for the rest of the evening... There is a quick break for the bar. The players circulate dutifully for a little bit, Roy slips off into the night and then some of the lads make a fairly theatrical show of yawning and stretching and pretending to be heading off to bed."

Instead they would drink till dawn and become "leglessly bonded" while Keane was left to brood.

There is a condition known as 'dry drunk', a term that describes the behaviour of a drinker who has quit but is still quick to anger and prone to mood swings. Without the release valve that alcohol has customarily brought, the dry drunk may be even more volatile than he was before.

Keane faced more than a month away from the things which kept him calm. He had no release valve and no escape unless he found one.

His autobiography, published in the autumn of 2002, was a story of drink, slightly romanticised perhaps by his ghostwriter. That summer Eamon Dunphy had to be taken off the air during a World Cup game he was analysing on RTÉ because — another euphemism — "he had been unable to fulfil the terms of his contract."

"I was not actually drunk," Dunphy insisted. "I had been."

Dunphy was not just a ghostwriter but a passionate advocate for Keane that summer.

So much in 2002 was being decided by people who were not actually drunk but had been. Paul McGrath was there too, flown out to work for the BBC and then flown home by the BBC after an incident on the plane to Tokyo in which he was reported to have insulted players' wives over their husbands' failure to support Roy Keane.

Keane and McGrath were friends, men who understood each other. Yet it's hard to believe that all this trouble could be caused by a bumpy pitch and some missing kit. Even the most wounding allegation as far as Keane was concerned — that he had faked injury to miss a play-off game in Iran — could hardly have resulted in all that chaos unless other impulses were involved. Unless other crushing phobias were knocking around.

In the aftermath of Saipan, the FAI commissioned a management consultancy to look into everything surrounding the affair. The Genesis Report was published in late 2002 but no report will ever be able to fully explain what drives one man to the edge, especially when drink is involved or not involved. Roy Keane returned, then went away again, this time quietly. Steve Staunton became manager with the understanding that he would harness some of the traditional values and when that failed the FAI turned to Trapattoni.

In Wiesbaden, the spa and casino town in which Dostoevsky had won and mainly lost, Ireland prepared for to face Georgia in Mainz (a game that had been moved from Georgia because of the conflict in South Ossetia).

On the night after the game, Andy Reid was playing the guitar which he had, as always, brought with him while around him teammates sang and drank in the traditional fashion. Suddenly Trapattoni appeared, armed with a rolled-up copy of *Gazzetta Dello Sport*. With this, Trapattoni embarked on a clash of cultures, swiping his newspaper at Reid's

head and telling him to go to bed. Trap's own version was that he had given Reid a paternal kick up the backside, sending him to his room as you would do an errant son. Reid was dropped from the Irish squads shortly afterwards and only returned after Trapattoni's departure.

Irish football and drink remain entwined. In the 2012 European Championship, Ireland's surrender on the pitch was contrasted by the spectacular nocturnal advances of the supporters, headed by the FAI's chief executive John Delaney. Delaney had taken part in a Drink Aware campaign before the tournament and many pictures circulated of him during Ireland's time in Poland relaxing in the company of people who were drunk and who were aware that they were drunk. Delaney said a night out was "something I'm entitled to do on the odd occasion when I'm there."

There had been rumours that his shoes had been stolen during his night out which Delaney also addressed: "It's a bit of folklore, a bit of fun. I'm coming home. Two hundred lads see me. They lift me up and they carry me up and lift me head-high to my hotel and they sing, 'Shoes Off for the Boys in Green'. And they handed me my shoes back and they handed me my socks back. Simple as that."

Delaney's story was simple but many weren't. Many were part of what Trapattoni called "the culture, the habit". Many were built on the need to say, "This evening, I am drink." This evening, I pursue oblivion. **Ⓑ**

ShotDead
in the head

FREE UK STANDARD SHIPPING OVER £50*

WITH PRIDE...

1878
THE BIRTH of FOOTBALL
NEWTON HEATH

MANC

VINTAGE CLASSICS

MEXICO 1986

FINGER Flickin' GOOD
SUBBUTEO

Football Special! 1980

HUGE RANGE OF TEAMS & DESIGNS
ACROSS MEN'S, WOMEN'S & KIDS' TEES PLUS HOODIES, SWEATSHIRTS AND MUGS

FORTUNE'S ALWAYS HIDING

106

Referees

"The Paraguayan league
has them as well."

The Final Whistler

Horacio Elizondo on the strategy of officiating, and sending off Zidane in the World Cup final

By Sam Kelly

Horacio Elizondo might be, excluding politicians, one of the most insulted people in South America. As one of the continent's pre-eminent referees, his two-decade long career took in three Copa Libertadores finals, countless Argentinian top-flight games and two Copas América as well as a World Cup. That last tournament was to put him in a unique position to comment on probably the most widely seen, and arguably one of the most controversial, red cards of all time; it was Elizondo who sent off Zinédine Zidane for his headbutt on Marco Materazzi during the 2006 final.

Since retiring — like Zidane, in 2006 — he has become a refereeing analyst for Argentinian media, and has worked with various government agencies on aid, education and sport programs. I met him one Monday afternoon, just after he'd finished a television spot for TyCSports, Argentina's main domestic cable sports channel, and was half expecting him to be in a rush to get away as we sat down in the lobby to talk. Not a bit of it.

🌐 *Let's start at the beginning. What made you want to become a referee — because I'd guess it wasn't a childhood dream?*

No, no... kids dream about other things! When I was a boy I dreamed about being a football *player*. I played in the Quilmes youth system, but when I was 13 or 14 years old, I realised there were lots of players like me, that I was going to be one more among the multitude and that the dream of getting into the first team was going to be almost impossible. So, I started dedicating myself to other sports — I played rugby, handball... until I got into athletics and decided I wanted to be a decathlete. I had really good personal bests in most of the disciplines, but there was one that I just couldn't do, which was the pole vault. I was afraid of heights! So from then on I settled into my strongest discipline, which was the javelin. I competed in that here in Argentina until the age of 22.

When I was 19 [in 1984], I started university, studying to become a Physical Education teacher and during my studies I had to referee a handball game, and... well, the teacher told me to referee and afterwards asked whether I'd ever thought of becoming a football referee — until that point, at 19, it had never crossed my mind — and I replied that no, I hadn't. Oh, he kept on at me for a long time! Telling me to take the [refereeing] course run by the country's handball association and I kept telling him no. Then one day, totally coincidentally, I was walking past the headquarters of the AFA [Asociación de Fútbol Argentino] and I saw a sign on the door saying "Enrolment open for refereeing course". Complete coincidence, you know? Because I didn't even know the AFA headquarters was there! I didn't know, and I walked past the door and saw that sign... and kept walking! Then at the corner of the block, I couldn't cross the road because of the traffic lights. So, what my teacher had been telling me — going on at me about — for all those months, plus that little sign... I said to myself, right then. Let's do it. It's only 50m away, let's go and see what it's all about. A little aside here which I like; that incident means traffic lights are something very important in my life, just as they were for the English referee [Ken Aston] who was inspired by traffic lights to invent red and yellow cards.

Anyway, I enrolled and after a few days I was already waking up and going to bed every day thinking about refereeing and all day in between as well. I had no doubt that this was my new vocation, and pretty soon I asked myself, "What am I going to do with this?"

🔵 *In a lot of countries, even top level referees aren't full time; many have a job during the rest of the week. What does a referee need to do during the days between matches, from a professional point of view?*

There comes a point in the career of any referee when he reaches a peak at which point he doesn't have much time for another job, unless he's lucky enough to have one which means he's effectively self-employed — I don't

know, perhaps if he owns a café or restaurant, for instance, he might be able to manage it somehow. But if your work depends on an employer, be it public or private, it becomes very complicated because you're not going to be able to meet every requirement. During the week, at least in my case (and there are those who don't do this — at least in Argentina), I trained every day of the week, I went to the gym, did my training at Ezeiza [the suburb in southern Buenos Aires where the AFA and some clubs have training bases], I learned to speak English [a requirement for referees who want Fifa approval to officiate international matches], went swimming... in my head, it was 24 hours a day of refereeing. My preparation was always aimed at doing things the very best I could on the field of play, so it took up all my time.

🔵 *When you started out as a referee, surely you couldn't have dreamed that one day, you'd be able to say you've refereed three Copa Libertadores finals, as well as the opening match of a World Cup and the final of that same World Cup [Elizondo is the only referee to be able to say the latter of a World Cup with knockout stages, although Englishman George Reader officiated both the opening match and the fortuitously decisive group match of the 1950 World Cup]. Was there any ambition as a referee that you didn't manage to realise?*

There's no short answer to that one. Looking back, when I realised that refereeing was becoming a big part of my life, I started to ask myself, "what am I going to do with all this?" I was 20 years old. The answer came very quickly: referee at a World Cup. That is to say, that was my objective, the number one aim. I knew from that moment that to get to that point a lot of things were going to come up and that I'd need to reach a lot of smaller goals along the way to arrive at that final point.

I actually had a big chance to go to the 2002 World Cup in South Korea and Japan, but in the end I didn't quite make it. At that point I started to think differently, asking myself, "I want to go to a World Cup, but until now I've never thought — what's a World Cup going to be like? What do I want to do [when I'm there]?" It's a point that maybe no one really knows, but that was when I realised that I wanted to referee the *final* of a World Cup. So from 2002 to 2006, everything was focused on imagining myself, visualising myself, preparing as if I was going to referee the final. That was the biggest thing — quite apart from whether it actually happened or not, because there are a lot of circumstances you have to rely on, which Horacio Elizondo couldn't take into account with his preparation. [For the organisers] there are a lot of political factors, a lot of strategic factors, performance-related factors... and comparisons with other referees at the same World Cup, of course. So, a lot of things to consider! Some officials were competing with me, some weren't. But the preparation — I want to make this clear — my preparation was always with the idea that I was going to be refereeing that match.

⊕ *Ironically, given what you've just said, I read an old interview of yours yesterday in which you said that your favourite memory from that World Cup was refereeing the opening match, not the final!*

Well, that was just... [blows out his cheeks] that match... it was so... it made me so happy! From an emotional point of view it was that match, yes. In the world of refereeing, remember, the refs who went to that World Cup had started to work towards it three years previously, in 2003. So of course, who's going to oversee the opening match? There are always two or three refereeing teams competing and before it started, on an entirely theoretical level, they said okay — we were the best. Just a little better [than the others]. So the satisfaction was enormous when we got that news, and on the day that I was going to referee the opening match... wow! It was as if I had a documentary entitled *My 22-Year Career* playing in my head, you know? So emotionally, that was the match which left me with the strongest memories.

⊕ *Modern football seems to depend more and more on the physical conditioning of players, which results in an ever faster game, at least in some countries. Does that mean referees have to meet requirements which didn't exist — or at least didn't have the same importance —when you started to referee? In terms of physique, or the ability to read a game that's getting quicker all the time...*

When I started refereeing compared with the football we see today... they're totally different games. Today it's a much faster and more dynamic game. For that reason, referees today need to work daily not only on their physical abilities, but also the techniques, tactics and strategies of refereeing. Referees need to train on all of these things every day of the week, just as the players do in their clubs, every day. This is something

I can't say I see very often — at least here in South America — a referee who's completely up-to-date with the professional world and who acts, shall we say, like a professional at all times.

⚽ *Related to this, do different styles of play from country to country present different challenges to referees? And is there a difference between refereeing an international match, a continental club match or a domestic league match?*

Absolutely. Of course, the rules of the game are always the same. You don't pick and choose, or tweak them depending on the context; the rules are always the same. What you *do* have to consider somewhat is your own strategy and tactics when kick off arrives. Why? Because if you compare our local league in Argentina, it's a game that, while it's got quicker, is frequently centred around the midfield. Everything is defined there. Whoever wins the midfield battle, that's the team who will have more opportunities to win the match. If you're going to referee a match in England, meanwhile, well, it's a lot faster. Players touch the ball once or twice at a time, and you're more likely to see quick, direct passes — lots of distance to cover! You need to be open to switching your refereeing strategy, then, because your job is going to need you to be able to read the game very quickly, so as to be able to get where the ball's been played to, only to almost immediately have to turn round and head back to the other penalty box. The game there is end to end, and is very dynamic. It goes from one area of the pitch to another very quickly. Whereas in Argentinian football, you have to be more focused on the players' tempers, on when they come

together. Why's that? Because the players really get stuck in in their attempts to win the midfield battle. That's their plan.

⚽ *So, when you refer to the "strategies and tactics of refereeing", you're talking about how you adapt to the strategies and tactics of the match...*

That's one element. Only one, because aside from that strategy and that tactic, you have to also consider what it means to work in a team, since referees work in teams. As they work on the technical side, the referee's technique is expressed in making good tactical choices when it comes to making a refereeing decision. Strategy is more complex than that, but you'd have, for instance, analysis of the game as an aspect of your strategy — as one part of it, not the whole thing. And then again, there's another difference when you talk about national team football. You're going to see a *much* more hard-running game, players who are physically well-equipped, *very* well prepared, and as a result you're definitely going to have to run more. There won't be as much 'friction' between players but you have to pay a lot more attention to the big decisions, because almost every match is decided in or around the penalty area. That means that in those matches, you have to be very precise when the time arrives to take your decisions, especially inside the box.

⚽ *Have you noticed any change in the media visibility of referees since you became a ref?*

Yes, a big change. Everyone looks at every match afterwards on television and decides whether you did well or did badly. Well, sometimes referees do make mistakes, and they should be responsible, they should work to get over those errors. Sometimes, on the other hand, there's a kind of journalism — at least here in Argentina — which isn't exactly overburdened with an understanding of the rules of the game and the factors affecting how referees make their decisions. That journalism can confuse the fans and spectators a lot, but well... that's how it goes. Whoever passes judgement on whether a referee is good or bad, from a TV studio, can be a very influential factor, and so you have to prepare yourself. Your preparation needs to be focused, so that during a game you're as close as possible to what everyone's going to see on screen.

⊕ *In England it seems like every time we go out of an international tournament, some of the press reaction is aimed at the referee in some way, for instance if an English player is sent off — Beckham in 1998, or Rooney... who you sent off yourself.*

[Chuckling] Yes, that's right... in Germany, in 2006.

⊕ *Do you see the same kind of reaction in Argentina, of blaming the referee?*

Perhaps a little, but we're a little more... more self-punishing. We're more likely to blame ourselves. If we go out of a World Cup, we'll say, "We're absolutely awful, we're good for nothing..." and then a little later we might find a way to shift the blame: "This coach can't carry on, he's done everything badly, the directors [of the AFA] have been awful as well"; or perhaps, "We're slipping from where should be, we want a change now, everything has to change..."

⊕ *Neither of those is very healthy, is it?*

Not at all! Both attitudes seem pathological to me. Most unhealthy.

⊕ *The reason I asked those questions is that you yourself are now part of the media discourse surrounding referees. Do you think that discourse affects how the game is refereed? Does it put more pressure on referees?*

It's a complicated subject for referees. In 2008, I was part of AFA's Directorship of Referee Training, where I was responsible for training the referees and one of the first things I told the ones I trained — because there were ex-referees who worked on TV and other media — was about how angry one gets as a referee towards that ex-ref who used to be his colleague and who now analyses him, criticises him on television, and I'd always tell them, "Don't worry about that stuff, sooner or later you'll realise why it's happening. Why is it happening? Because at one time that person was a referee, but he's not any more. Now he's an analyst, and he has to do his job, which is analysing. I can like him or not like him, I can like or not like what he says, I can agree or I can disagree, but he's not a referee any more. That's in the past. Now he's an analyst. And one has to have the intelligence to keep learning. And of course, you should also take on board the analysis of an ex-colleague, because as well as his capabilities and understanding, he's also lived the experience of being on the field of play — he knows the things that happen to a referee, what a referee feels, what he thinks — and it's much preferable that suddenly an ex-colleague analyses you, than that you're being analysed by a journalist who doesn't have quite the same understanding of that stuff, who hasn't had the experience of being out there on the pitch.

My idea, now that I'm an analyst myself, isn't to be down on the referee, kill or criticise the referee, but rather to look specifically at the *decisions* the referee takes, how he takes them, and look at *why* this or that referee has had a good or a bad day.

● *The second part of this question was whether there's anything you'd like to change — or that you do try to change — in how the media cover refereeing decisions.*

People say, "Hey, I think this, I feel this way, I believe..." No. "Belief" is about the game. But there's something in common for everyone: the laws. If we take the laws of the game as the starting point for the discussion, we'll be able to have a much more encompassing theory of it, and we'll be able to come to an agreement much more quickly. If everyone keeps seizing on, "No, I believe this," or, "I think whatever..." No. There's no "I". The rules of the game are what decides what needs to be done. Part of how I approach my media job is precisely that, making people understand that it's wrong to talk in such a personalised way in these discussions. That is, the idea isn't to be a god of refereeing but to keep up-to-date with the rules of the game so that you can communicate them more clearly.

Also the fan, the television viewer... we help *them* to analyse and they can analyse it with us, not because I'm the holder of The Truth, but because the viewer analyses *me*. My belief is that if I can introduce that idea to television,

it changes the discourse a little. Why? Because when one is a reference point in the world of refereeing — through being in the media, and for people, for society, I mean — one can say, from a refereeing point of view, whether a point is a good one, or a bad one, or an okay one. So, I try to use that fact to teach people as well, to instruct... so they get a sense of how complicated and difficult it is when the moment arrives to take a decision, how that process can be trained in referees to aid their decision-making, the quantity and quality of their decisions — the lot.

● *Now, back to the 2006 World Cup. It's late on during the final. You're putting your hand into your pocket to take out the red card and show it to Zinédine Zidane. What thoughts are going through your head? You must have known already that it was going to be a huge incident...*

You know something? At the time, I really didn't. With the act of refereeing matches — and the *number* of matches I'd refereed — well, you just try and take the best decisions possible. Why? Because just as players score goals and celebrate those goals, when a referee makes a big decision, for us that's like scoring a goal, you see? For ourselves. The ref feels happy enough with the rules to be able to make a good decision. Totally independently of what the decision might be, of which players it involves or of where it's made. It could be in the domestic league, in an international match, in the local club round the corner from your house, but the important thing is to take those decisions — and make them better decisions every time. That way, you're always scoring more goals!

So at that point, no. Obviously, after the match I realised that it had been an *enormous* decision, thanks to the big media reaction to it. But right now, as I'm showing him the card, no. Showing him that red card, or showing the red card to Rooney, or showing... oh, there was one to a Czech Republic player [Tomáš Ujfaluši] during Czech Republic v Ghana... or showing a red card here in my own country. It's just a player on a team... pfff. It's the same.

⊕ *Obviously, that decision was correct. A headbutt to the chest — no room for doubt there! But discussion has continued about the role of the fourth official in that decision. In 2006, did you get a word in your ear from the fourth official?*

[Standing up to pace around the lobby, as if he's back on the pitch] It was all done over the headset. When Materazzi fell to the floor, the ball was up the other end of the pitch and of course I was keeping up with play over there. I whistle for a handball and give a free-kick. Then play switches and goes back into the half of the pitch Materazzi was lying in, but on the other wing, and I remember it was at that point that I saw him lying on the floor. I wait to see whether he gets up — he doesn't get up... doesn't get up... doesn't get up — and I stop the match. From where I was to where Materazzi was, was a walk of about 25, 30 metres. So immediately I ask my assistant, Darío García, [touching a finger to his ear to indicate the headset] "Darío, did you see anything? What happened? Why's he on the floor?" He tells me, "I don't know, I see him there on the floor but I didn't see what happened." Then I ask Rodolfo [Otero, the other assistant referee], who was on the other touchline, in the other

half of the pitch — without much hope, because he was a long way away — and he tells me, "No, me neither." And that's where I start to think... [blows out his cheeks] I had a lot of doubts, clearly something had happened, but if no one saw what it was... and then Luis Medina Cantalejo's voice [the fourth official] appears in my headset, and he says, "Horacio, Horacio, I saw it," he says to me. "A really violent headbutt by Zidane on Materazzi, right in the chest."

So obviously, when I get to the spot, I already know Zidane is on his way. I got to the spot, to where Materazzi was, and the Spaniard [Cantalejo] had already told me what I needed to know to make the decision that Zidane was going to leave the pitch. What I then asked [Cantalejo] was, "Why did he headbutt him?" — whether he'd seen whether Materazzi had done anything beforehand — and he replied, "No, honestly I don't know. I just saw the headbutt." And when I got there, I realised that the players didn't know what was going on either, apart from [Gianluigi] Buffon who was protesting to the assistant, pressuring him, and [Gennaro] Gattuso, but the others saw almost nothing, just like me. And the noise in the stadium... the crowd just went silent, as if to say, "What's going on? Why is that player lying on the floor?" And me in the middle of it, thinking, "Right then... how do I make this decision clear? Zidane's going, he's standing there calmly."

It didn't seem very correct, to me, to just *BANG!* take a red card out like that, as if from nowhere, with the crowd and players all having seen that I'd been in the other half and hadn't seen anything. So, since the headsets were only new, you can see if you watch it on video that I go over to Darío García... I went over to Darío, but I knew Darío didn't know anything! So, why? Well, because that *is* understandable. Everyone understands if you go over to the assistant that it's because the assistant is going to tell you something to help you make a decision. So I get to Darío, and I just say to him, "Focused!" — I say it to him and I say it to myself, to remind us both, "there are still 10 minutes to go, stay focused." — I turn around and go to Zidane and take out the red card.

 Even though he hadn't been the assistant who told you...

No, he didn't tell me anything. How could he, if he didn't know? When I realised I needed to get the card out I thought, "Right then, let's see, how can I make this easily understood?" And I say to myself, "If the assistant calls you over, everyone knows that's because he's going to tell you something. It was a little bit of a disguise, but it contained some truth as to how the decision was taken.

 One of the questions that's continued to be asked since is whether the fourth official, Cantalejo, saw it happen on a television replay, or live.

At every point, the [fourth] referee was standing on the halfway line. The one who started this complaint, saying that he saw it on the video was [Raymond] Domenech, the France manager. Why? Well... at World Cup matches, between the two benches, there's a monitor of sorts. It's between the two banks, but set back from the pitch. That is to say, the fourth official has to walk about 10m to see that monitor and then come back

to pitchside. If the fourth official had done that, it would have been easy for anyone to spot. And the fourth official was always on the halfway line. When I spoke to Luis, I asked how he'd seen it, to be sure. That is, going back to the game, when he tells me, "I saw it, I saw a headbutt," right there and then. After the match I asked him again, whether he'd seen it on the monitor or on the field of play, and he told me, "No, I saw it on the pitch. The monitor didn't come into it."

 Following on from that, I wanted to ask as well whether you'd like referees to be allowed to use—

Ah, technology! I believe that when there's a case where the doubt and confusion is that big, that important and involves something that's going to affect the development of the match in such a major way, I think so, yes. Why not?

 Only for fouls, or if there's doubt as to whether the ball's crossed the goal line, or...?

Let's see. Technology today is a very useful tool. Football is — the rules of football, for the most part are — totally subjective, not objective. That is, there are very few things in football which you can measure. Goal or no goal, ball on or off the pitch, those are things you don't have to *interpret*, whereas whether a foul was inside or outside the penalty box, or offside decisions — was he off when he received the ball or not? But in which *phase*? Because when the referee has to decide to sanction an offside that was about a player moving into position to distract an opposing player [without receiving the ball], it becomes interpretative. It's become subjective.

So there are very few things and maybe you could add to the list, I don't know, aggression, a stamp behind the referee's back so that he can't see it. There are very few things that can be measured.

In terms of all the rest of the laws of the game, it's very interpretative. I mean, can the referee interpret whatever he wants? No. He's got a law to interpret and the standards that spring up from that law contain a concept which you have to interpret according to what's written down.

🔵 *Would you like to see any other change in how matches are refereed and rules applied?*

No... for me, the rules of football are just fine. I'd like to see just that, how technology could be used a little to see whether football can incorporate it within the rules of the game — to start with, how technology and those rules can live with one another, how they adapt, and afterwards, going forward, to see whether we can use it for other points in the game, perhaps.

🔵 *As well as technology, there's also the example of the officials behind each goal, as we saw in the Europa League and the Champions League...*

The Paraguayan league has them as well.

🔵 *And here in Argentina, there's the aerosol spray to mark out where the wall needs to stand at free-kicks. I sometimes take foreigners to games here and they always say, "What a good idea!"*

For me the aerosol isn't really that important for a referee. Why? Because

the only thing it does — the only positive it has — is that there's a line and everyone can see that line, not just the referee and the players but also the fans and therefore see whether the wall creeps forward or not. The thing is, there's nothing to indicate whether the referee's made a mistake in drawing out the line — whether it's at 5 metres from the ball, say, or 9 metres. Plus, there's no guarantee the line will actually be respected, because, well, it's Argentinian football... they'll kick the line away so it disappears or they'll just stand in front of it. So, using that aerosol spray isn't going to help improve the standard of officiating.

The officials behind the goals, I think have good and bad points. The down side is that instead of four officials, you've got six. That makes reaching an agreement and working in a team much more difficult. That's point one. Point two: what needs to be asked about and measured out is whether the quality of decisions inside the penalty box has improved with those two officials behind the goals, or whether it's remained the same. I think it's remained the same. They haven't improved. Also, to transfer that to South America, for most of South America [aside from Paraguay], it would require a lot of preparation — we'd need to train up a huge number of new referees and get them all up to Primera División standard just for that job, and the budget that would require would be... well, it'd be a big investment, and it doesn't seem like that big of a deal to me. It seems to me more like a kind of marketing strategy. They look really nice, don't they, standing behind the goal? But it must be said that they offer greater security because there are more people "controlling" the game, and who knows, the players maybe think, "Okay, I've got another pair of eyes looking at me now. He'll call a foul if he sees it, he'll punish me..." I don't know about that, really, but I suppose it would be one more person watching.

⊕ *No one's perfect. You must have taken a decision, at some point—*

[Laughing] Loads! Awful ones!

⊕ *—and then, on seeing it on TV, realised it was mistaken. What does a referee think when that happens? And does the size or importance of the match affect those thoughts? If you'd realised later that evening that the red card you showed to Zidane had been unjustified...*

No. A mistake is a mistake. Committing a mistake in a World Cup final, in the local league or in a continental competition is all the same. It's a mistake. It could be more or less noticeable for the media, more or fewer people might see that mistake, that's all circumstances, nothing more. But the mistake always lives on with you, no-one likes doing anything badly, no-one likes being wrong and much less to see on the television when you've messed up a decision, because, well, you think about the other person — that is to say, you think of the player, who's trained so hard, put in so much effort, of the manager, the fans, and then you made one wrong decision, which might even have thrown the result of the match totally — and you feel awful.

When you first sit down afterwards, after a while you start to realise that everyone makes mistakes, that you're a human being and that everything you do, you do in good faith, both the correct decisions and the wrong ones. And then you can start to take that pressure off, because at first you feel *so* guilty.

⊕ *Do you remember any of your decisions in particular that were just awful?*

Hmm, which ones should I tell you... I remember in a Ferro v River match, I awarded three penalties. Not one of them should have been given! [Laughs] Let's see, other matches... whenever you look at really controversial incidents... when they're within a certain range of being correct or being a mistake, it's like this: some people think you've messed up and others don't, they say you were right. There was another one in the Primera División, Unión de Santa Fe against Newell's Old Boys, a short player, there was a shot on goal, he was standing on the line, little short guy, and he jumped up with both hands. I give the penalty, because he'd touched it over with his hand. But he hadn't — the ball had hit the crossbar, never touched his hands, they were at the same height as the bar, but the ball hit the crossbar *between* his hands, he had them wide open. That was a mistake which caused a lot of anger, partly because [having given the penalty] I had to send him off and apart from that he was a nice kid... yes, so many mistakes! [That late penalty gave Newell's a 2-1 win].

⊕ *What about the Ferro v River game, who did you give the penalties to?*

Two of them to Ferro, one to River. Does that make me a Ferro fan?

⊕ *Don't worry, I won't tell anyone. To finish, you have two boys—*

And two girls. Two sons, two daughters.

Of course, I'm sure you want all of them to live their own lives, but if one of your sons does go into football, what would make you happier: that he become the next Elizondo, or the next Messi?

No question, every single time the next Messi! For so many reasons. First, because as a player he'd have a lot more people who would look up to him. Albeit it can't be entirely easy to live like that, because there are so many things that must just stop being private, perhaps you're not left with much freedom to just do what you want. But of course, if he feels happy with that life, I'm happy for him. Wanting to be an Elizondo would be more complicated, partly because he'd always have hanging over him the fact that everyone would compare him with me. Are you better or worse than your father? That can't be fun. Sons [of famous fathers] are always going to live being compared, from that point of view, and I don't think it would be a very productive comparison for my sons, I think at some point that you need to make a cut between father and son — my father was that, but this is what I am. But without a doubt, if he's able to become a Messi instead of an Elizondo... [Grins broadly]

The First Modern Ref

Refereeing a Cup final cost Harry Nattrass his job but he became the greatest official of his age

By Alexander Jackson and David Toms

In the week before the 1936 FA Cup Final between Arsenal and Sheffield United, the appointed referee was sacked from his job for spending too little time at work. Unlike many top-flight referees, Henderson (commonly known as Harry) Nattrass didn't work in an office, school or other middle-class profession, he worked down the pit. A coal miner since the age of 14, he worked at Seaham Colliery, near Sunderland. It was owned by Lord Londonderry, one of most aristocratic coal owners in the country.

That an unemployed miner refereed the Cup final may surprise many. Until they professionalised recently, referees were one of the last remnant of the Victorian amateur tradition that was such a strong feature of British sport until well into the 20th century. David Elleray, Harrow schoolmaster and referee of the 1994 FA Cup Final would seem to have more in common with one of the linesmen in 1936, Dr AW Barton, a Cambridge University graduate and schoolmaster at Repton, than he does with a pitman-referee from the economically depressed North East.

Normally, telling Harry's story would be impossible. In contrast to the vast numbers of books about clubs and players, referees and refereeing attract little attention outside of their own circle. But Harry's story can be told here because of a wonderful donation to the National Football Museum by his family. From an archive of newspaper cuttings, letters, telegrams and other personal mementoes kept by Harry it is possible to offer a rare and fascinating insight into his refereeing career.

And what a career it was, for Harry was a very special referee. A frail child, he apparently never kicked a football and took up refereeing after his wife suggested it as an alternative to watching games. The youngest man to referee a Cup final before the Second World War, his appointment caused controversy as more experienced referees were passed over in favour of an official who helped pioneer the diagonal system of refereeing which is still used today. Held in high esteem, he not only refereed Scotland v Germany, when the Swastika flew over Ibrox, but several times for the Irish Free State. Respected as one of Britain's top referee's Harry quite literally stood out from his contemporaries. Wearing a plum-coloured outfit, he earned the nickname of 'Natty Nattrass' for his bright and distinctive dress. This then, is the story of Harry Nattrass.

"Seaham Harbour is like no other town I have ever seen. It is a colliery town on

the coast. It looks as weird as a cart-horse with scales and fins." JB Priestly, English Journey, *1933*

Harry Nattrass was born in 1897 in Seaham Harbour, a mining town in County Durham. Employment revolved around the coal mines and harbour owned by the Londonderry family. When JB Priestly visited in the middle of the depression he described a town, "almost entirely composed of miner's cottages, laid in dreary monotonous rows. They were so small that they made the whole town look diminutive, as if it were only playing in a miserable fashion at being a town."

In one cutting from the *News of the World*, Harry described the origins of his interest in football and refereeing. "As a schoolboy, attending the elementary school at New Seaham, I was lightly built and of poor physique," he said. "Not being strong enough to play football I had to be content to follow the 'doings' of my own school team, from which emanated the ex-Huddersfield and English international centre half-back, Tom Wilson.

"At the age of 14 I left school and went to work in the mine at Seaham Colliery. Wages were small, and quite naturally 'pocket money' was in proportion. The train fare from Seaham to Sunderland was 9d. This, plus 6d I had to pay to see the game, just about brought me to the end of my resources. As I got older I attended the games at Roker Park more frequently, and took an interest not only in the players, but in referees, all the time learning the finer points of the game, and acquiring a sound knowledge of the rules of the referee's chart.

"It was purely out of interest in the game that I did these things. I had no idea about qualifying as a referee, until one day my wife, who had grown somewhat tired of the attention that I devoted to the game remarked: 'As you appear to be so keen on football, why don't you take up refereeing?' It gave me an idea, and in July, 1921, I went to Sunderland and sat an examination under the Durham Football Association, I obtained a certificate for proficiency, and I applied to be placed on the list of Seaham and District referees the following season."

Between 1921 and 1930 Harry worked his way up the pyramid of North Eastern football, before earning a chance to become Football League linesman in somewhat unusual circumstances. The original nominee from the Sunderland area was not Harry but his friend Michael Combes. However, in a Newcastle v Sunderland referees football match Combes broke his leg and Harry replaced him for the 1930-31 season.

In 1933-34 he was promoted to the Supplementary List of Referees and his first game in the Football League was Blackburn Rovers v Arsenal, a game that he recalled as "the finest League match I ever controlled." By the start of the next season he was on the Full List of Referees. Within two more he was striding out onto the Wembley turf after becoming one of the most controversial appointments to a Cup Final.

"You take my breath away! Is it really true?" Northern Echo, *April 1936*

Harry was not just being modest when he asked the reporter from the *Northern Echo* to repeat the news of his appointment to referee the 1936 FA Cup Final: he was probably genuinely surprised. For at the age of 38, Harry became the youngest man to take charge of the Cup final.

Usually, the honour was given to a referee of considerable experience and this departure from protocol was not well received by all. One critic of the FA's decision was the former referee JT Howcroft. Arguably Britain's leading referee of the early twentieth century, he refereed in the Football League between 1899 and 1925, overseeing the 1920 FA Cup Final and 18 international matches. Later a regular contributor to the press, he criticised the decision in the *Sheffield Green'Un* on the eve of the Cup final in an article entitled "The Cup Final Referee: Plain Words to the FA — A good man chosen, but why are long-service experts passed over?"

Calling the decision a "bombshell", Howcroft argued that the FA's abandonment of protocol threatened to undermine the wider importance of the appointment. Appealing "for a broader view", he argued that the "obvious inference in the FA's action is that nowadays, if a man can have some luck and enjoy a good time for a season or so, he is as likely to get the first prize open to referees as a man who has given the very best service to the game for tens of years... I still consider that injustice has been done in passing over so many men who were eligible to the Wembley prize."

While Howcroft may seem uncharitable, he did have a point. Of those Cup final referees appointed between 1919 and

1935, only one other referee had been appointed so early in their career; J Davies in 1921 — he was on the Football League list for only two years. Otherwise, no other referee was appointed to the final without at least four years on the Full List. Indeed, several referees waited for a decade or more before getting the final. Among the letters that Harry kept was one from another referee called Bert Bowie, who had spent 10 years at the top. It wished Harry well but also expressed Bert's disappointment at missing out. Why, then, did Harry get the game?

In part, Harry indeed had had a very good couple of years. At the end of the 1934-35 season he ran the line at Hamden Park before a crowd of 130,000 for Scotland v England. The following season he was selected to referee the English League v the Irish League, Scotland v Ireland and Ireland v Wales.

Of the Inter-League match Harry wrote, "I have little doubt that this match proved a big step on my way to Wembley. I believe I had a good match, and as a result I was chosen to referee the international Scotland v Ireland, at Edinburgh. After this game I was congratulated by Mr Fleming, the president of the Scottish FA, and was also complimented in the press of the following days.'

Harry had earned an unusually rich series of top-level appointments. The praise bestowed on him would not have been lost on Stanley Rous, a former referee and the newly appointed secretary of the FA in 1934. And here, perhaps, lies the key to Harry's surprise appointment.

A former grammar-school teacher, Rous was a genial but determined moderniser, seeking consensus rather than confrontation. While he helped oversee a raft of changes in his time at the FA, one of his most enduring was one of his earliest projects; the diagonal refereeing system. This was a response to the difficulties faced by referees after the change in the off-side law in 1926 made the game faster and faster. Used across the world, it still remains the standard way of organising the responsibilities of the three officials for maximum efficiency.

Although who exactly invented it is uncertain, Rous certainly played a key part in establishing it, having both used it during his refereeing days and then pushed for its adoption as an administrator. Publishing an FA memorandum on how to apply it in January 1935, Rous oversaw its eventual incorporation into the Referee's Chart in 1938-39.

However, Rous faced some opposition from Charles Sutclifffe, secretary of the Football League and a former referee himself, who favoured an alternative scheme of two referees, one in each half. Although now consigned to the realms of amusing what-ifs, Sutcliffe's proposal was, in its own way, an intelligent, if different response to the problems faced by referees. The idea of two referees may now seem surreal, but in the mid-1930s it was genuinely considered as a possibility. Sutcliffe had lobbied for it for nearly a decade and in 1935 had managed to get the FA to arrange two trial matches. Although Sutcliffe's scheme received mixed reviews, it was still alive and kicking in 1936.

What Rous probably wanted at this time was a referee who could show off the diagonal system to best effect. One cutting revealingly notes that "the FA people are keen to have the busy referee on their side: the man who doesn't loll through a game, the man who has the pace to chase up and down and keep in direct touch with the incidents of play. Nattrass is a lean kind: he can run and he can command."

Harry's command of games was based on a thorough, even professional approach to his craft. Clifford Webb, one of Britain's leading sporting writers of the 1930s remarked after one game that "Last year's Cup final referee is recognised as being one of the best at his job. Maybe that is because he treats refereeing with all the importance that it deserves. He invariably takes stock of a pitch before a match starts and 'arms' himself accordingly. He knows all the players' methods of ankle strengthening, bandaging for quicker turning on the field, and things of that sort, and uses them himself."

He was also thorough in his dealings with his linesmen, a crucial factor in using the diagonal system well. WG Gallacher of the Daily Record wrote in 1938 that Nattrass "told me that he made it a habit prior to every game, of having a conference with his linesmen to whom he explained his ideas of what their duties should be, with the request —perhaps I should say the instruction — that they operate accordingly."

One of Harry's most distinctive features was his dress sense. Referees were not governed by any strict rules on what they could wear and where possible, Harry turned out in maroon jacket and shorts or a white shirt with red cuffs and collar to help him stand out.

Sports writers loved it and many of the clippings that Harry kept commentated on his dress, with one writer calling him "Natty Nattrass." One artist even based a cartoon match report around him, noting that "Positively the nicest thing in referees was on view at the Grimsby match (H Nattrass, Esq). His suit was a symphony in heliotrope. He outshone Cleopatra's barge for colour."

If the controversy over his appointment weren't enough to daunt him, Harry was then sacked from his job at Seaham Colliery. On the one hand, the colliery had some cause for complaint as Harry had apparently only been able to work 11 days in 1936. The coal industry was still suffering from the depression of the 1920s and in the uproar over Harry's dismissal not all sided with him. One writer to the *Northern Mail* complained that "many a man would have welcomed Mr Nattrass's opportunity to work at the pit, with five shillings a week for rent and free coal. These seem to me matters that deserve consideration before any man takes on jobs that prevent him doing his own regular work." *The News of the World* reported his sacking and, within 24 hours, presumably to avoid further bad publicity, Harry was offered his job back at the end of the season, although Harry said he would consider his options before accepting it. In the end he took a job as a Colliery Welfare Official which took him out of the pit and into the office.

Despite all the controversy and stress, it was normal pre-match nerves that kept Harry Nattrass awake all night before the final. On arrival at the stadium, though, he would no doubt have been moved by all the messages of support sent by his friends, family and colleagues. These are perhaps the most touching items in the collection as you try to imagine Harry's reaction as they were passed to him in the build-up. Perhaps he enjoyed a smile as the Sunderland Referee's Society told him to "take hold a Northeast grip. Best of luck."

To referee at Wembley before a crowd of 93,384 was something new, even to Harry, and in the Newcastle *Sunday Sun* he described "how impressive the vast sea of faces seemed when I went out for the first time on to the Wembley turf. I had never previously even been to the Stadium to witness a match, far less officiate at one and the sight was awe-inspiring." Endearingly honest, he wrote that "I don't mind admitting that I was a bit 'windy' when I first came out but I soon found my bearings... after the first 10 minutes, however, I was quite OK. Everything went along swimmingly and I felt entirely at home. Never did I have the slightest difficulty in controlling the game."

The game was a tight one with a single goal from Ted Drake giving Arsenal the Cup but it passed without great controversy and Nattrass publically thanked the players for their sportsmanship. In turn the *Topical Times* praised him in terms that would have gratified both him and Stanley Rous. "There was no argument in this game. The goal brooked no complaint. Referee Nattrass, of Seaham, signalled the goal and all through the game he showed his infinite capacity for doing his job thoroughly and well; without flourish of whistle or trumpeting; without semaphoring and with sense. It was one of the best final tie referee displays ever given, and the pace of the man with the whistle kept him right on the spot where things were happening."

One of the first men to salute Harry after the final whistle was the Arsenal manager, George Allison, who had actually written to Harry before the game to congratulate him on his appointment — something he asked him not to mention. Sheffield United's manager, Teddy Davison, also tried to find him after the game but on missing him wrote to thank Nattrass for the "splendid and efficient" manner in which he controlled the game and commented that "the way in which you carried out your duties must have satisfied all and sundry that you thoroughly deserved the high and proud distinction which has been conferred upon you." As Harry put it in one newspaper, "these things — particularly a letter from the manager of the losing side — are things that any referee can appreciate."

"Who is the Busiest Referee?"

Harry had little time to take in his Cup final achievement for within the week he was refereeing the Channel Islands Cup Final, being presented with a crimson scarf. This kind of constant travel was a feature of a referee's career. At his peak in 1936 one paper estimated that he was refereeing two games a week in Britain and Ireland. While the Cup Final was the "blue riband" event of his refereeing career, he still enjoyed a distinguished career throughout the 1930. As well as refereeing regularly in England he was also popular at the international level in Scotland and in particular, Ireland, where he also refereed many club games.

After the Cup final, the next big game of Harry's career was equally controversial but for different reasons. Scotland v Germany in 1936 was the second visit of a football team representing Nazi Germany to the UK and the first between England and Germany in 1935 had attracted a storm of protest from the TUC and anti-fascist groups. Protests were planned in Scotland and a copy of the *Scottish Daily Record* that Harry kept records that five men were arrested for chalking anti-fascist slogans on walls while two other men were arrested at the game for shouting "Down with Hitler" and carrying a banner with anti-fascist messages. The view of the newspapers and the SFA was that football and politics should not mix and they tried to downplay the political dimensions of the game. Pathé News made similar efforts in their newsreel, with their commentator ignoring the striking opening images of a swastika fluttering over Ibrox and the German team giving the Hitler salute to all four sides of the ground. What Harry thought of it all is not recorded but he gave another good performance as Scotland won 2-0, although one paper called his disallowing of an early German goal for offside "a doubtful decision to say the least."

To cap an outstanding year Harry was then selected to referee a game between the Irish Free State and Hungary. This marked a new high in a distinctive part of his refereeing career. From around 1936 to 1939 he became a highly popular figure in Irish football refereeing three international games (all against Hungary), several Inter-league games between the Irish League of Northern Ireland and the League of Ireland from the Republic, and a number of FAI Cup-ties, Free State Shield and Free State League games. As a leading English referee, his views were eagerly sought by the Irish papers, especially when his interpretation of the laws differed from those in Ireland. After his first international match he told the *Irish Independent* that "Ireland might have got a second penalty in the second half when your inside-left was fouled, but he was in a scoring position and I played the advantage and he failed to use his chance." His use of the rule was questioned the next day in the same newspaper when it noted "few, if any of our referees here know of the advantage rule, or seldom employ it."

It wasn't the only time that Harry caused consternation with his decisions in Ireland. In 1938 he officiated the third attempt to settle a FAI Cup quarter-final tie between Bray Unknowns and Shamrock Rovers. Bray lost 2-1 and Nattrass was involved in Rovers' first goal when he stationed himself in the area for a corner kick. A clearance rebounded off him and in the scramble the ball was forced home. More theatrically, in a game between Cork and Shelbourne, a linesman flagged for a corner kick but Nattrass ignored him, whereupon the linesman dropped his flag and stormed off the field to be replaced by Tom Aungier, President of the League of Ireland.

Despite having achieved so much so young, Nattrass was still robbed of nearly half the top-flight career he might have enjoyed in normal circumstances. He refereed during the war, although exactly how often is unknown. He retained his natural enthusiasm for the game, which led to him being banned by the Durham FA for refereeing three games without renewing his referee's license. Even an appeal failed, much to disgust of one newspaper reporter who called Harry "one of the best ambassadors of

football we have ever had." Despite this he returned to top-flight duties for the 1946-47 season. At the end the Football League retired him "in order to give younger referees a chance," whereupon he quit refereeing altogether.

Still working for the newly nationalised Coal Board, he continued to be involved in football. Almost immediately he was signed by Barnsley and later Newcastle United as a scout. His most successful recommendation was the full-back Irving Nattrass (no relation) who played for Newcastle in the 1970s.

Harry lived out his passion for football but, as his granddaughter Helen Nattrass points out, there was a social cost at home. "The household suffered significant absences as he travelled to match locations around the country and abroad," she said. "I guess my grandmother would have had concerns about money at certain times, especially at the time Harry lost his job as a miner. As a consequence of all this, my father was never really interested in football and I can never remember him ever going to a match. However I do have clear memories, as a child, of Harry visiting our house in York when he had been on nearby scouting trips. He would arrive in the early evening on a Saturday and settle down quickly to write his reports in large angular writing. He was always wary if any of us had a cold. But he could always be tempted by the offer of one of our sweets."

It was refereeing for which he was remembered, though, and, when he died in 1974, aged 77, Nattrass's obituary noted that "his rise to prominence as one of Europe's top referees was unprecedented."

B

The Psychologist

Tom Henning Øvrebø on man-management and that game at Stamford Bridge

By Ben Lyttleton

This is a bit weird. I'm listening to classical music, sitting in the waiting room of Norwegian health centre in a smart district in central Oslo. There are tasteful pictures of female nudes on the walls and jars filled with condoms placed on every surface. It's not where I would expect to meet a former Uefa referee.

Tom Henning Øvrebø spends most of his week here. The centre specialises in helping teenagers cope with pregnancy (hence the condoms) and Øvrebø, on whose door is written his name and 'Psykolog', is a trained clinical psychologist who rents his office from the Centre. Two afternoons every week, Øvrebø works with athletes at Norway's Olympic training camp to improve their mental conditioning and it just so happens that on this particular afternoon, that's where he is.

Øvrebø is currently recovering from a knee injury but is still an active referee in Norway. For some reason, I did not expect him to struggle with his time-keeping, but when he eventually arrives, he is full of apologies. He is wearing jeans, a pink T-shirt and Converse trainers — again, something of a surprise (though I knew he wouldn't be wearing black shorts and a black T-shirt).

He is personable, charming and immensely proud of his refereeing career. In his office, there is a world map dotted with pins to indicate where he has taken charge of games. There are a lot of pins. He understands, though, that despite all the games in Norway, Uefa competitions and international football — he refereed two games at Euro 2008 and made the 14-man long-list, but not the final 10, for the 2010 World Cup — the one match he will be remembered for was the worst of his career. He laughs at how it works: for players, the memories are made from great moments, but for referees, from the mistakes. "That's the way it goes," he says. "I understand that and I don't mind it at all. In fact, I learnt a lot from that game myself."

Before we focus on the events of 6 May 2009, I want to ask Øvrebø about the psychology of the decision-making process under pressure. Between his two jobs, if he doesn't have an idea about it I don't know who will.

* As a psychologist trained to understand behaviours and motivations, did you feel at an advantage when you were on the pitch?*

Sport is a lot of psychology, with emotions, conflicts and communication, so it's not a disadvantage to have the theoretical background. You can understand the different psychological reactions of players and yourself but despite that, I still feel the same pressures and make the same mistakes as everyone else.

What came first, refereeing or psychology?

Refereeing! I started when I was 14 and my psychology studies began when I was 22 at university. I have been a referee for much longer. I played a lot of football and other sports when I was younger, and by coincidence I helped out as a referee and found it fun. From there it has gone step by step.

Why do you think northern Europe has produced so many elite referees in recent years?

Sweden has a good tradition of referees, so do Denmark and Norway, but it's hard to tell why. I think we all like to work very hard, we have a professional attitude, like all referees from other small countries who are at a high level, we are always very well prepared off and on the pitch.

How would you describe your style as a referee?

I tried to get a good dialogue with the players. I would smile and be proactive, maybe I was a bit... not soft, as I had to be strict, but I tried to get good communication as it made it easier for me and for the players. The most important thing for a referee is to take the correct decision: if it's a wrong decision, it's still a wrong decision whatever your style.

In many ways, referees are like players: they make choices under pressure on the pitch and constantly have their performances assessed. Why is there not more support between the two groups?

They are not necessarily against us, but nor are they very supportive. In the heat of the game, when you think of all that's involved — prestige, money, the high risks for the players — it's not like their main thing is to support the referee. But the biggest difference between players and clubs and countries is all about how they behave towards the referee. You find differences in some countries, where it's more okay to cheat the opponent and cheat the referee: for example, in England, they don't like simulation but in other countries it's more accepted.

If a player has a reputation as a diver, do you then take that into account if, say, he has been brought down in the box?

When you're a referee at the top level, you have to be well-prepared and know how different teams and players behave. Some players may have the tendency to simulate more than others, and that's a part of the referee's preparation.

At what point does it become hard not to be prejudiced against a certain player?

That's very important. Sometimes you have to take a decision in a split second, and you don't think about which player is involved. At other times, if you know a player has a history of simulation and he has a situation in the penalty area, it can be that you have some of that history with you when you take that final decision. It could be that it sways you.

⊕ *What about when players appeal for a decision: does that have any impact on you?*

If I give a penalty, my attitude is you have to be 100% sure, not 50% or 60%. If it's a free-kick in midfield, you could give it if it's a 'maybe, maybe not'. In the penalty area, you know that the consequences can be much bigger so I have to be 100% sure. It doesn't help if players again and again try to appeal for penalty. The referee still has to be 100% sure. The assistants can help here: that co-operation is important and I have had incidents when they have given a signal if I haven't seen it, or told me not to give one.

⊕ *The difference between players and referees is that players are allowed to make mistakes, and referees aren't. Why is that?*

It's hard to say but it's certainly true that referees make mistakes like everyone else. It's not just that the referee is the man in charge, the pilot, of the game but also important that he treats both teams equally. So if you make one mistake with Team A, you have not treated them equally. So what do you do with Team B? Is it correct to make a mistake with them too? Referees are not allowed to make mistakes and must treat everyone fairly. When I go out and referee, the players want to do their best but they make mistakes in every game: it could be a bad throw-in, free-kick, a foul or more serious, a penalty or sending-off. It's part of football but hard for people to accept it when it's a referee. If you're a referee

and you start to become afraid of making mistakes, then you're in trouble. Your focus will be all wrong.

⊕ *How would that affect your performance?*

If you're scared, you will think too much about the consequences and not have the courage to take difficult decisions. You may always try to play safe and that can be wrong sometimes: instead of taking the right decision, you maybe take the easiest decision. As a referee, that's the wrong perspective to have.

⊕ *How important is body language for a referee?*

Very! Of course if I make a decision and it's clearly wrong, then I will be in trouble but in my experience, it's not the decision itself that gets you into trouble but the way you sell it, if you like. The way you sell it will to a large extent be influenced by your body language, your posture, your eye contact. Sometimes you can smile a little, but it's not wise to stand there smiling if you've given a controversial penalty or as you show a red card. That would not go down well. You can use a smile when you give a decision to calm a player down or look away if you don't want a player protesting against you. Using body language correctly is a big part of it. I remember when I was a new referee, there was a game at Brann Bergen, who have fanatical fans. It was on TV and I gave a penalty. But as I awarded it, I was biting my lip. There was a picture in the paper of it and my appearance makes me look unsure about the decision even though I wasn't.

Body language, players protesting and making mistakes: it's hard not to talk about your most famous game as a referee, the Champions League semi-final between Chelsea and Barcelona.

There's a good picture of me from that game with [Michael] Ballack running after me appealing for a penalty. In that picture, it's not very confident. I don't look like the pilot of the game. When you look like that for every decision, it won't be very easy to sell that decision.

I sensed that the more the Chelsea players appealed, the more it had the opposite effect and the more you wouldn't give the decisions...

I can answer this not as a referee but as a psychologist: maybe the decision can go a bit in the other direction, to show, "I'm not influenced by the spectators." If you say, "I shall not be influenced by the crowd, I will be extra strong," it will still influence you one way or another. But it can be a negative influence for the team tying to appeal.

The Ballack appeal came after you turned down a fifth penalty appeal for handball against Gerard Piqué and it seemed the one most likely to be given. If that had happened in the first 20 minutes, before the atmosphere had become so hostile, would the decision have been different?

Unfortunately we will never know: I could have or I could not have! That's the fascinating thing about refereeing. It's all about the heat of the moment. In psychology, I can talk to my colleagues if there's something I'm not sure about — maybe we should give this medicine

or try this approach. But in football you need to take an instant decision in a split second. Sometimes that decision turns out to be wrong, but luckily most of the time the decision is correct.

We all know what happened after the game. Didier Drogba called the defeat "a fucking disgrace" and you were whisked out of the country in disguise and became the victim of threats from Chelsea fans. Did that affect your performances?

After the game, it's hard because the media always remind you, call and contact you. Referees at international level are not allowed to speak to the media. We speak to the media [after league games] in Norway, after we have a shower, and I think the relationship between the media and referees is okay, we don't have that much trouble here. In other countries, it's harder to have that relationship. With international matches, you are not allowed to speak and in many ways it's a positive, but it can also sometimes be a problem. The media can chase the story and not quieten it down immediately. Uefa says that if anyone did speak, there might be language problems with the quotes being mistranslated and with different football cultures, that could cause problems. So they decided to be strict. As a referee, I am loyal to that decision but sometimes it can be, well... To have a statement that says, "I've now seen the decision, I support my decision or unfortunately it turned out to be the wrong decision," would be good. I've done that in Norway and the media and the supporters accept it. Maybe there will be some headlines on the Monday but on Tuesday the story is quiet. If you say nothing, the story carries on. If a star player missed an important penalty in a big tournament, it would be easier for him to release a statement the same day, instead of not speaking to the media, as that will continue to give focus on him and the story will last longer. It's part of the job and I understand it, though. It's like in psychology: I must conduct myself in silence. It would be interesting to speak about my clients, I have some fantastic stories to tell, but I can't. Our employers don't want us to.

Are referees better now than 30 years ago?

I hope so, but players have developed too. There is more emphasis on fitness and personality, on knowing the laws of the game more correctly; there are more courses, more fixed teams of referees and assistants now. Like the players, referees are better than 30 years ago, also when it comes to preparation, but do referees now make fewer mistakes? I don't think so. The game has more speed, the players have more power, more money, are bigger stars, but if you look at the referees now and then, overall they are much more professional now.

Ben Lyttleton was speaking to Tom Henning Øvrebø for his book Twelve Yards: The Art and Psychology of the Perfect Penalty Kick *to be published in spring 2014.*

Limited Edition
Football Periodic-table Art Prints

On A Sixpence design neatly-structured art prints to depict renowned football teams and great football managers. Inspired by traditional football wallcharts, we spend a great deal of time researching, categorising and arranging key metrics relating to each subject in a periodic-table and then using an appropriate colour palette to reflect the history of the topic.

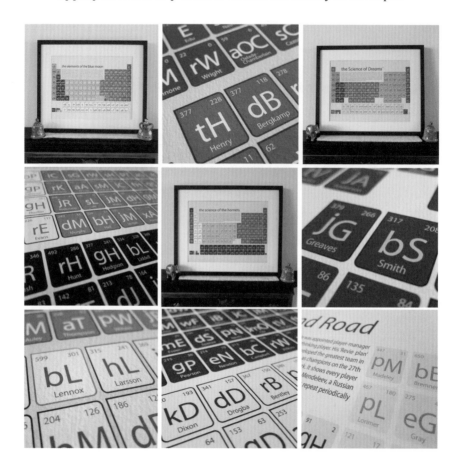

The 'Professor of Science' print, for example, shows every player to be selected by Arsène Wenger in his 17 completed seasons. Each cell includes the initials of the player with information on appearances and goals. Each image is a high quality giclée print, on a luxurious heavy weight Hahnemühle fine art paper. Prints can be personalised to include an additional cell with the name of your choice.

Prints include: Arsenal, Manchester United, Liverpool, Spurs, Chelsea, Manchester City, Fulham, Leeds United, Nottingham Forest, Crystal Palace, Celtic, Barcelona, England and Italy.

Recently featured in The Guardian's 'Beautiful Games' series

Available from www.onasixpence.bigcartel.com

131

Exile

"How was it possible that a man who had made football history in a country where the game is as loved as in Italy could be forgotten?"

The Lost Legend

Árpád Weisz was one of Serie A's first great coaches. He was also Jewish.

By James Horncastle

They came for Árpád Weisz, his wife Elena, son Roberto and daughter Clara in the early hours of 2 August 1942. A truck turned into Bethlehemplein, the square in the centre of Dordrecht, a Dutch town of no more than 50,000 inhabitants, and pulled up outside No.10, the house the Weiszes called home. Gestapo officers got out, walked up the steps leading to Weisz's door and knocked.

The noise roused neighbours from their sleep. Some switched lights on, others peered from behind their curtains. What they were witnessing was to become an all too familiar sight. The Weisz family were loaded into the back of the truck, as other local Jews would be, and driven away. They were gone, never to be seen in Dordrecht again.

Weisz had feared that this day would come. He had desperately hoped that it wouldn't. But it had long felt like only a matter of time, an inevitability. Nazi Germany had invaded on 10 May 1940. Five days later, following the bombing of Rotterdam and the threat of similar action over Utrecht, the Netherlands surrendered.

The racial laws introduced by the Nazis at the Nuremberg Rally in 1935 — laws which had already led Weisz and his family to leave Italy — were gradually imposed by the Reichskommissariat Niederlande, the occupying government, and its collaborators. This time there really was no escape. Weisz could have paid the price the Nazis were asking for safe passage out of the country, a price that rose from 20,000 to 50,0000 then 100,000 Swiss Francs within a year. But it's thought that, like many, he couldn't afford to. So the family stayed in Dordrecht and there they were stripped of their rights, one piece of legislation at a time.

Things began to get personal on 29 September 1941. That was the day the local police sent a letter to Weisz's place of work, DFC Dordrecht, one of the Netherlands' oldest football clubs. He had been their coach for two and a half years, but that was an end of it. The letter conveyed that, after seeking legal advice on Weisz's position, it was strongly recommended that DFC Dordrecht not appoint or retain any Jews in their service or else there would be damaging consequences for the club. The decision was ratified less than a month later.

Weisz was prohibited from attending Dordrecht's games and following their training sessions. The Nazis had made it impossible for him to coach. They had forced the club's hand. Dordrecht's chairman, a man by the name of Van

Twist, had little option but to relieve Weisz of his duties. He did so with great regret.

No one had achieved the kind of success at Dordrecht as Weisz had, not even Jimmy Hogan, the former Burnley and Fulham inside forward, who, frustrated at a lack of opportunities in England, had become a pioneering coach on the continent, one of the most influential there has ever been. Bottom of Eerste Classe West-II, one of the five regional groups Dutch football was divided into — with the winners of each playing-off to be named national champion — this small-town club was struggling in the spring of 1939. They were in need of a saviour and found one in Weisz.

Just how he came to Dordrecht's attention isn't clear. Briefly in Paris and unable to find work, it's thought that he wrote letters to football associations across Europe seeking opportunities. Perhaps one reached the KNVB. Its future chairman Karel Lotsy — who the journalists Frits Barend and Henk van Dorp would later claim collaborated with the Nazis and excluded Jews from Dutch football — was apparently the one who, on learning of Weisz's situation, reached out to him on Dordrecht's behalf, proof perhaps of how complex these times really were.

Lotsy's horizons were much broader than the Netherlands and it's possible that he'd heard of this great coach's achievements already. After a couple of meetings in Paris, thought to have been held in February and March 1939, Lotsy and Weisz struck an agreement. This was an extraordinary coup for Dordrecht. Not that many people outside of football's then tiny class of international cognoscenti realised it at the time. It was still a small world. Weisz was massively overqualified for the job. But the circumstances in which he found himself gave him little choice but to take it.

With Lotsy apparently acting as his interpreter, Weisz didn't take long to get his message across to Dordrecht's players, nor to impress on them that he was something very special and belonged on benches far more prestigious than theirs. Improbably, considering how late in the campaign he was appointed, he ensured they survived. And a year later perennial relegation battlers Dordrecht claimed the scalp of Feyenoord and finished fifth, exploits they'd repeat the following season. It was just incredible.

Weisz had completely transformed Dordrecht. "Some of us began to realise that he must have been a really great coach," Nico Zwann, one of the team's players, recalled. His methods were completely new to them, from how he physically prepared the team to his hands-on approach to training and the team meetings he held in a hotel the morning before games to go over strategy. Remember that football in the Netherlands was semi-professional until 1954. Tactically it was decades behind the best of Europe. But for the two years or so that Dordrecht were under Weisz's guidance, they were ahead of their time within their local context.

The players claimed not to be aware that he was a Jew. It didn't matter to them. It did, however, to the Nazis. Weisz's dismissal was sought and obtained. He was replaced by Ferry Triebel and although Van Twist apparently offered

Weisz financial support, money alone wasn't enough to help him out of a situation that was becoming more and more desperate.

His wife Elena had been forced to sew the star of David onto their clothes. His children, Roberto and Clara, were made to leave school. Jews were prohibited from shopping or using public transport between two and five o'clock in the afternoon and a curfew was imposed between 10 at night and six in the morning. The circle around Weisz and his family was closing tight. There was no way out. There was only a fateful knock at the door and a warrant for their arrest.

They were transported to Westerbork — the same transit camp Anne Frank would be held in a couple of years later. Then on 2 October 1942, Weisz and his family were placed on a train to the east. A day later, it pulled into Cosel, one of the sub-camps of Auschwitz and here, a selection was made. Around 300 men were ordered to disembark the train and forced into labour as part of the Nazi war effort. Fit and able, a man of sport, it's thought that Weisz was among them.

He was separated from his family and must have had to say an unimaginably sad and heartbreaking goodbye. The train that Weisz watched leave Cosel carried onto Auschwitz. Within hours of their arrival, Elena, Roberto and Clara were all killed in the gas chambers. Weisz would survive longer but not long enough to be alive when the Soviet army liberated Auschwitz at the end of January 1945. By then, he'd been dead almost a year. The cold and the exhaustion, it seems, had claimed him.

We know all this because someone had the curiosity to ask what had happened to Weisz and when the answers weren't forthcoming, resolved to go looking for them himself. That someone was Matteo Marani, the editor of *Il Guerin Sportivo*, the world's oldest football magazine.

"'Do you know Árpád Weisz?' I repeated in front of tens, maybe even hundreds of bewildered faces," Marani wrote. "For more than a year, that question accompanied me consistently. The more I came to realise that the story was unknown, however, the more the passion to discover, to excavate it grew. Above all I pushed to bring the final part to light, the part that wasn't written in the almanacs: his life after football. The end. How had Árpád and his family died?"

What Marani found was to shock him and the readers of *From the Scudetto to Auschwitz*, the book he wrote which would win Italy's national prize for literature. How was it possible, he asked, that a figure as influential as Weisz, a man who had made football history in a country where the game is as loved as in Italy, could be forgotten?

"The reality is that, 60 years after his death, all trace of Árpád Weisz had been lost," Marani explained. "And yet he had won more than anyone of his time, a glorious time in football, conquering Scudetti and trophies... much more than many acclaimed coaches today, coaches who make the front pages every morning and the news in the evening. Could you imagine if one of them were ever to disappear? It happened to Weisz."

Weisz was born in the Austro-Hungarian Empire on 16 April 1896. He grew up in Solt and would attend law school an hour or so's drive north in Budapest only for his studies to be interrupted by the First World War. Details are sketchy but it's been suggested that he was taken prisoner by Italian soldiers during the battle of Caporetto.

After the end of the conflict, Weisz returned to Hungary and, although he held down a job in a bank for a while, football was his calling. Tall, thin, with striking eyebrows and hair that brings to mind the film director David Lynch, he was an outside-left, apparently gazelle-like in his way of bounding up and down the wings for Törekvés and Makkabi Brno, with whom he played alongside Ferenc Hirzer, the first foreign player signed by Juventus following the club's acquisition by the Agnelli family.

Both were good enough to represent their country. Weisz, for instance, was in the Hungary side that drew 0-0 with Italy in Genoa on 4 March 1923 and it was there that he supposedly came to the attention of directors from Padova. They agreed to sign him a year later after the Olympic Games in Paris. Although Weisz didn't play in either Hungary's victory over Poland or their defeat to Egypt in France, just being a part of that squad and sharing the experience with his teammates must have been formative.

One of them was Béla Guttmann, a fellow Jew who, unlike Weisz, would evade the Holocaust and go on to have a long and peripatetic career as a coach, greatly influencing the development of the game in South America and twice winning the European Cup with Benfica. He was a strong personality and led something of a mutiny at

the 1924 Olympics. Incensed by the choice of hotel, its location in the noisy Montmartre district and the number of officials sent to accompany them, he led Weisz and the rest of the squad on a rat-catching exercise. They then tied their prey to the door handles of the various officials' rooms. How much Guttmann and Weisz learned from each other and whether their vision of football was formed over the encounters they had together is unknown but the thought of it captures the imagination as both men would do so much to shape the game over the years that followed.

Soon after the Olympics, Weisz left Hungary and went to Italy to play for Padova. He scored on his debut, against Andrea Doria, but would make only six appearances in the 1924-25 season. Opportunities to prove himself were few and far between.

New to Italy, perhaps for a time Weisz thought that it wasn't for him. There was a club there, however, that had been founded precisely with players like Weisz in mind — foreign players. They called it Internazionale. Weisz could identify with this team. He fitted in.

But after a promising beginning to his career in blue and black, Weisz was struck by grave misfortune. He suffered an injury from which, at a time when surgery was not sufficiently advanced, there was no coming back. Not yet prepared to hang up his boots but aware that it would be at least a year before he'd be in a condition to attempt to resume his career, it's been claimed (without great certainty) that Weisz put his time out of the game to good use and went on a sabbatical. His destination was apparently South America. And more specifically, Uruguay.

Why there? Well, perhaps the team he'd watched win the Olympics in Paris had made such an impression on him that he wanted to know more about them. *La Celeste* were recognised as the best side in international football at the time and would demonstrate it again by winning the 1930 World Cup.

What Weisz did across the Atlantic is shrouded in mystery. There have been suggestions that he made his first tentative steps in coaching in Montevideo with a brief spell at América, a club that no longer exists but, again, reports are unconfirmed.

Faced with the prospect of retirement, it seems fair to assume that he must have been contemplating a move into coaching. And if he weren't already, he would definitely have done so on his return to Italy when Inter made it clear that they didn't believe he was capable of playing again. A new chapter of Weisz's life was about to begin: within it he'd write many of the most important pages in the history of Italian football.

It started with a short apprenticeship as assistant to Alessandria coach Augusto Rangone. For the previous four years, Rangone had also been a member of the Italian federation (FIGC)'s technical commission and, following the failure of the national team at the 1920 Olympic Games in Antwerp, he had been concerned with raising the standard. Open to new ideas, it's thought he held a profound appreciation for the Danubian school.

Indeed, Italy looked to it over the twenties and thirties for inspiration, so much so that by 1935 seven of the 16 clubs in Serie A were coached by Hungarians. It was over this period, for instance, that József Viola became the first coach [followed by Giovanni Trapattoni and Alberto Zaccheroni] to work at each of Italy's Big Three. As trainers, the Danubians were highly-regarded, a perception that Weisz would enhance.

After a couple of months working as Rangone's No.2, he went back to Milan to become coach of Inter in the summer of 1926. By then the club was known as Ambrosiana, a name imposed after a merger with the financially more stable US Milanese by the Fascist government in accordance with its diktat against the use of all foreign names and words. Ideologically speaking, Internazionale had socialist connotations that didn't sit well with the regime. Weisz also had to Italianise his name to Veisz. But whatever the regime wished to call the club and its coach, it wasn't long before Italians were referring to them by a different title: winners.

In 1930, the inaugural year of Serie A as a single-tier league rather than one divided into regional and inter-regional rounds, Inter were crowned champions of Italy. Weisz became the first foreign coach ever to win the *Scudetto* and, at 34, the youngest too, an honour he still holds (although many cling to the mistaken belief that the record is held by Trapattoni).

Top of the scoring charts that season for the first time was a player who'd define the era — arguably the greatest Italian footballer of all time — a future double

World Cup winner, after whom they'd later rename the stadium. Giuseppe Meazza found the net 31 times. He was only 19.

Weisz had taken a chance on him after he'd been rejected by Ambrosiana's rivals AC Milan because he was too thin. He bulked Meazza up with steaks paid for by the club and got him training in front of a wall, kicking the ball against it to improve his technique with both feet.

When Fulvio Bernadini, Inter's striker at the time of Meazza's emergence, revealed with great tactical awareness that he felt better use could be made of his own skills in midfield, Weisz was all for it. "Now I can play the kid," he replied. Meazza was given his debut against Como in the Coppa Viola and so began a career in which he'd score 272 goals.

Bernadini was a player who would later develop into a great coach himself. No trainer other than 'Fuffo' has ever won a *Scudetto* with two different teams based outside the traditional centres of power — Milan and Turin: he did it with Fiorentina and Bologna. He'd later acknowledge Weisz's part in the formation of his ideas on coaching. As would Gipo Viani, another of his players at Inter, who'd become a three-time *Scudetto*-winning coach at Milan and is credited by many as the father of *catenaccio*.

Weisz's contribution to the tactical evolution of football can perhaps be gauged by the reaction to *Il Giuoco di Calcio*, the book he co-wrote with Aldo Molinari, Inter's director of sport. It became a reference point among his peers. The preface was written by none other than the *commissario tecnico* of

Italy, Vittorio Pozzo, who remains the only coach to lift the World Cup twice.

His respect for "my two friends, who harmonise their efforts of instructing and guiding Ambrosiana, the most technical of Italian teams" shines through. Weisz was considered someone of the *avant garde*. His teams played a W-M, the invention pioneered by Arsenal manager Herbert Chapman in the same period. Bearing in mind that there's no evidence they ever met or saw each other's teams play, it's safe to assume that Weisz had the same intuition as to the best way to react to the 1925 change in the offside law.

Other innovations attributed to him include the *ritiro*, the assembling of the team at a hotel or a training camp the night before a game, which would become a mainstay in Italian football. At Bologna, Weisz would persuade the president Renato dall'Ara to subcontract a Turin-based company, De Bernardi, to maintain the pitch at the Littoriale to his specifications. He'd request that the dressing-rooms be heated and a treatment room established so that a club doctor might perform tests on the players, ascertain their condition, what their potential was and how they might recover from injury.

A moderniser, Weisz was doing the unheard of in Italy and at Bologna he'd achieve the unprecedented.

After leaving Inter in 1931, he took a step down to coach the Serie A debutantes Bari, whom he saved from relegation in a play-off against Brescia. Inter missed Weisz so they brought him back. But the arrangement didn't last.

Their new president Ferdinando Pozzani — or 'General Po', as he was known — was a precursor of the *mangia-allenatori* ('coach-eaters') that would become a feature of the game in Italy. In seven years at Inter, he went through seven different coaches. Pozzani was one of those presidents who liked to interfere. He wanted to have his say on the team's composition and configuration. And when he had the nerve in 1934 to bring in another coach to work with Weisz, undermining his authority, their relationship came to an end.

Weisz then accepted a post with Novara. They were struggling in Serie B but he managed to turn things around and steered them to fourth place. This was his one experience outside the top-flight. It was only a matter of time, with a reputation like his, before he was offered a chance to be back among the elite.

The spring of 1935 brought with it a call from Bologna. They were an establishment club and had friends in high places, as illustrated by the way they'd become *campione d'Italia* for the first time a decade earlier, an achievement remembered as the *Scudetto delle pistole*. At the time Italian football was divided into regional and inter-regional leagues. The winners of the two northern leagues played off with the winners facing the victor of the central-south region in a championship game.

And so Bologna had come up against William Garbutt's Genoa, the holders. The two teams couldn't be separated. Bologna won at Marassi and Genoa won at the Sterlino meaning a third play-off was necessary, to be held on neutral ground in Milan. What happened there was scandalous.

Genoa were 2-0 up with half an hour to go. The tie, it seemed, was over. Only it wasn't. Bologna's striker Giuseppe Muzzioli forced a save from Genoa's goalkeeper, the great Giovanni de Prà. It led the referee Giovanni Mauro to signal a corner, which unexpectedly provoked a pitch invasion. From nowhere a number of thugs, supposedly armed and wearing black shirts, descended on to the pitch and surrounded Mauro. He was coerced into thinking that Muzzioli's shot had crossed the line before De Prà had got to it. To the disbelief of the crowd, Mauro blew his whistle and awarded a goal. Bologna equalised soon afterwards and there was outrage.

Fingers were pointed at Leandro Arpinati, a Bologna fan and local leader of the Fascist squads who'd brought "order" to the left-leaning city after the First World War. He was apparently in the stands that day and it's supposed that he organised the chaos. If the FIGC's rules had been followed, then Bologna would have forfeited because of the pitch invasion. Arpinati, however, ensured that they weren't, practically standing over Mauro's shoulder as he wrote a report downplaying the incident.

The play-off went to a fourth game, played in Turin. After it ended in another draw, tensions rose further. There was a stand-off between Bologna and Genoa fans at the city's Porta Nuova station. Shots were fired. Blood was drawn. Two Genoa supporters were hit. As a consequence, Bologna were fined, leading to protests and a campaign against the FIGC.

In the meantime, Turin refused to hold a fifth play-off because of the risks to public order. And so it was decided that it would take place instead on the outskirts of Milan. A date was put in the diary for September and Genoa's players relaxed. After all, there were supposed to be two months between the games. Except Arpinati somehow heard different. It was to be held on August 5.

Bologna therefore stayed in training and when they met Genoa behind closed doors at seven o'clock that morning on a pitch surrounded by carabinieri on horseback, they were in better shape. It showed. They won 2-0 and went on to claim the championship, beating Alba, one of the capital clubs who'd be fused to form AS Roma in 1927.

Referred to as *la stella rubata* by Genoa supporters, that *Scudetto* would have been their 10th and worthy in retrospect of a star, the special commemoration introduced by Juventus president Umberto Agnelli in 1958. Robbed of it, Genoa would never get as close again.

A year later Arpinati became mayor of Bologna — ascending to the office unelected — and would be named president of the FIGC, a position he held not without controversy. When he revoked the *Scudetto* from Torino in 1927 after they were alleged to have fixed a derby with Juventus, his intention appeared to be to award it to the runners-up, Bologna. He thought better of it, though, and left the title unassigned for fear of being accused of bias.

Although Arpinati left his role with the FIGC in 1933, his presence still loomed over Bologna. The Fascist party, as

was their wont, thrust clubs on local businessmen. And so it was that Renato Dall'Ara became president of Bologna in 1934. Deferential but by no means a political puppet, he'd run the club more or less as he saw fit until his death in 1964. Some decisions were beyond his control, but before we get to them, let's return to Weisz's appointment.

He replaced a compatriot of his, Lajos Nems Kovács, midway through the 1934-35 campaign, inheriting a difficult situation. Results were initially shaky but he managed to stabilise them and secured a respectable sixth-place finish. Juventus, meanwhile, won their fifth straight *Scudetto*, a feat that the Grande Torino would repeat between 1943 and 1949 as Inter would between 2005 and 2010. The Old Lady seemed unstoppable. But not to Weisz. Looking at his squad, he dared to dream.

There was Angelo Schiavio, the striker who had scored the winning goal for Italy in the 1934 World Cup final. There was Raffaele Sansone, a quintessential Latin lothario from Uruguay, who'd marry a local waitress but wouldn't allow himself to be tied down. On the other side of midfield was his compatriot Franciso Fedullo. They were interchangeable, so much so that the pair of *mezzale* became known as Fedone and Sansullo.

Positioned between them was another man from Montevideo, Michele Andreolo, the *regista* of Bologna's play, a real leader. His teammates would follow him everywhere — supposedly even to the brothels around via Indipendenza on nights spent drinking late and playing cards.

At the back, replacing the captain Eraldo Monzeglio, a friend of Benito Mussolini's who moved to Roma where, when he wasn't playing, he taught tennis to il Duce's children, was a kid from the academy, Dino Fiorini. An agile defender, he would involve himself in the National Republican Guard once Italy became engulfed in the Second World War and be killed by partisans in 1944.

It was a team that Weisz, together with Filippo Pascucci, a former gymnastic instructor on cruise liners, took little time to get into shape and into contention. Bologna would leave Juventus in their wake — breaking a cycle — and edge Roma and Torino to the *Scudetto*, the club's third and its first for seven years. They clinched the title with a 3-0 win against Triestina, an own-goal from Nereo Rocco, one of the defining managers of the future, bringing jubilation.

In August 1936, Weisz and his players would be granted an audience with Mussolini. It was a photo-opportunity and little else. Still one wonders what Weisz must have been thinking as he stood before the man who during the preceding year had allied himself with Nazi Germany. The regime had begun its spiral into oblivion. Mussolini's hunger for an empire, the invasion of Abyssinia, the sanctions and pariah status conferred on Italy by the League of Nations, had led him to turn to Adolf Hitler, bringing about an acquiescence with his hate-filled view of the world. Weisz can't but have noticed that the atmosphere around him was beginning to change.

Perhaps to distract himself, he threw himself into his work. Schiavio, Bologna's all-time top scorer, retired that summer. His loss, heavy though it was, wouldn't weaken Weisz's team. Far from it. They'd long been grooming Carlo Reguzzoni as Schiavio's successor and he wouldn't disappoint. Bologna comfortably retained their title, an accomplishment that, prior to them, only Juventus had realised.

At the end of the 1936-37 season, they were invited to participate in the Tournoi International de l'Expo Universelle de Paris. It featured the champions of France, Olympique de Marseille, the Coupe de France winners, Sochaux, the champions of Austria, FK Austria Wien, the champions of Czechoslovakia, Slavia Prague, the DFB Pokal winners, VFB Leipzig, the now defunct Hungarian side FC Phöbus Budapest and Chelsea, admittedly a mid-table team in England, one that had never won a major trophy, but a representative from the revered home of football nonetheless.

The competition was considered a forerunner to the European Cup, which would only come into being in 1955. As such it was treated with the utmost seriousness and Bologna reached the final, knocking out Sochaux and Slavia Prague. Once there, they blew away Chelsea 4-1, Reguzzoni scoring a famous hat-trick. This was a moment of great significance.

Weisz's Bologna had triumphed on the continent. By doing so, his team became the first side from Italy to defeat an English club in a competitive match. They entered folklore as "the team that shook the world". A lesson had been given to the masters of football and that lesson had been taught by Weisz. It was the source of huge personal pride, the highlight of his career, the zenith. He deserved recognition as one of the greatest coaches of his time. What he'd achieved, however, would earn him no favours, nor did he ask for any.

After joining the Axis Powers and withdrawing from the League of Nations in late 1937, the Fascist regime in Italy published the Manifesto of Race in the summer of 1938 and began to enact it in the autumn. A census of foreign Jews living in Italy was carried out and printed. Weisz and his family were on it. For a time, it looked as though they wouldn't have to leave the country. Those foreign Jews who had been resident in Italy prior to 1933 would be permitted to stay. Mussolini, however, amended that in August so that only those resident before 1919 could stay.

The discrimination against the Weiszes began to tell. Roberto had to leave school and his father was compelled to resign from his post at Bologna. His last competitive game in charge was a 2-0 victory over Lazio on 16 October 1938. He had to say goodbye to the country that he'd called home for the previous 15 years or so. The family had been notified of their obligation to leave Italy within six months of 7 September 1938. They had to pack their things, hand over the keys to No.39 via Valeriani and go. They were being deported, cast out. It was the beginning of the end: the starting point of a sorrowful and harrowing journey to Auschwitz via Paris and Dordrecht.

Weisz's exit was barely commented on in the local papers. There was a line here and there but little else. He was forgotten. Writing in a book to celebrate Bologna's 90th anniversary in 1999, one

of Italy's most prominent journalists of the last century, Enzo Biagi, a passionate fan of the club, reflected on the team of his teenage years and its coach. "He was called Weisz," he wrote. "He was very good but also Jewish and who knows what happened to him?"

Marani found out, in part, by consulting the archives of Roberto's old school. He obtained a list of his former classmates and set about contacting each of them. "Did you know Roberto Weisz?" he asked. One of them answered: "Yes... He was my best friend." His name was Giovanni Savigni. He'd kept in touch with Roberto after the Weiszes left Bologna, corresponding by letter, as their mothers did too. The last one that Savigni received from Roberto was dated 14 December 1940. It wished him a Happy Christmas.

The rest of their story Marani pieced together by consulting state and municipal archives, those of Yad Vashem, Dordrecht and of course Auschwitz. He became "a detective of memory", solving the case. But Marani didn't stop there. He sought recognition for Weisz.

In Bologna's centenary year, the city put up a plaque at the Stadio Renato dall'Ara commemorating him as "among the greatest coaches and innovators of his time". Another would be unveiled at San Siro in 2012 and on the occasion of Inter and Bologna's Coppa Italia quarter-final last season the players walked out wearing T-Shirts on which Weisz's image was printed. Underneath it was the slogan "No to racism." It marked how, within Italian football and society as a whole, Weisz has become a powerful symbol for tolerance.

His story is as relevant as ever. It appeals to our humanity and reminds us of the sentiments conveyed in a stanza of the "Canto of Ulysses" from Dante's *Inferno*, which Primo Levi, writing in *If This is a Man*, recalls desperately trying to remember in his effort to teach the assistant Kapo, Pikolo, some Italian while collecting a soup ration in Auschwitz:

Think of your breed; for brutish ignorance
Your mettle was not made; you were made men,
To follow after knowledge and excellence

Commit those words to memory and, with them, the great Árpád Weisz.

Closure

Travelling through Siberia with Avram Grant to find the graves of his grandparents

By Igor Rabiner

The Mi-8 helicopter flew over the never-ending taiga of the Komi Republic. We'd been passing over the green, gold and crimson tops of the trees for half an hour already, and there was nothing else: no roads, no cars, no rivers, no people. Only at such moments do you realise quite how vast Russia is.

One of the passengers stared out of the window. A year and four months earlier, Avram Grant had led Chelsea to a Champions League final against Manchester United, but Russia for him was not just Moscow, where that final took place, but something immeasurably greater. Sometimes Grant closed his eyes and it seemed that he was sleeping, but he was thinking — thinking that one of the main goals of his life, something he had been determined to do since the age of 15, was soon to be achieved.

One night he had heard a terrible scream coming from the next room. It was his father, Meir, shouting out in his sleep at some nightmare. His mother was sick that day and for the first time in years she was sleeping in a different room to her husband. Grant realised that nightmares had tortured his father every night but that his mother had known instinctively when he was about to shout out: just a touch and he had woken up, the horrors receding. It had been going on for years and Grant had had no idea.

Meir was an easy-tempered, lively, optimistic man. Sometimes he spoke briefly about his adolescence, and Avram heard about the mysterious land of Komi, where his grandfather, grandmother and two of his aunts were buried. But he had been sure that belonged in a distant past for his father. Meir, with his joyful nature, never made a cult of the past but lived for the present and the future.

Only at night could he not control himself. After hearing his father scream that night, Avram vowed that he would find out everything about what had happened to his family — and find the lost graves of those relatives who were buried in far-off lands.

And now he was flying to those graves.

Two days before he had set off, Meir came out of a coma he had been in for seven weeks. Doctors had given him a 1% chance of recovery.

This story is also about chance, which governs us all.

I met Grant in May 2009 thanks to German Tkachenko, his friend and a well-known Russian football executive. The Israeli hadn't given a single major interview for a year since his hugely disappointing sacking from Chelsea, although dozens of British and Israeli papers and even the *New York Times* had asked for one. He just didn't want to speak and that was it.

This time, though, for some reason he agreed.

Before the interview, Grant didn't know me and he didn't know the questions. He probably thought that I would be talking only about football.

As I was preparing for the interview, I pondered for a long time what I should begin with. A first question is extremely important for setting the tone of the whole conversation. Then I remembered the words of the Russian poet and musician Vladimir Vysotsky, that quarter of Israelis are "our former people", and decided to ask whether Grant had any roots in Russia.

What if I hadn't remembered Vysotsky's quote? What if, knowing that Grant doesn't speak Russian, I hadn't asked the question, but had focused on something more urgent? What if Tkachenko hadn't introduced me to Grant? What if Grant hadn't agreed to an interview? After all, I was from neither his native Israel or England, where he had made his home.

But Tkachenko introduced us, Grant agreed to the interview and I asked the question. Everything coincided. During our trip to Komi, Grant often repeated that without that question, none of this would have happened. In his answer, he told me the story of the deaths of his grandfather and grandmother and added, "I've never been in Komi, and my dream is to go there one day and to find their graves."

Grant couldn't have imagined that his dream would come true in just four months. The interview came out in the national daily *Sport-Express* on 22 May 2009 and on September 20 the old Russian TU-134 plane — "Are you sure we'll get there?" Grant asked when he saw it — took off from Vnukovo airport with Grant on board, bound for Syktyvkar, the capital of Komi. A day later, Grant took his place in a helicopter, flying from Syktyvkar to a settlement in the Koigorodsky area called Rabog.

It's a settlement that doesn't exist.

Grant left his passport at the hotel, so at first staff in the VIP area of the airport in Syktyvkar didn't want to check him in. He offered his English drivers' licence but the official on the desk asked how he would check in to return. It wasn't easy to explain that in Rabog there is no check-in, no airport. There is nothing. Nobody has lived there since the fifties, and the settlement doesn't appear on maps from 1956 onwards. In 1960, the last stables there were burned down because of an infection that had killed calves. In the seventies the occasional shepherd would build a hut there, but that was the last trace of habitation. By the eighties, as the Russian idiom has it, people had even stopped chasing calves there.

The nearest populated area to Rabog is the village of Uzhga, 20km away. There is no road between them, just forest, forest and more forest.

Komi is vast. It's 24 hours by train from south-western Syktyvkar to north-eastern Vorkuta, the same distance as from Syktyvkar to Moscow. It wasn't simply a matter of going there and hoping to find a clue as to the location of the graves. When Grant and I, after returning from Rabog, visited the head of the republic, Vladimir Torlopov, I said to him, "Thank you for not being indifferent. All great things in this life happen because somebody is not indifferent."

Torlopov couldn't be indifferent. His father was from Komi and his mother was Russian. His whole family was exiled to the wilderness during Stalin's regime. His grandfather and grandmother died there, as Grant's grandparents had. That, I guess, is why he took on Grant's quest as his own.

The Komi Republic was the first to include in its budget a separate section for remembering the victims of political oppression. In Syktyvkar, there are already nine volumes of the martyrology *Repentance*, listing the names of all those who died in gulags in the republic. One of them includes the names of Grant's relatives. Torlopov presented Grant with that volume and gave him the documents certifying his grandparents' deaths.

On June 23, I received an email from the press secretary for the Komi region, Konstantin Bobrov. A passionate football fan in his early thirties, he dedicated himself to finding the graves of Grant's grandparents and then organising his visit to Komi. In less than three months we exchanged more than 50 emails and even more text messages as Bobrov told me about every step in tracking down the graves.

First of all he went through the archives of registry offices and the Ministry of Home Affairs. He discovered that on 5 January 1941 somebody called Abram Ertselevich Granat had died in Rabog of myocarditis and that on May 31 his wife Ruda Granat had died of pneumonia. Bobrov asked me to check with Grant whether these people were any relations.

He confirmed that his family had been called Granat before losing the second 'a' and that his great grandfather was Ertsel. Moreover, Meir Granat remembered exactly the dates of his parents' deaths and they coincided with the data from the Komi registry office. After that it was only a technical matter to find the burial place. As Bobrov noted, one of the few advantages of the horror of the gulag was the strict bureaucracy. If anyone of *spetspereselentsy* ['special settlers', as they were called] disappeared, they would have been severely punished, perhaps even shot. That's why the archive contains documents about all 8800 refugees from Poland who found themselves in Komi.

But it is one thing is to discover the theoretical burial place, quite another to find it — especially in impassable taiga, where nobody has lived for more than half a century.

The expedition had been organised. From Syktyvkar to Rabog is about 200km, or 50 minutes by helicopter. The first expedition sent by the Komi government went by jeep, but got stuck in the mud as the roads, such as they were, disappeared. What was meant by the term 'road' in the north we learned the evening before our flight, driving half an hour to the borough of Chernam for a dinner in honour of Grant. In that area the Russian writer Sergei Dovlatov guarded prisoners. The well-known Israeli journalist Roni Daniel, who was covering Grant's journey with a film crew from Israeli TV, a man with a stern face and an amazing sense of humour, looked at the roads and muttered, "Now I know why Napoleon lost."

The first expedition completed the last 10km of the journey to Rabog on foot, walking through the forest and the weird mud. Thigh-high boots had been provided for us, but fortunately it was dry and they weren't needed. Our expedition was accompanied by old locals who remembered the way to Rabog and found a huge field where the settlement had once been. Nearby, they found a neglected graveyard. Only a fence, a wooden cross and shallow trenches where people were buried without coffins offered a reminder of what it had been. The grandparents of Avram Grant were among them.

When you tread in this space, it's hard to find words to express your feelings. If no one of my family were lying there and I felt that, what must Grant have been feeling?

Sometimes there are unbelievable coincidences. You already know about one of them: Meir Grant coming out of coma just two days before his son's trip to Russia. You know about the second one: the similar fates of the grandparents of Grant and the head of the Komi administration.

Here's the third. When Grant arrived in Syktyvkar, he was immediately told that

the bodies of the parents of his former boss Roman Abramovich lie in the town cemetery. Abramovich's father was killed on a construction site when his son was a baby. Grant asked if he could see the grave. A friend of Abramovich's father, Yuri Cheremisin, was quickly found and, carrying a large bunch of flowers, led us to the cemetery. As we chatted, it became apparent that Abramovich's grandparents had been deported to Komi from Lithuania in 1940 — the same year Grant's were exiled from Poland. The fates of the two Jewish families ran in parallel and almost six decades later their grandchildren met in London and almost won the Champions League together.

I looked into the eyes of Grant. It was clear that after all the coincidences he was in a state of shock.

When we flew to Rabog, it was other coincidences that concerned him. Grant's grandfather, after whom he was named, died in Komi at the age of 54; Grant was 54 when he visited his place of death. Grant's daughter was 13 when he made the trip, the same age Meir had been when his parents passed away in early 1941. Meir had dug their graves in the frozen soil with his own hands, then buried them. The historian Mikhail Rogachev, who travelled to Rabog with us, told us that the dead would, at best, have been wrapped in a sheet of material, but that usually there was nothing and corpses were put in the ground without any covering.

Grant's son at the time was 15. At that age, Meir had been an orphan for two years, living at Rabog alone. He stayed there for another two years. Only he really knows how he survived. "He is the most optimistic and joyful man I ever met," Grant said. "He didn't have a choice, going to Komi or not. But he chose how to live beyond that. He could have gone into the shell of his memories and become gloomy and unsociable. But he had left the past in the past. Only in the nights was peace denied him."

When, in 2001 Grant found in Poland the place where his family had lived before the war, Meir remained indifferent. The father grumbled at his son: "Why do you drag me into the past all the time? I want to live in the present and the future." But when the manager told his father in June 2009 that the cemetery with his parents' graves had been found in Komi, Meir couldn't believe his ears: any form of registration, for the living or the dead, seemed impossible in those conditions.

But it was possible. And when Rogachev, who wore a baseball cap with the Champions League logo, told Grant, who was interested in every detail, what had happened at that time, the Israeli regularly exclaimed, "It's exactly as my father told me!"

At first Avram didn't tell his father that he was flying to Komi. He decided that, two days after coming out of a coma, the excitement might be too much for Meir, even though he had fully regained consciousness.

The next day, doctors allowed Grant to tell his father where he was. As he did so, his voice shaking, tears falling from his eyes, Meir asked simply, "Is it cold there at this time of year?"

In winter in Rabog, the temperature regularly fell to -40° C, but there were no warm clothes for *spetspereselentsy*. There were no doctors. People there were dying in their hundreds, in their thousands.

The Grant (or rather Granat) family lived near Warsaw until 1939. The war forced them, like many other Jews, to flee to the east of the country, to Białystok. Several weeks later it was occupied by Soviet troops after the Molotov -Ribbentrop pact divided Poland between the USSR and the Third Reich. The border was immediately closed.

The Granats didn't want to take Soviet citizenship. They wanted to go back home. But the Germans would not allow Jews to return. As Rogachev noted, ultimately that saved them, because if they had ended up near Warsaw they would almost certainly have ended up in the gas chamber. But, avoiding Hitler's hell, Grant's family in 1940 entered the hell of Stalin, the predicament captured by the start of Andrzej Wajda's film *Katyn* in which people running from the Nazi tyrant meet at the bridge people running from the Communist monster.

Grant's father had nine brothers and sisters. One of them was killed in a bomb attack and two others disappeared — probably killed in a concentration camp. A fourth took shelter at a Catholic priest's house and, when he was found after the war, didn't know he was a Jew. Another brother and sister managed to escape and ended up in Canada and the USA. Grant's grandparents, with Meir and their two daughters, fourteen-year-old Sara and four-year-old Rachel, were packed with thousands of other Polish Jews in special trains and taken to Komi to chop down the forest.

Locals were prohibited from contacting and helping *spetspereselentsy* but they nonetheless worked together and the people of Komi secretly taught them how to hold an axe correctly, how to cut trees and boughs. Meir Grant spoke kindly of these people, but it hardly mattered if they sweated their guts out for 10 hours a day waist-deep in snow if nobody could give them boots instead of their usual shoes. They had to wear light clothes in bitter frost. It's amazing that any of them stayed alive.

Before September 1941 they were effectively prisoners. Later a partial amnesty was declared and theoretically *spetspereselentsy* could have moved to any town in Komi — but nowhere else. But how could they leave? On what would they travel? And where would they go?

According to the rules, at least 100 families should have lived in such a settlement, but there were only a couple of wooden barracks. Each person was allotted an average of three square metres.

The food rations were even worse. There was no provision made for children: let them die, the policy effectively ran; there was no use in extra mouths. Those who could work officially received salaries but only if they achieved a certain level of output. The threshold was set so high that even a strong man would have struggled to achieve it, never mind the exhausted, the starving and the sick.

The only food available was flour. People boiled it, mixing it with the needles from conifers and sawdust. There was no river, so there was no clean water. Dysentery and other diseases became endemic and there were no doctors

for *spetspereselentsy*. They gathered berries and mushrooms from the forest. But for people from the city that could be dangerous: Sara Granat died from eating a poisonous mushroom. It's said that later in life Arkady Abramovich, the father of Roman, couldn't bear to look at mushrooms because that was all he'd eaten through those dreadful years.

Meir Granat told his son that for every day of his four years in Rabog, he woke up and from morning to evening thought about food and looked for it. Most often it was in vain.

When his parents died, Meir should by law have been taken to an orphanage. But the Jews did everything they could to prevent that: as Rogachev said, even if a kid had lost his parents, their friends would hide him. Meir lived alone from the age of 13 to 16.

How did he live? How did he pass the days? How was he able to retain the belief that there would be a happy ending to the horror? Grant reflected upon that in the time we spent in Komi. "Now we know that it ended in 1944," he said. "But my dad didn't know that. I always tried to imagine him, a 13 year old, in that situation. And to understand how he managed to turn into an inveterate optimist with a great sense of humour."

"'Everything that doesn't kill us makes us stronger', as the famous quote says?"

"Exactly."

We passed through the enormous field and reached the graveyard.

Grant asked everybody to leave him alone. He prayed for a long time. According to Jewish custom, he poured earth from holy places in Jerusalem onto the ground. He lit candles. He took a handful of Rabog soil as an act of remembrance.

Did he cry? To me it looked as though he kept everything inside. "The guys from Israeli TV, who followed me through a camera, reported that I cried," he later said. "But I don't remember. I was thinking about my father and my dead relatives. I didn't feel whether the tears flowed or not."

Later he and the chief cantor of the Moscow and St Petersburg synagogues, Baruch Finkelstein, said a memorial prayer for each of his relatives who died in Komi and also a prayer for the victims of Nazism and Stalinism. The Grant family united both themes.

The Jewish prayer rang out in the middle of the Russian taiga. Israeli journalists shook their heads. Again and again, I caught myself during those days wondering at the feeling of unreality all around. "It's as if a load that I carried all my life has been taken off my mind," Grant said later.

In the helicopter he immediately fell asleep. Rabog had sucked so much energy out of him that devastation came. The emotions came back so strongly that the next night he couldn't close his eyes. As soon as we got back to Syktyvkar, the rain began to pour as though it had delicately waited until the holy mission was fulfilled.

During those two days Grant was busy. He spoke at a local Jewish cultural centre, where children dedicated beautiful dancing to him. He watched young footballers training and answered their questions. There were some tricky ones: "Was it hard to work with Abramovich?" Grant replied diplomatically. "You have to be proud that there is a man from these parts who has achieved so much," he said. "He should be an example for you that it's possible to achieve anything."

Grant took part in an opening ceremony of an indoor football tournament between teams from orphanages, which was held in the excellent new palace of sports. One of the kids impressed him so much with his sincerity and artlessness that Grant wanted to invite him either to Israel or to an English Premier League game. After the visit Grant asked me about him dozens of times, but things have changed in the Komi administration. Vladimir Torlopov and his press secretary Konstantin Bobrov resigned and the new authorities didn't show any interest in making it possible for the boy to travel abroad.

Why did Avram want to do that? Because his father also became an orphan very early and he never forgot that. He saw how his family, neither poor nor rich, always gave a tenth of its income to charity, as the Jewish tradition demands.

It also demands that Jews should fight for their land and their freedom. In 1944, the surviving Polish Jews were allowed to move from Komi to Ukraine and, in 1946, Meir left by ship for Israel. The boat, though, was stopped by British authorities, and all its passengers were interned in Cyprus.

"How it was there?" Grant asked his father.

"Like a five-star hotel," Meir replied.

When in 1947 he finally reached Israel, he went to Jerusalem straight from the ship to fight for independence. Soon, already in peace time, he met his future wife, a refugee from Iraq. And the a little later Avram Grant appeared on earth.

In Komi he often said, "Thanks to football." What, I asked, was the connection to the game? The manager explained that if there was no football, there wouldn't have been an interview in *Sport-Express*. Then the head of the republic wouldn't have learned about Grant's family and wouldn't have started the search. And the passionate people who completed the process wouldn't have been found.

"If your father fully recovers from his illness, would he want to go to Komi himself?" I asked Grant.

"I know him and I don't think so," he said. "He never liked to live in the past. But he'll look attentively at the pictures and won't miss a detail from the story. But I'll bring my kids here for sure. Because I experienced here, in Komi, one of the most exciting moments in my life. I'll never forget it."

Meir Grant never had the chance to go to Komi. A month later he passed away. But he had time to learn that his son had found the land where his parents were buried. Ⓑ

The Survivor

Emmanuel Schaffer escaped the holocaust and took Israel to the World Cup

By Shaul Adar

"I know I'm mad," he said to a friend who had asked him why he curses so much. "You must understand that anybody who was there and survived came back mad. Those who think they are normal, they are mad. We all became mad. Nobody came back from there sane."

"He" was Emanuel Schaffer and "there" was the holocaust, the years when Schaffer, a Jewish German-Polish teenager, fled and suffered years of hunger and loneliness. It was a burden he had to carry for the rest of his life and fame and success did not make it any lighter.

But Schaffer was a survivor by nature. He managed to see the end of the war and rebuild his life. "Football was his life," said Eran Schaffer, his son, in the family house in affluent Ramat HaSharon, to the north of Tel Aviv. "Football helped him survive during the war, football helped him back to life and gave him fortune and fame."

In the summer of 1970, football gave Schaffer his place in history when he led Israel as manager to their first and only appearance in the World Cup finals. It was his proudest moment when Israel played against world powers like Italy and Sweden. In many ways he owed that success to the nation that had hurt him

so deeply. Football and Germany were the two factors that shaped Schaffer's life and his personality.

Schaffer was born on 11 February 1923 in Poland and moved with his family a month later to Recklinghausen, in the Ruhr area of Germany. He grew up in Germany but, in 1936, three years after Adolf Hitler took power, the family was expelled to Metz in eastern France near the German border. As anti-Semitic persecution grew, the family contemplated emgrating to Palestine, but Schaffer's father chose in 1937 to move to the village of Porohy in Poland where he had relatives.

When the war broke out, the region where the Schaffers were living was under Soviet rule according to the Ribbentrop Molotov pact that divided Poland between Germany and the USSR. For a time, they were safe and Emanuel was sent to school in Drohobycz where he lived with his uncle and aunt. There he began playing football with the Jewish club of Beitar Drohobycz.

In June 1941 the war came to the USSR when Germany attacked its former ally. German forces stormed through eastern Europe and millions of Jews fell under

Nazi rule, their lives placed in constant danger. Schaffer, who heard rumours of the hardship of Jews in Nazi territories, fled to the east while his family stayed behind.

"Eddy [his nickname in Germany] escapes behind Russian lines by pure good fortune," explained an article in *Anstoss*, the magazine of the artistic and cultural programme for the 2006 World Cup. "For many months he suffered from typhoid, diphtheria and deficiency diseases before finally overcoming them."

Schaffer, still a teenager, reached Baku in Azerbaijan and later wandered further east to Alma Ata [now Almaty] in Kazakhstan, where he worked in a shoe factory producing boots for the armed forces. He escaped the Nazis and the fate of his people but life was extremely hard for the young boy in Stalin's country. There were nights when he had to share a bench in a park with his cousin whom he met there. Many times he went without having a proper meal and later in life when he became a successful manager he didn't forget those days. "I must have a loaf of bread everyday," he told his players, "just so that if I die tonight, I won't die a hungry man".

During those days his personality was forged. His work at the factory hardly made ends meet, but his luck was about to change. One day he saw a woman carrying a bag of *pirozhki* — Russian pasties. "The smell must have tortured him," said his son Eran. He followed the woman and offered her a hand carrying the sack. She agreed and when they reached her destination she gave him a *pirozhok*. The fresh, warm pastry was a rare treat but the young Schaffer was too resourceful to waste it. Despite the huge

temptation to devour it, he managed not to eat the *pirozhok* and instead sold it in the local market for a greater quantity of plain bread. From that day on he waited for the woman every day and helped her in return for one pasty.

"Even early on in life he knew how to survive and how to do business," said Shoshanna, his widow.

Life became easier when he joined Dynamo Alma Ata, the NKVD (secret police) team and it was then that he received the news from his aunt that his parents and three sisters had been killed in the holocaust. When the German army advanced east, the Jews in the village were rounded up and sent to Stanisławów ghetto (today Ivano-Frankovsk in the Ukraine). There they lived in horrendous conditions until they were murdered by Germans and Ukrainian collaborators in the Jewish cemetery. The tens of thousands of bodies were thrown into mass unmarked graves.

The shock and grief followed him to his final days but Schaffer had found a new purpose in life. With a friend, Zvi Zimmet, he returned to Poland, to Bielawa where his aunt lived, having survived the war thanks to a Polish woman who hid her. There he founded a Jewish football team — ZKS [Jewish Sport Club] Bielawa.

While working as a salesman in a clothes shop he honed his skills acting as organiser, coach and player. The team won promotion to the second division of the Polish league but that wasn't the only achievement of ZKS, which was much more than a football club. "The work we did at the club helped people who had their heads down," said Zimmet. "It helped them a lot. It was also a social club with dancing and singing in Hebrew and Yiddish, songs that people remembered from before the war. It uplifted the morale and once the gentiles saw a different kind of Jew it changed their perception."

In 1950 the club activity was terminated by Soviet orders and Schaffer, having been called up to the Polish army, decided to emigrate to Israel, which had been founded in in 1948. With his football connections he got a job in Haifa port and a place on the wing at Hapoel HaNamal Haifa [Haifa Port Worker]. Later he married Shoshanna, a Holocaust survivor from the same Polish village, although they met for the first time in Israel, and moved to Hapoel Kfar Saba. He had a decent career, winning eight national caps before an injury forced him to retire in 1957. The next year he forged a friendship and understanding that changed his life.

It was only 13 years after the war. The wounds were still open but Schaffer decided to attend a coaching course at the acclaimed German Sports College in Cologne. He was only the second foreign student and there, under the guidance of Hennes Weisweiler, he was awarded his badges to become the leading Israeli coach in the world.

For an Israeli to go to West Germany wasn't a simple matter. The reparations agreement between Israel and West Germany was signed in 1952 and led to great turmoil in the young and traumatised state. In January 1952,

while the Knesset, the Israeli parliament, debated the agreement, Menachem Begin, the leader of the opposition and later prime minster, led a demonstration and addressed crowds in Jerusalem's Zion Square. "They say there is a new German government that we can talk to, that we can negotiate and sign an agreement with," the charismatic Begin said. "Before Hitler came to power the German people had voted for him. 12 million Nazis served in the German army. There no one German who didn't murder our fathers. Every German is a Nazi. Every German is a murderer.

"Today I will give the order: Yes! It will be a war to the death," cried Begin and his supporters reacted. The protest turned into a full-scale riot in the streets of Jerusalem.

The parliament building was stoned and some members were hurt while others fled the scene. The debate was cut short for the only time in the history of the Knesset.

The relationship has improved over the years. The state and survivors received compensation and German products started entering the Israeli market. But for many Israelis it was too soon, especially when it came to culture and sport.

Music by Richard Wagner, an anti-Semite and the Nazi regime's favourite composer, is taboo in Israel to this day and Hungary's defeat to West Germany in the 1954's World Cup final was mourned in Israel, almost as a national disaster. When, in 1965, a former Wehrmacht officer was appointed as the German ambassador to Israel the old pains resurfaced. The new ambassador was greeted with stones and a mass demonstration.

In 1966 a broadcaster on state radio refused to read an ad for Volkswagen cars, saying she could not morally aid the distribution of German products in Israel. To go and live in Germany in 1958 was a bold move. "For him it was the best school in the world," explained Eran Schaffer. "He thought that German football after the 1954 World Cup was the best in the world and as a perfectionist he had to go there. He made the distinction between football and the past."

He still had some difficulties. "He once went out with a friend, journalist Yehoshua Sagi, to a German restaurant," says his son, "and there was a big queue. He said to Sagi, 'Let's go out of here. I've been made to queue for food by the Germans before; I'm not doing it again.' He found it hard with old Germans, the thought of where they'd been during the war was always at the back of his mind but that was the place to learn football. Weisweiler was the Alex Ferguson of the time. He turned Borussia Mönchengladbach into a European force."

"It always surprised me," said Amatzia Levkovic, his assistant in Mexico 1970, "but he spoke German and adored their football. It was the best school and it was his homeland."

Germany wasn't just the fatherland: it was the land that rejected him in the most brutal way and categorised him as sub-human. For Schaffer to be greeted back there was sign of acceptance and even revenge. His life mission was to present a different image of Jews and football was his weapon.

He became Weisweiler's friend and was chosen by the rest of the year at the school as one of the two best students; the other was Rinus Michels. Schaffer had a number of offers in to work in Germany but his family was the priority. "He went to visit Recklinghausen," said Shoshanna, "and wrote to me that a woman from the Jewish community said that he could live and work in wonderful conditions there. I told him that I would not let my son grow up in Germany and I wouldn't have a German nanny for my son, no matter how much money he was offered."

When Schaffer came back to Israel, he rose from coaching the youth team of Hapoel Kfar Saba to become manager of the Israel national youth team in 1964 and, on the eve of the 1968 Mexico Olympic Games, he was promoted to lead the senior team. It was the start of the best two years of Schaffer's career, and the best two years in Israeli football.

Israel began the 68 Olympics with a 5-3 win over Ghana and secured a place in the second round after a 3-1 victory against El Salvador. A 2-0 defeat to the eventual winners Hungary in the third game led to a quarter-final match against Bulgaria. Georgi Christakiev scored for Bulgaria after four minutes but Israel levelled through Jehoshua Faigenbaum in the final seconds. Extra-time brought no further goals and so the game went to the drawing of lots. Bulgaria won. "I'm sure the two pieces of paper both had Bulgaria written on them," said Mordechay (Motalle) Spiegler, the Israeli captain, half-joking. As a result, Israel missed the chance to win their first Olympic medal.

The game had major implications for Israeli sport and world football. Israel had to wait 24 years to win their first Olympic medals, claiming a silver and a bronze, both in judo, in Barcelona in 1992, while the heads of the Israeli FA, in their frustration, tried to come up with a better and fairer way to decide the outcome of draws. In a letter to Fifa, they suggested a penalty shoot-out.

It was the start of a revolution in Israeli football. At the time, as far as the sport went, Israel was a primitive outpost. Players had day jobs, football was heavily politicised and most grounds outside Tel Aviv and Haifa were just a bare pitch between dusty hills or makeshift stands.

Schaffer brought his German values, science, systems and demands and the result was a culture shock. "We will have three training sessions," he said to his players in one of their first meetings. "Three sessions a week?" complained one of the players. "Even in our team we don't do that."

"No!" shouted Schaffer. "Three times a day".

In broken Hebrew, a language that he never fully mastered, he set rules that stunned the players. Food and fitness were key issues. He controlled their diets, threw away cakes and cream from the tables and checked the players' weight regularly. The stars of the team were outraged but he had history on his side.

Israel, in the years after the Six Day War of 1967, was a bastion of self-belief and the army was a model for Schaffer as he looked to install the mentality of an elite unit. When Israel qualified for the Mexico World Cup of 1970 (through Oceanian qualifying), Schaffer successfully demanded long periods to work with the

players. In the year before the World Cup he had 170 days of training with them, far more than their clubs had.

He galvanised the team with a speech about what it meant to play under the Israeli flag. "We have the best army in the world," he said. "We have the best engineers in the world. There is no reason why we won't have great footballers too. They have two legs as we do, but we have better brains." One player even volunteered for reserve service on the deadly shores of the Suez Canal when he got back from Mexico.

In Mexico, Schaffer told David Lacey of the *Guardian* that "whatever the results, our aim is to prove to the world that what we have achieved in our home with the army we can achieve on the football field."

His personality also brought crisis after crisis to the team. He was a perfectionist, a demanding man prone to flying into a rage at the slightest provocation. His poor Hebrew didn't help and he used his assistants and some of the players to ease tensions after those eruptions. "They were all my children," he said in later life, trying to defend his outbursts. "We are a team of amateurs," he told Lacey, "and that means that I have to be tough. There is no other way. Not all of my players love it but that's the way it is. I would rather be a good coach and a tough guy than a bad coach and a good guy."

The language barrier and the strict discipline led to some misunderstandings that found their way into Israeli folklore. "I want to see you tomorrow at half eight," he said, translating from German and so meaning 0730. One player was up and booted by 0400. The players whom he took to the World Cup weren't the best players in Israel but the ones he could work with and whom he deemed dedicated enough for the mission. The sensitive, lazy and unfit were left out. "He picked the most reliable rather than necessarily the best players," the goalkeeper Yitzhak Visoker told the Israeli journalist Uri Misgav. "He saw us as his soldiers and he wanted only those he could count on.

"What was great about us was that we completely agreed with his German approach." That meant man-to-man marking, attacking full-backs and operating as a unit with a work-rate never previously seen in Israeli football. Only two players had creative licence: the playmaker Gyora Spiegel and the Russia-born winger, Motalle Spiegler. Spiegel, a member of a football dynasty, was wonderfully talented but was also slow and not keen on running up mountains, and was the hardest player to fit into Schaffer's Spartan style. "I found the fitness sessions hard not just because of the difficulty but also because nobody bothered to explain why it was so important," he told Misgav. "I rebelled and had lots of discussions with Schaffer and it wasn't pleasant. I really struggled with the long-distance runs. I was way behind and didn't make a real effort to catch up with the rest. I asked him to tell me why it was so important but he didn't like it because it would have broken the distance between us. In the end he just used to say, 'Shut up and do as you're told.'"

Those were the years when the relationship between Schaffer and his old mentor, Weisweiler, became closer. Borussia Mönchengladbach took their winter breaks in Israel and, in February 1970, played against Schaffer's Israel. At half-time, Borussia, inspired by Günter Netzer, led 3-0. "Eddy," asked Weisweiler, "shall we keep on playing like this or should we drop down a gear?"

"I told him to keep on playing like this," said Schaffer. "I wanted the players to know what they were up against in Mexico."

Drawn in the same group as Uruguay, Sweden and Italy, Schaffer feared a series of heavy defeats. He brought a lieutenant-colonel from the Israeli army to work on fitness and took the team to the heights of Ethiopia, Switzerland and Colorado in preparation for playing at altitude in Mexico. Alamosa in Colorado was, according to David Primo, a tough defender, "a satanic hell hole, a shitty miners' town up in the mountains."

"Our lungs were on fire," said the defender Menachem Bello.

Amid the turmoil, players and coach found a way to work together. "We heard him but did things our way," said Spiegel. "On the pitch we played as we thought we should do and usually it worked. Motalle and I understood that in football you need moments of spontaneous inspiration and unexpected moves. I use to leave myself some space, to keep some energy so that in the decisive moment I'd be sharp enough to score or give the crucial pass. Schaffer wasn't stupid: he saw that and shut up. He gave a little, we gave a little and met each other half way."

On 2 June 1970 Israel played their first World Cup game in Puebla against

Uruguay. Goals from Ildo Maneiro and Juan Mujica didn't tell the whole story. Uruguay were comfortable 2-0 winners and Spiegel and Spiegler didn't wait long to voice their opinions. "We are strikers, not centre halves," they told Israeli TV and began crisis talks with Schaffer.

Israel looked like they didn't belong in the World Cup. "Israel intended to rely on set pieces, corners and free-kicks but against the tall Uruguay defence that availed them little," reported the *Guardian* but it also had positive words about the manager: "Schaffer's fierce urgency of manner has been welcome effervescence in the pervading moroseness of the group. He has communicated a great deal of it to his players, many of them pitifully innocent of the simplest tactics of modern professional football."

The team was on the back foot, timid and passive. It was their worst game under Schaffer and he blamed the Israeli FA who hadn't let him travel and spy on the South Americans. "I saw Sweden and Italy and I knew what was in store for us. I didn't see Uruguay, so they were unknown and that's why we lost," he said.

Five days later in Toluca, Israel faced Sweden. It was one of the most violent and brutal games in World Cup history, with both teams exchanging kicks, elbows and grapples. It suited the Israelis and, with their nine fighters and two artists, they took the game to Sweden. Tom Turesson scored in the 54th minute (from an offside position, claimed Schaffer) but two minutes later Spiegel found Spiegler who equalised with a beautifully struck shot from 20 yards, Israel's first ever goal on the world stage.

Back in Israel it was hailed as a historic point won.

Against Italy, the European champions, Israel came as a different team. If for the first game the players couldn't believe they shared the same stage with Pelé, Moore and Müller and against Sweden they came to "kick the hell out of them" as one player commentated, against the team of Riva, Rivera, Mazzola and Faccheti, they came to play. "We played in a smart way," said Spiegel. "It wasn't just being back in our box. We played slowly and held the ball. We made it to the halfway line in 20 passes. They were used to a much faster pace and it rattled them."

Italy had two goals disallowed and hit the woodwork but Spiegler also had a golden chance saved by the goalkeeper Enrico Albertosi. Physically, the Israeli amateurs held their ground in Toluca and both teams were happy to hear the final whistle. After Middlesbrough in 1966 and the shock defeat to North Korea, the Azzuri didn't mind how they got out of the group. Italy made it safely to the second round and later to the final and Israel left Mexico with two points and a decent performance.

In Israel, the results were received with joy. "There is no doubt that yesterday we made history in world football," said a piece in *Maariv* newspaper. "We took a point from a superb Italy and we finished our performance at the World Cup with an achievement we didn't dare to dream of: two draws against the lions of the group... You should have seen our players, all of them bar none. How they battled, how they fought and how they threw themselves to the ground when it was the last option. And for this I have two words: Well done!"

"Everyone should play according to his abilities," Schaffer said. "When you play against a similar team you can attack like we did against Ghana [in 1968]. When you play against the mighty Italy you need to be tactically disciplined."

The players were given a vacation in Acapulco and $100 as a bonus for their efforts and Schaffer fulfilled his life's ambition to represent Israel on the world stage but the euphoria was short lived. A bitter dispute with the FA, who demanded that players be called to the national team on basis of the political affiliation of their clubs, led to Schaffer's resignation a few months later.

By then Schaffer was the German football ambassador to Israel. The Borussia Mönchengladbach of Netzer, Vogts, Heynckes and Simonsen visited Israel nine times in the seventies and was greeted by Schaffer each time. West Germany's defeat of Holland in 1974 was still regarded as a national disaster but thanks to Schaffer relations between the two football federations grew closer. Over the years people like Franz Beckenbauer and Otto Rehhagel used to have coffee at the Schaffers' house when they visited Israel.

Apart from raising generations of Israeli coaches, Schaffer stopped working as a coach and despite not having a proper education became a successful manufacturer for Adidas. Business trips to Germany were part of everyday life and after one such trip he heard about the death of his old friend. "In 1983 we went to the airport to pick him up," says Eran, "and on the way it was announced that Weisweiler had passed away. Dad landed, we told him the news and on the spot he bought a ticket and went back to Germany that day. They were the best of friends."

Before the 1980 Olympics he was tempted back to the head post of the national team but the old magic was missing. The clubs and players were much stronger, he could not keep the players away from their teams for long periods and they reacted badly to his harsh manner.

Football remained a great passion and he kept going to domestic games and international tournaments. In 1997 he suffered a stroke while in Germany and for a while couldn't speak. "First to come back were the languages he acquired first," said Eran. "It was in that order: German, Polish, Yiddish and Russian and only in the end broken Hebrew. When we got him back home after he was released from the hospital, a German journalist called and asked to speak to him about football and then, suddenly, his memory came back to him. We were amazed. He remembered games and dates like nothing had happened to him, like his brain lit up again."

In December 2005. he was given one final honour, as the German football federation (DFB) presented him with their Golden Award for his outstanding services to international and German football. "Through this award the DFB thanks the honouree for his valuable cooperation and the many proofs of friendship and affection which he has shown German football," the organisation announced. "In the post-war years and beyond he has at all times furthered the idea of reconciliation between Germany and Israel through his actions.

"We express our gratitude to Emmanuel Schaffer and his substantial effort for the solidarity and the cohesion of the international football community."

Schaffer passed away on 28 December 2012. On his death bed, drifting in and out of consciousness, he kept calling for Cila, his elder sister who had been murdered seven decades earlier.

FLAGSHIP STORE NOW OPEN

SPIRIT, STYLE AND QUALITY FROM THE BIRTHPLACE OF THE BEAUTIFUL GAME

FROM SHEFFIELD, UK, THE BIRTHPLACE OF THE BEAUTIFUL GAME, COMES GOALSOUL'S FLAGSHIP STORE... A UNIQUE CELEBRATION OF THE WORLD'S FAVORITE GAME

GIFTS FOR ALL SEASONS

ALL GOALSOUL ARTWORKS ARE AVAILABLE ON STYLISH, HIGH-QUALITY CLASSIC JERSEY TEES, OR STUNNING GICLÉE ART PRINTS AND BOXED CANVAS'. ALL ARE AVAILABLE ONLINE AND INSTORE AT GOALSOUL.

NEW! BIELSA PEP TALK
INTENSE ATMOSPHERIC PRESSURE

NEW! ZBIGNIEW BONIEK
THE BEAUTY AT NIGHT

NEW! LAURIE CUNNINGHAM
3 DEGREES OF SEPARATION

KEEPING THE GAME BEAUTIFUL ONLINE AND INSTORE

WWW.GOALSOUL.NET

GOALSOUL . 283 SHARROW VALE ROAD . SHEFFIELD . S11 8ZF . +44 (0)114 266 3374

goalsoul

161

Fiction

"He had big feet as well. And girls
like boys with big feet."

The Handkerchief

Young love intervenes between a goalkeeper and his chance of glory

By David Ashton

The mirror of the wardrobe door was long and thin — the same shape that Robert Agnew took up, standing before it, arms outstretched — ready to divert the ball as it hurtled towards the top right-hand corner of the goal.

His cat, Miffy, a born thief, crouched under the sofa and plotted its next exploit as the boy shifted, knees bent, eyes narrowed, coiled like a panther while he waited for the next shot.

Robert, 10 years old, an awkward collection of skin and bones, did not flinch as his father walked into the big room with the Saturday paper neatly folded to the racing page — some selections already ticked in biro. Andrew Agnew paid little attention to the crouching form though a slightly puzzled look flashed across his face before he sat at the window where his beloved geraniums overlooked the West Station and yearned for a glimpse of sun.

But this was Greenock — Renfrewshire, Scotland, Great Britain, the World and the Universe — where it forever rained.

The mirrored Robert was never sure if the Milky Way came into the equation but slid off to the side as a low sneaky effort spiralled towards the goal, losing sight of his own image as he sprawled across the new carpet — an imitation Axminster his mother's pride and joy.

His father spared a glance from perusal of the 2:30 where a horse called Wee Jinkie had engaged his attention. "Thought you were a right-back," he observed.

But Andrew had been to Middleton Camp where the class had gone for a school holiday, where Robert had howled in the cold shared showers and the man had said, "Ye're no' much use without yer mammy, are ye son?" — where he had gone every day into the small forest to hide and thrash armies of stinging nettles with a gnarled bent branch till they were beaten to the ground and he was covered in welts of retribution — what was he beating on?

Where he had watched other boys join together in gangs, missed his best friend Ian who had not been allowed to come because his mother had delusions of grandeur and wanted to go to Dunoon for the Fair — where Robert had never ever felt so isolated — was that what he was beating on? We all hammer away upon the anvil of disappointment.

Yet where — where — in the absence of Mearns Street School's designated keeper whose family had gone with Ian's to climb the greasy social pole of Dunoon

— where — on a hockey pitch with appropriately small goals that doubled for fitba' — Robert had been shovelled into service and performed a series of saves that bordered on the miraculous.

In one of the opposing teams, Ardgowan School, was Charlie Cooke who went on to play for Greenock Juniors, Aberdeen, Chelsea, Scotland, the World and the Universe, but even he — even he — could not get the ball past the inspired custodian.

Is there a moment in life when a greater energy takes possession? The Daemon? Where you become the number one son of Charlie Chan? Every time Robert waved his hands the ball landed and stuck there like a Chinese bun.

Or was it just down to the fact that he was, as one of Charlie's team mates shouted in disgust, "A fuckin' hockey keeper!" Cooke just nodded — when dimensions altered he'd be on hand; it is always thus with great players. They bide their time.

Mearns Street had won the tournament but Robert did not remember a feeling of triumph just bewilderment. As if it had happened to someone else.

Back at school the legend grew and even his best friend Ian Cameron had muttered, "Whit happened tae you?"

For Robert did not fit in. Rake-thin with bizarre co-ordination — at a hint of violence he bled from the nose, was second cleverest in the class and — hereby hangs the tale — was next to useless with girls.

I wonder if any of you out there, realise the pain of not fitting in? It never leaves,

like a shadow on the wall. Especially with — as it is termed — the opposite sex.

The ritual of pigtail pulling, yelled insults between playgrounds and in the case of Wee Willie McFarlane, masturbating while spitting at the same time was beyond Robert's reach.

And so, sadly, was Mary Capaldi.

She was small, dark-featured, and beautiful. To watch her throw a ball up against the wall and twirl around in the girl's playground was poetry in motion — but — she was also claimed by Donald Kennedy, a tall, athletic, hawk-faced leader of men who had not been at Middleton Camp otherwise Robert would in no way have sniffed the reduced rectangle.

For Donald was true guardian of the posts in the Mearns Street football team — his old man was a police inspector and according to Robert's communist father, a fascist by any other name.

Ian's father was also in the force but was the police billiards champion and only a sergeant so that made him, in Robert's supposition, a lesser fascist.

Political considerations aside, Donald had the inside track with Mary because of an ability to pluck balls out of the air with hooked unwavering hands. He was also first in the class and next year heading for Dux Boy.

He had big feet as well. And girls like boys with big feet.

The odds were stacked against our hero for Donald and Mary were, according to rumour, 'winching', which did not mean lifting a load off the ground — although maybe it did, come to think of it. They were often seen at the library, looking into the same shelves.

So Robert's chances had so far been about as promising as Wee Jinkie's but this Saturday might tell a different tale.

For a trial was to take place where the lesser lights of the school were mixed with the top players and Agnew, potential runner-up Boy Dux, had been chosen, due to his heroics at Middleton Camp, to stand in goal for the "A" team, the defence of which was marshalled by Ian Cameron, a tower of strength at centre-back.

Donald was relegated to keep the faith behind a very leaky "B" team fortification but their attack was lethal, led by the bandy-legged John Doig.

How these events had coincided was no doubt to do with the fickle finger of Fate but this might be Robert's chance. If he kept a clean sheet? Anything is possible with a clean sheet.

Saturday morning was usually two bacon rolls, the *Adventure*, *Rover*, *Wizard* and the *Hotspur* but he sacrificed the comics, gulped down the rolls, left his father frowning over the 3.30, his mother deep in her latest Max Brand cowboy story, *The Lone Rider of the Purple Sage*, and belted up the hill towards the Murdison Park where a full-size football pitch spread out like a vampire's cape.

He got changed, wearing Tam Donnachie's spare football boots since Middleton Camp had been in sandshoes and Robert had never needed proper footwear until now. Tam was the hard

man of the class. "Don't pee on them," he warned. "Or Ah'll hammer ye senseless." He had a soft spot for Robert.

He was given a lime-green goalie's jersey, potentially Papist and not blessed; Donald at the other end, had a dark-blue woolly effort that contrasted with his fair hair — contrasting in turn with Robert's dark, tangled, thick, unruly locks.

He could make out the petite figure of Mary behind the opposition goal along with her pals — but though she sometime favoured him with a sideways glance in class — she did not wave.

How many times have we waited for a wave? Across the Great Divide.

The game began and so did the rain, heavy, monotonous, baleful. The ducks in the Murdison Dam above watched morosely as large chunks of sodden doorstopper bread floated past into oblivion.

By half-time, Robert dared to hope. Though a muttering Ian Cameron had to take the goal kicks due to his inability to propel the ball beyond 40 yards, the defence held firm, marshalled by the centre-back, and Robert had only to field a few long-range shots that were no patch on Davy Crockett.

But their attack had managed to boot in a single goal scored by Wee Willie in his tackety boots as part of a twin terrorising spearhead with Tam. Willie balanced his lack of dribbling skills by petrifying the opposing centre-half Colin MacMaster, who was the janitor's son and therefore an easy mark.

Donald tried to insinuate offside but Mister Harvey the gym teacher with red thinning hair and pale blue eyes — who had picked the teams and been booked by Inspector Kennedy for speeding in his Hillman Minx with a blonde not two weeks before, blew first his nose and then for the goal.

The rain however fell on all without favour and when they changed ends, Robert was thrilled to see that Mary had stayed put underneath a big golf umbrella that one of the girls had no doubt borrowed from her father and was striped like a barber's pole. She was now behind his goal with Donald a long streak in the distance.

And the rain fell.

Robert could now hardly see through the downpour but Ian's rangy figure intercepted, tackled and bawled instructions in language that would have shocked the denizens of Dunoon. "These bastards are no' gettin' by us — a clean sheet or nothing fucking doing!"

While Mister Harvey pretended deafness, the captain turned to his drenched and drookit last line of defence. "Aggie — you keep on the qui vive!"

Aggie. A hated nick-name. The girls behind giggled. Wee Willie kicked Colin MacMaster into a crumpled heap and the referee blew for a reluctant foul.

The ball was now so heavy it could have been shot from a cannon.

The rain fell and went on falling.

His hair was dripping large, unwholesome, splutters of water into his eyes and Robert began to panic. A goalie needs vision.

The ball hurtled over from a corner and he plunged bravely forward but Ian's head lamped it to safety. "Stay on the line Aggie," he advised. "That's where ye belong."

"Robert?" A more enticing voice cut through the wet. Mary had slid round to the post and offered a small white handkerchief, already knotted at the four corners. "This'll keep ye dry."

For a moment their eyes met. Hers were unscathed from under the umbrella, his blinking away the heavy hair-dripped watery gobbets — he solemnly accepted the favour and like a gallant knight, put it upon his head. More giggles but Mary seemed all solicitude.

The hankie sat on his head like a skullcap but it did a half-decent job. It was now only five minutes to go and glory beckoned.

How often have we thought this? Money riding on the likes of Wee Jinkie, breath caught short by a wild hope.

The bandy legs of John Doig emerged in the pelting rain but once again Ian Cameron had moved to cover and, in disgust, the forward took a whack at the ball from 25 yards. It dipped to hit a muddy patch and skittered goalwards. An easy save. Approaching glory.

Yet as Robert stooped down to collect the trundling ball, the handkerchief slid deceitfully from his head to fall over his eyes and, blinded by the material which clung on like some sort of treacherous ectoplasm, he was left to grope with desperate but futile intent. The ball smacked onto his hands like the teacher's belt and then squeezed between his legs.

For a second there was an eerie silence and then cheers plus howls of derision rose to the black clouds above.

His first sight on scraping the perfidious hankie aside was that of the ball in the net. And as the old fitba' saying would have it, "Once the ba's in the net, not even Moses can help ye."

Robert fished the thing out and booted it up the field, then suffered the cold unforgiving stare of his centre-back. "There goes the clean fucking sheet," said Ian.

Hardly time for kick-off before the final whistle blew.

As the sparse crowd left the scene, some still laughing, one person stayed in place for a moment. Charlie Cooke. He lived close to the Murdison Park, had bided his time and now witnessed the downfall of a flash in the pan.

Cooke shook his head dismissively and turned to go but somewhere behind him, Robert thought to have glimpsed his own father's figure among the departing.

When he turned back, the girls and Mary had vanished. The field was also uninhabited save for Wee Willie who sat whistling cheerfully in the downpour as he examined the toe-end of his tackety boots. "Ah pit a dunt in it, kickin' that bastard MacMaster," he announced — and then, "Hey? Ye want tae hear the latest?"

"I suppose so," replied Robert.

"Big Donald and Mary — they're winchin' hard!"

"What does that mean?"

"Big Donald tellt me. Got his hand up. Right intae the hairy bits!"

Willie roared with laughter as Robert walked on, clutching at the handkerchief, his cup of misery near to overflowing.

"Hey Aggie?" Willie shouted. "By the way — ye're a shite goalie!"

Robert sneaked into the changing room, grabbed his belongings and ran for it — he'd give Tam back his boots on Monday but could not face the merciless barrage of scorn.

He walked home bareheaded, studs slipping on the pavement — a drowned rat from a sunk ship. Then he saw his father standing in front of a tobacconist's the top of Dempster Street.

"Away in and get me 10 Capstan extra strength," said Andrew.

'Were you at the game, daddy?" asked Robert with some dread.

"Certainly not. Here you are." A silver half-crown changed hands. To a certain extent this made sense to Robert; his father was dead shy and had been known to wait outside a shop for hours until he was certain it was empty of customers. "There's an auld biddy inside the place talks 90 to the dozen. Away ye go — I'll haud the clothes ye can keep the change."

But as Robert entered the shop and the door pinged, the old woman went out past him and he was left looking at a bear of a man with buck teeth, running a bit to fat, thinning hair, two massive paws resting on the counter while behind him, John Player's, Capstan and the Wild Woodbine cigarettes lined up for the long season.

Jimmy Cowan. A genuine hero — the Greenock Morton keeper who had single-handedly defied England at Wembley: The Prince of Goalkeepers, who'd prowled the line like a tiger.

"The usual, Robert?" he asked.

The boy nodded. In his desolation he had forgotten that the Prince had long retired and this shop was his wee nest-egg. He was teetotal so a pub was out of the question.

Coin given, change and cigarettes accepted, Jimmy took in the bedraggled figure before him and indicated the lime-green sweater. "I had one that colour," he said quietly. "Never let me down. How about yourself, son?"

It was then the tears flowed and Robert told the whole shameful story.

Jimmy's slightly hooded eyes never left the boy's face. He was a gentle soul and fame had left no scars upon him. "The goalie always gets the blame, Robert. Hold on."

He disappeared into the back shop and returned with a flat bonnet that looked like a squashed pancake in his huge hands. "I wore this a few times. Take it. Bring you luck and keep the rain out of your eyes, eh?"

"I'm no' playing again, Mister Cowan."

"You never know. Take it — if it's too big ye can stick some newspaper in."

Robert wiped his face with the sodden, knotted handkerchief, took the cap, nodded a polite and grateful thanks for the precious gift, then left with another ping of the door.

Jimmy sighed. Andy Agnew had been at school with him — never much good on the wing just the one trick, but his classmate had nipped in before to warn Jimmy that there might be a broken heart to mend. Well, he had done his best.

"The goalie always gets the blame," he muttered to the Wild Woodbine.

The rain had finally stopped by the time Robert and his father had reached their close at the West Station. Andrew suddenly handed the boy a line from the bookies.

"Away and collect that."

"Collect? But you never win, daddy."

"Wee Jinkie. Came in at 10 tae one. Don't tell your mother — she'll want tae buy a ranch."

Andrew looked down at his son. "Whit was the result anyway, for the game?"

"It was a draw," Robert replied carefully.

"Six more and you've won the pools. Away ye go then!"

Robert stuck the cap on his head. It was too big right enough but for the first time he felt like a real goalie. The boy turned smartly and walked off while his father feinted and then side-footed a stone into the gutter — his one trick.

As Robert walked past Auld's the Bakers where the wee cock-eyed woman always dithered over doughnuts, he felt the dampness of the handkerchief in his trouser pocket. He'd have to unpick the knots and ask his mother if she could spare the time from the Purple Sage to wash and iron the piece of cloth — then give it back to Mary Capaldi.

Not her fault that a sweet gift turned sour but girls were a menace. Maybe it would be better to wait a bit later in life before he tackled them full on.

He turned and saw himself reflected in the bakery window. The women inside smiled and thought he was looking at them or the cream buns.

But he was looking — he was looking — at a goalkeeper.

169

Greatest Games

"I don't think I played... but I was so bevvied that I've no idea."

Dundee 1 Dundee United 2

Scottish Premier League, Dens Park, Dundee, 14 May 1983

By Richard Winton

Amid the haze of time and booze that has obscured their recollections, the one thing they all remember is the clock. Even 30 years on, Paul Hegarty swears it stopped at 4.30pm, while the Dundee derby veteran Hamish McAlpine confesses it was only that afternoon that he first noticed it hanging above the tunnel at Dens Park. It is no longer there, having apparently been removed on safety grounds, but it retains a special place in the memories of the players who earned Dundee United their solitary Premier League championship title.

It was on 14 May 1983 that Jim McLean's side won the league at Dens. They beat their city rivals 2-1 to hold off the challenge of Celtic and Aberdeen, who had celebrated a trophy of their own just three days earlier — Alex Ferguson having led them to Cup-Winners' Cup glory against Real Madrid in Gothenburg — and would go on to secure the Scottish Cup the following weekend. It made for a remarkable climax to the campaign, the top three being separated by just one point having scored 256 goals between them, with the prospect of a play-off to decide the champions remaining alive until the final few seconds of the season. As it was, United's victory ensured that they were the ones flying the flag, Aberdeen's 5-0 skelping of Hibernian and Celtic's 4-2 triumph over Rangers at Ibrox being rendered moot by the Tannadice side's 24th league win of the campaign.

Yet while the venue of their coronation made it even more special, their succession only came after a fraught finale in front of 29,106 wedged inside Dens. "It was very tense and nervy and was a game I didn't enjoy," said the winger Eamonn Bannon. "And I remember just being physically and mentally drained. You see players go mental after they win leagues but I was very subdued. We didn't play well and it was a real anti-climax for me. I just felt shattered."

Such emotions are understandable in the circumstances but the game had started better than the league leaders could ever have imagined, Ralph Milne marking the weekend of his 22nd birthday with a goal so breathtaking that it has since become immortalised in song.

On the 14th of May, 1983,
Six minutes into the half,
The ball soared over Kelly's head,
And it was Happy Birthday, Ralph.

The lyrics do not do justice to the moment. Davie Narey won the ball in the United half and guided it into the centre-circle for Paul Sturrock, who pivoted and shunted a pass into the path of Milne. The winger, almost reluctantly, assumed

possession near the halfway line and casually shuffled past Stewart McKimmie before ambling forward, his strides lengthening as he advanced. Eventually, he seemed to tire of such exertions, instead glancing up and nonchalantly chipping the ball over the goalkeeper Colin Kelly from 25 yards.

It is perhaps difficult for English readers to reconcile the description with their memories of a player ridiculed for his abject stint at Manchester United — indeed, Ferguson recently selected Milne as his "worst-ever signing". Yet, given the notorious drinking culture at Old Trafford in the mid-to-late 80s, there was no worse place for Milne to be, his extraordinary talent — talent that ripped apart an Aberdeen side tutored by Ferguson and considered one of the best in Europe — having already been diluted by drink. This, after all, was a man who could run the 100m in 10.1 seconds "while wearing old trainers" and who scored 15 European goals during a spell in which the only opposing midfielder who outshone him was Falcão, the Brazilian hub of the AS Roma team who edged out United in the 1984 European Cup semi-final.

McLean, understandably, was infuriated by the way in which the winger wasted such talent but, even now, Milne remains bitter at what he considers a lack of recognition from his manager. The wounds run deep; the player was omitted from Scotland's 1986 World Cup squad, apparently on McLean's advice, and instead spent that summer working in a polythene factory to supplement his wages.

Not content with wasting only his talent, Milne sadly seems to be doing the same with his life. Now 52, he has twice appeared in court charged with assaulting his girlfriend Fiona Spence, who earlier this year described his daily routine as "drinking cider at 6.30am, going to bed drunk at 10am, getting up again at 2pm then drinking again". The pair have both been hospitalised after violent incidents of domestic abuse but remain together, even though Spence has admitted fears that "it's only a matter of time till one of us dies."

The bloated and bitter figure of Milne today bears scant resemblance to the lithe, if somewhat scruffy, talisman upon whom the United players converged that day in 1983. Usually deployed on the right — although equally adept at playing off a central striker — the Dundonian was a key tactical pawn in McLean's innovative formation, something Sturrock describes as an early 4-5-1 in which many of the components were adaptable. "Jim McLean was a genius as far as I was concerned," Sturrock told the *Scotsman* earlier this year. "His training was revolutionary and his coaching transformed me.

"When I joined the club, I was a running-type striker, all left foot. He said I had to do extra work on crossing and shooting with both feet and getting the ball fed into me. I worked so hard on it, three afternoons a week for three or four years, that I could run you into the channel, I could come short or I could turn you. I was probably three strikers rolled into one. A lot of players will be very thankful for the work he did with them. As for

his man-management skills? Well, that's another debate."

McLean, after all, was a man who withheld his side's £50 entertainment bonus after a 7-0 win over Kilmarnock in the December of that season, reasoning that, having scoring five times before the interval, they did not do enough in the second half to keep the crowd. "We weren't best pleased but that's just the way he was," said McAlpine, chuckling. "We'd all played together for a few years and our success was built on that spirit. We were all on the same wages, which I think was the lowest in the league, but the bonuses were great so you had to win to get some decent dosh."

It was not the first, neither would it be the last, time that the manager employed such a tactic. However, such methods helped fostered a togetherness among his young squad, who banded together against a manager whom they all respected but very few actually liked. Take Bannon, for example, a favourite target for McLean's ire. He was too clever for his own good, the manager thought, and too willing to defend himself when criticised; so much so that former teammates recall jostling for seats to the winger's right because of the manager's habit of working round the dressing-room in an anti-clockwise direction when berating his players.

Indeed, McAlpine recalls that even during the interval that day at Dens, Bannon was upbraided for missing a 17th-minute penalty kick, even though he reacted quickest to lash the rebound past the prone Kelly. "I was never nervous taking penalties," the winger recalled. "But I remember having to wait three or four minutes to take it and there was all sorts going on around me. I made the mistake of changing my mind and the keeper saved it but I was lucky it came back to me and I whacked it in."

Regardless of such fortune, the two-goal advantage appeared to confirm that the title was heading to Tannadice. Not yet, though. Iain Ferguson — who would score a winner for United when they came from behind to beat Barcelona at Camp Nou four years later — rifled past McAlpine before the break to haul Dundee back into the game and set United nerves jangling. "It really rattled us," said Bannon. "We got anxious and starting booting the ball rather than passing it."

The game remained delicately poised. "Your deadliest enemies could stop you winning the league; can you imagine the pressure? You had to live in the town; if they had been able to do that, it would have become folklore," said Sturrock, who had been unable to train during the previous couple of months because of a pulled hamstring, but played every game during the run-in it finally ruptured that day. "It felt like another 90 minutes," he recalled of the half hour he spent watching from the bench. "Every time the ball went in the box you were cringing. I couldn't watch the last couple of minutes, it was so nervy."

So much so that, even the phlegmatic goalkeeper was panicking. "I kept shouting to the dugout 'how long to go?' because we were hanging on," said McAlpine, a penalty-taking, crossbar-swinging, cult hero. "The final few minutes seemed like an eternity."

That it took until the last few moments of the campaign for such doubts to creep in

were a consequence of United thinking their title hopes were over after losing 2-0 at Celtic Park in April, the defeat leaving them three points off the pace with another trip to Parkhead pending. "At that point, I honestly believed the league was beyond us," McLean later admitted. "In fact, it's a miracle that we've won this title. At the start of the season, I certainly didn't believe we'd be champions, simply because we have no depth of pool. 12 players, the 12 who played against Dundee at Dens, have achieved this tremendous success."

The manager was being a little disingenuous with his claim, given 20 different players made league appearances for United that season, but the statistics were remarkable enough to need no exaggeration. Only 14 men played more than five times over the course of the campaign; six were native to the city — 10 had come through the youth ranks — and transfer fees were paid for just two, £192,000 being lavished on Hegarty and Bannon. McLean had spent 12 years building a team to win the championship and spent a further decade attempting to emulate them, but in that one glorious season it all fell into place. "That United team, it was an exceptional side," says Sturrock. "People forget that the following season we got to the European Cup semi-final and then found out that the referee had taken a bribe. So we could have been in the final against Liverpool. I mean, Dundee United? It's incredible really."

The same could be same of the conclusion to their campaign, United's shallow squad rousing themselves to win their final six matches and overhaul both Celtic and Aberdeen. Each of those games, including three consecutive 4-0 wins ahead of the decider, were vital but one in particular stands out: having lost at Parkhead in April, United returned to Glasgow and secured a surprise 3-2 victory, despite the dismissal of Richard Gough. "That was the turning point, a real game changer because it put us a point ahead having been written off," insists Bannon. "All of a sudden we had our noses in front and we kept winning from there on in."

For all that he recognises its importance, Bannon's recall of the game is sketchy. "I remember the pitch being like a beach, big Goughie getting sent off and Ralph scoring a great goal but beyond that... did we get a penalty?" They did. And he scored it, adding to Hegarty's opener before another virtuoso effort by Milne, who took a cross on his chest and lashed a 25-yard volley past Packie Bonner. The winger had also scored twice before being sent off in the win at Pittodrie a few weeks earlier. "Ralph, that season, was fantastic," recalled Hegarty. "There were games that either he or Paul Sturrock won almost by themselves."

The triumph in Glasgow moved McLean's men within a point of Celtic and they went top for the first time that weekend, towsing Kilmarnock while Celtic were losing to Aberdeen, who were four behind with two games in hand. The failure of Alex Ferguson's side to win at Easter Road seven days later, coupled with another thumping United win at Morton, ensured it was in their own hands. "It clicked for me that we had a right good chance with about five games to go," said McAlpine. "But that game at Cappielow is the one that stands out for me because I remember the club organising buses for the fans."

"Aye, that was a nice move by Wee Jim," added Bannon. "It was like rent-a-crowd and it made a massive difference because our lack of away support meant we were at a disadvantage compared to Rangers, Celtic and Aberdeen and really had to win games off our own back. That makes it even more remarkable."

So, too, does the fact United played a chunk of that match without a recognised goalkeeper after McAlpine went off injured. "I got a stud above my hip, which left a hole above the bone and seized me up a bit," McAlpine recalled. "But I hung on until we were 3-0 up before I went off and we always knew Heggy was more than capable anyway..."

"It didn't feel that way at the time," said Hegarty, who pulled on the gloves and maintained United's clean sheet. "I was almost as nervous as the day at Dens, worrying about what Wee Jim would say if I let one in..."

By then, the superstitious McLean was already riven with anxiety, the tension having built to such an extent that he steadfastly refused to arrange any official celebrations before the title was won. Hegarty recalls the players leaving Dens and wandering the 100 yards or so down Tannadice Street for a drink in the United boardroom, before being obliged to attend a supporters' function in Coupar Angus, then retiring to Frank Kopel's house, the defender and his wife having decided to host an impromptu party that continued until the early hours.

Bannon was there, too, but still nurses a sense of regret that "Wee Jim was too miserable to rent a place" for a proper party. "It was very subdued afterwards and everything was off the cuff and a bit low key. I wish there had been an organised event as a club. Years later, when I was a coach at Hibs, we lost the League Cup final to Rangers but still went back to a hotel in Edinburgh and had a great night. I wish we had done something like that."

Not everyone had such a restrained night, though. Sturrock has a hazy memory of the manager, dressed in his pyjamas, kicking him out of his house at 7am; something that McAlpine also remembers. "Ken this, I couldn't tell you most of what happened because we had a right few bevvies," he says. "God knows where we went but I know we were in Wee Jim's house for a while and Luggy reckons he was given a swearing."

"I know this much," Sturrock added, grinning. "We partied big time. For about four days solid, we were never home."

The party continued at Station Park the following afternoon, McLean having committed to taking a strong team to play a benefit match for Billy Bennett and John Clark. Almost every member of the league-winning side played some part despite many of them being barely able to stand, never mind run, with the injured Sturrock despatched by his hungover teammates to find food to soak up the alcohol. "I was sent to find a man who had a shop that sold bridies," Sturrock said. "Some boy told me where the guy lived so I knocked on his door. I don't know if he was the baker, but he had a key, and he went round to heat them up. That was my job for the day,

bringing back pies and bridies for all the players. The subs were even eating them in the dugout.

"We lost the game 2-1 and Wee Jim wasn't too happy. If I remember rightly, he picked near enough every player that had played the day before. It was quite incredible. Half the players couldn't stand up. They had been drinking all night. We were pished out of our minds."

"I don't think I played..." added McAlpine, hesitantly. "But I was so bevvied that I've no idea. I do remember Wee Jim asking at half-time if anyone wanted to come off and everyone put their hand up."

Bannon was one of the few absentees, nursing his own hangover while being kicked up and down Easter Road by John Brownlee in a testimonial for Jim McArthur. "I could have seen it far enough." he said. "I was hungover and it was unbelievably wet; the roads were flooded. John was on trial for Hibs that day after breaking his leg at Newcastle and was right up for it. Two minutes in, he clattered me, which was the last thing I needed because I was just trying to get through it."

Meanwhile, in Forfar, his colleagues were suffering just as much. "There were one or two thick heads and bleary eyes but I don't think anyone would begrudge us," said Hegarty, who remembers surviving the 90 minutes. "I dunno how we got on, to be honest... but I don't think we did particularly well. Just like the game the previous day, it seemed to go on for ever." **B**

Stroke is the third biggest killer and the leading cause of severe adult disability in the UK.

Behind much of the Stroke Association's unique work are people just like you – people who want to do something powerful and lasting through their Will.

To find out more about leaving a gift in your Will please call us on **020 7566 1505** or email **legacy@stroke.org.uk**

stroke.org.uk

Registered as a Charity in England and Wales (No 211015) and in Scotland (SC037789). Also registered in Isle of Man (No 945) Jersey (NPO 369) and serving Northern Ireland.

177

"Who could have imagined a 36-year-old journeyman, who had been mocked for his weight problems throughout his career, could outstrip the most expensive player in the world?"

Unexpected League Leaders

A selection of minnows who, briefly, found themselves at the top of the tree

By Michael Yokhin

 **Norwich City
1992-93**

Four years before the famous "Arsène who?" question, many pundits wondered "Mike who?" When the local favourite Dave Stringer resigned as Norwich manager after narrowly avoiding relegation in 1992, Mike Walker, a largely unknown Welshman who had spent the majority of his playing career at Colchester, was surprisingly promoted from the club's youth academy to take over as manager. With Walker on the bench for the inaugural Premier League season, their chances of survival looked slim, especially when their main striker Robert Fleck was sold by to Chelsea — seemingly against the manager's wishes — for a club record fee of more than £2 million.

Norwich went to Highbury on the opening day and were soon trailing 2-0. Then the unthinkable happened. Mark Robins, the Manchester United outcast who had famously scored the goal against Nottingham Forest that supposedly saved Alex Ferguson's job, came on as a substitute and netted a brace, bookending a burst of four goals in 15 minutes. Norwich ran away with a 4-2 win; they never looked back.

Walker's team oozed confidence, displaying their gung-ho approach wherever they went. The defence was fragile, with the goalkeeper Bryan Gunn seeming to appeal for offside every time the opponent attacked. Blackburn thrashed them 7-1, Liverpool put four goals past them, and their local rivals Ipswich defeated them at Carrow Road. But that didn't stop Norwich from leading the table until Christmas. Their swift short-passing play was brilliant at times, while Gunn, who lost his daughter to leukaemia during the season, became a hero.

Almost every player seemed to improve under Walker's management. The winger Ruel Fox, bench material for so many seasons, became a star. Ian Crook cruised from box to box, making crucial contributions in his best personal season. A young Chris Sutton scored eight goals in his first year in the starting line-up, while Robins added 15 goals of his own.

After nine games, Norwich had seven wins and enjoyed a three-point lead over Coventry. While the Sky Blues faded, the Canaries were relentless. They scored 34 times in the first 19 games, by which point they'd extended their lead over second-placed Blackburn to a hefty eight points, even though they only kept a clean sheet once during that period and their defensive record of 31 goals conceded was the third-worst in the league. The fans didn't care: as far as they were concerned, Walker could have walked on water. They believed the championship was possible.

The first crisis came in December as Norwich went five games in a row without scoring and dropped to third, but remarkably they managed to come back. In late January, having beaten Everton 1-0 at Goodison Park, they led the table again, largely thanks to Ipswich beating Manchester United and Aston Villa losing at Southampton on the same day. After 26 games, the gap between the Canaries and the bottom club Oldham was just 21 points, as opposed to 48 separating United and QPR at the same stage last season: the league was far more competitive two decades ago.

It soon turned into a three-horse race and Norwich had to win at Villa in late March to keep their hopes alive. They did so, but their aspirations were ended in their next game as United scored three goals in the first 20 minutes at Carrow Road. Tottenham then put five past them and Walker's side eventually finished third, qualifying for Europe for the first time — with a negative goal difference.

The Canaries' adventure in the Uefa Cup proved memorable, including the famous 2-1 win against Bayern Munich at the Olympiastadion. Walker seemed the brightest managerial hope in the country, mentioned as a possible successor to Graham Taylor as England boss. Fed up with the chairman Robert Chase, Walker left for Everton in January 1994, only to fail spectacularly. Without him, Norwich fell apart and were relegated in 1995.

 **MSV Duisburg
1993-94 season**

This story is probably the weirdest of them all, given the newly promoted minnows managed to lead the table until as late as February, with a negative goal difference.

Ewald Lienen, arguably better known as left-wing activist than a footballer in his playing days, took over as manager, his first coaching job, in March 1993 and guided MSV to a promotion. The squad was thin, though, and the Zebras were expected to go straight down. Their major acquisitions during the summer did little to inspire hope — Uwe Weidemann, a 30-year-old East German playmaker and Peter Közle, a striker who spent all his previous career in Belgium and Switzerland and had barely been heard of in his homeland.

Duisburg's philosophy in their magical season was based on tigerish defence and very fast breaks. The first opponents fully to experience their power were the champions Werder Bremen, who sensationally conceded five goals in 20 second-half minutes in late August. Duisburg won 5-1, and were given the nickname 'Konter-Könige' — Kings of the Counterattack.

This was a bizarre adventure. MSV didn't lose until mid-October, but failed to win any of their home games during that period. When defeat did come, it was a 4-1 thrashing at Borussia Mönchengladbach. Winfried Schäfer's Karlsruhe crushed them 5-0 a month later and Stuttgart won 4-0 against them. But while everyone expected them to disappear, Duisburg also claimed numerous hard-fought wins. Weidemann's passing proved a revelation, while Közle rattled in 13 goals.

Közle, not Roberto Baggio, was the Divine Ponytail for MSV fans. He suddenly became one of the most talked about players in the country and enjoyed enormous popularity in Duisburg. The charismatic striker opened his own pub, called Cash, and even participated in recording the club's anthem — his voice can still be heard at the stadium every match day.

This was one of the tightest Bundesliga seasons ever. At the winter break, with 20 games played, Duisburg were seventh, but just two points behind the leaders Bayer Leverkusen and Eintracht Frankfurt. When the league resumed, MSV won 2-1 against Leipzig thanks to a goal from their captain Torsten Wohlert, a no-nonsense centre-back. That took them fourth. Then, on February 18, history was made.

It was a Friday night, the opening game of the weekend. Duisburg hosted Bremen, level on points with them, still favourites to retain the title and eager to take sweet revenge for the shameful defeat in August. The visitors dominated the game for long spells, but Lienen's players held firm and, with 15 minutes to go, Közle struck once again on the counter. 1-0 to the Zebras, and suddenly they were top.

This was a huge moment, but Eintracht and Leverkusen still had games to play on the Saturday afternoon. Amazingly, both lost. Eintracht succumbed at Karlsruhe, while Leverkusen wasted an early lead against Hamburg. Duisburg stayed top. After 22 games, their stats read: 27 points, 29 goals scored, 30

goals conceded. They were the strangest leaders German football has ever known. The local newspaper published a photo of a jubilant Közle shouting, "Look, we are number one!"

A week later, Bayern Munich — then second, a point behind Duisburg — hosted the leaders and that's where the fairytale was brutally ended. The Bavarians scored four goals before the break, won 4-0 and MSV never recovered. They only recorded four more wins and eventually finished ninth, albeit just eight points behind Bayern who took the title. Even the dream of qualifying for Europe was not achieved.

The following season went from bad to worse for the Zebras. They never left the relegation zone, and Lienen, still considered a legend, was sacked in October. Közle stopped scoring and started drinking too much. His pub was smashed by angry fans and he fled the town before the season ended. The team went down without a fight.

This summer, Duisburg were demoted to the third division over financial irregularities.

Excelsior Mouscron
1996-97

The Mpenza sensation in Belgium was stunning. When Mouscron, promoted for the first time in their history via the playoffs in 1996, signed the Kinshasa-born brothers, Mbo and Emile, from second-division Kortrijk, they could never have expected such an explosion. A tiny club whose Canonnier stadium could house just 9,000 fans, Excelsior played football of astonishing intensity and quality. They feared no one, took the game to their opponents and attacked relentlessly. Destined to finish rock bottom according to the predictions ahead of the season, Mouscron went unbeaten in their first seven games, scoring 15 goals in the process.

Their coach Georges Leekens never had a good reputation in his country, even though he had had short spells at numerous top clubs, including Anderlecht and Club Brugge. At Mouscron, he unexpectedly fulfilled his potential, and as weeks went by the country became addicted to watching the most exciting team Belgium had seen in years.

Mbo Mpenza was 19 when the season started, Emile just 18. Their mutual understanding was telepathic, each of them scored 12 goals, and their youthful energy had the whole squad believing they could go all the way to win the title. Mouscron led the league from the first day of the season and continued their surge to be crowned winter champions.

Sadly, Leekens wasn't patient enough to wait for his project to bear fruit. He was enjoying his sudden fame and when the Belgian football federation asked him to replace Wilfried van Moer as national coach in February 1997, he walked away from Excelsior. Geert Brouckaert, who replaced him, failed to maintain the momentum, and Mouscron's challenge faded away. Leekens promoted the Mpenza brothers, as well as the veteran stopper Gordan Vidović and the midfielder Dominique Lemoine to the national team, but at the same time they only won three times in their last 11 league games, finishing third, 12 points behind the champions Lierse, led by Erik Gerets.

The Mpenza brothers left for Standard Liège in the summer of 1997. Both later left continued to bigger leagues and Emile had an especially prolific career at Schalke, where he went painfully close to winning the title in 2001. Mouscron were never top again, but remained a significant force in the first division before going bankrupt in 2009. Mouscron-Peruwelz, a new club built on their remains, are doing fine in the second division this season.

 ## SC Sedan Ardennes 2000-01

Cédric Mionnet enjoyed his moment immensely. In the last minute of the game between Sedan and Paris St-Germain on 2 December 2000, he received the ball in the penalty area, expertly fooled the keeper Lionel Letizi, then proceeded to make fun of Éric Rabésandratana before slotting the ball into the net from a tight angle. It was a goal of rare beauty from a striker who became the darling of France that season, the icing on the cake in a 5-1 win that helped Sedan to go top of the league.

Like many of his teammates, Mionnet had never dared to dream of becoming a "real" footballer. When he joined Sedan in 1997, aged 23, they were a tiny third division club, with semi-professional status, on the brink of bankruptcy. Most of them stuck around and went on an unbelievable journey.

In 1998 they were promoted to the second division under Bruno Metsu, the man who was later responsible for the Senegal sensation at 2002 World Cup. Metsu left that summer, but the team achieved a second successive promotion without him, while also making it to the Cup final, where they unluckily lost to Nantes thanks to a controversial penalty.

Sedan finished a respectable seventh in their first season in the top flight in 1999-2000, but a year later, things got even better. With a new coach in Alex Dupont, playing at the newly built Stade Louis Dugauguez, named after the former player and manager, the Wild Boars in green shirts produced an effective and attractive style of football.

Olivier Quint was the brightest star with his mazy runs down the left flank. Salif Diao, soon to become one of the most memorable Anfield flops, bossed the midfield. Up front, they used a combination of two short strikers, both just 5'8" tall. Mionnet and the Cameroonian Pius N'Diefi each scored 10 goals that season.

It all started with a 1-0 win at Auxerre, and Sedan gradually became stronger as weeks went by. At the beginning of November, after a 3-0 triumph at Guingamp, they topped the first division table for the first time in their history. A week later, with the whole country watching, they dismantled Marseille 2-0 with a very assured performance. Suddenly, they were legitimate title contenders.

Dupont's team then went three games without a win, but the clash with PSG revived their challenge. N'Diefi scored a magnificent hat-trick and then came Mionnet — a likeable, humble, down-to-earth guy with whom every fan could identify. Two weeks later, another home win against Strasbourg saw Sedan return to the top of the table for the final time.

Eventually, they just were not consistent enough. The most crucial game came in March when the leaders, and eventual champions, Nantes, hosted Sedan who trailed them by three points. The Boars were thrashed 4-1 and, more significantly, lost Mionnet who tore cruciate ligaments after a mistimed tackle by Nicolas Gillet. Not only was his season was ended, his whole career was ruined. Heartbroken, Sedan only finished fifth, some 16 points behind Nantes.

Henri Stambouli, who replaced Dupont in the summer of 2001, totally changed the system, breaking up the team, and Sedan were relegated in 2003, only to reappear in the 2006-07 season. They went bankrupt this summer and are now playing in the fifth division.

 **Sokol Saratov
2001**

They were unheard of before, and have never been heard of ever since, but during the first months of 2001 Sokol Saratov were the biggest story in Russian football. Sokol means 'falcon' in Russian and the team suddenly soared after their first promotion to the top flight. After eight games, they were amazingly leading the table with a squad of nobodies.

Their debut in the top division was away at the Luzhniki stadium, against then seemingly eternal champions Spartak Moscow. The hosts were expecting a record win, but the Sokol coach Aleksandr Koreshkov secured a goalless draw by packing his entire team behind the ball. Thereafter, Saratov won five consecutive league fixtures against lesser teams, all by a one-goal margin. During that period, the team also recorded their most famous victory, beating Spartak 3-1 away in the Cup quarter finals with a hat-trick from Andrey Fedkov, a 29-year-old journeyman, who made such an impression that Oleg Romantsev called him into the national team almost immediately.

After recording a 1-1 draw at Dinamo Moscow, the stage was set for Sokol to feature in the most bizarre top-of-the-table clash ever played in Russia. Krylya Sovetov Samara led the table with 19 points, Sokol had two points fewer. The Saratov outfit duly won 1-0 and went top, with the whole town gleefully delirious. Could they stay there?

They couldn't. Saratov's fourth visit to Moscow ended with a 6-2 defeat at the hands of Torpedo, and the team never recovered. They lost 12 more games before the season ended and finished in eighth place.

Sokol were relegated in 2002 and sank without trace. Fedkov, though, still managed to make more headlines in his career, scoring the winning goal for Terek Grozny in 2004 Cup Final.

 ### Chievo Verona
2001-02

Gianluigi Buffon became the world's most expensive goalkeeper in history when Juventus paid Parma €51 million for him in the summer of 2001. But in the third week of the season, Buffon committed one of the most bizarre errors of his career, making a terrible mess of a simple corner kick and allowing Massimo Marazzina to score into the empty net. When Marazzina then made it 2-0 to Chievo at Delle Alpi, expertly finishing a team move of the highest quality, the country was shocked. Could the Flying Donkeys be for real?

The nickname was derived from the song sung by fans of Hellas Verona, Chievo's bigger city rivals, who claimed that donkeys would fly before they faced their poor neighbours in Serie A. Who could blame them? When Preben Elkjær led Verona to the *scudetto* in 1985, Chievo were still in the fifth division. They were promoted to the fourth a year later, made it into Serie C in 1989 and quite unexpectedly rose to Serie B in 1994. The biggest promotion of them all, which followed in 2001, was a sensation.

This was a team representing a tiny district on the outskirts of Verona, owned by a family of bakers. No significant signings were made during that summer, which left as their best striker Marazzina, who returned from a loan spell at relegated Reggina, where he had scored four goals in 29 games. Nobody doubted that Chievo were destined to go straight down.

From the very first day of the season, though, the Flying Donkeys became the neutrals' favourite team. Their coach Luigi Delneri gave his little-known players a free hand to improvise, and Chievo flourished. Fiorentina were beaten 2-0 at the Artemio Franchi and Chievo triumphed by the same scoreline against Bologna on their home Serie A debut. Juventus were the only other team to start the season with a maximum six points and so the clash at the Delle Alpi became a top-of-the-table event.

Then, with the whole country watching in disbelief, Marazzina struck twice. It was a miracle.

Juve fans apart, Italy was brokenhearted when Juve eventually came back to win 3-2. But that was only start of the story, as Chievo went on to win four of their next five games, drawing the other one and scoring 12 goals in the process. It was November and the Flying Donkeys were leading the table. Although they suffered a few setbacks, such as a 3-2 defeat to Hellas Verona, who were eventually relegated, in the derby, they remained top until mid-December. When Marazzina and his lanky partner Bernardo Corradi scored in a 2-1 win against Inter at San Siro, it was no longer a surprise. The Italians learned to love and respect Chievo and some even believed they could actually go all the way and win the title.

It wasn't to be. The defending champions Roma condemned Chievo to their first home defeat, beating the Donkeys 3-0, and they never regained the top spot. Delneri's troops recorded just five wins in 19 games in 2001, and eventually finished fifth, missing out on the final Champions League berth by a single point. Marazzina ended with 13 goals, Corradi got 10.

Delneri became the most wanted managerial talent in Italy, but stayed at the club until 2004 and many of the stars, like Simone Perrotta and Eugenio Corini, also remained loyal for the following season. Chievo never challenged for the title again but they are the only team of the eight presented here who showed any sign of stability. Unluckily relegated in 2006-07, they immediately came back and have remained a well-respected midtable outfit

ever since. And the derby is back this season, as Hellas Verona finally returned to Serie A after 11 years in the doldrums.

7 Leixões SC
2008-09

Looking at the badge of Leixões, you see a basketball, a tennis racquet and a cricket bat — but no football. That's because the club, established in 1907, only played those sports until football was introduced in 1926. Tradition is very important in Matosinhos and so the logo was never altered.

Matosinhos is a small fishing town just north of Porto. The tiny club could never have competed with the Dragons, but the fans are extremely proud of its history nevertheless and memories of Portuguese Cup triumph in 1961 are passed from generation to generation. The 60s were the golden era of Leixões, when the majority of the players were homebred, and so received their nickname of *'Os Bebes'* (The Babies). There has been very little to celebrate since then, apart from the Cup Final appearance in 2002 that led to qualification for Uefa Cup. Aspirations were always minimal, but that changed in the autumn of 2008.

Promoted in 2007, Leixões only survived in the top division in injury time of the last game of the season. They then appointed José Mota, a promising coach from Paços Ferreira, who was noted for his adventurous style of football. That attitude seemed to backfire when his debut ended in a dismal 3-1 home defeat at the hands of Nacional, but the team responded by going on a phenomenal run. Nobody could ever explain how these anonymous players managed to do it. It was beyond logic.

Leixões had only managed to record four wins during the previous season, the first of them coming in December. In the autumn of 2008, they amassed five away wins in a row — all of them by a one-goal margin. Porto, champions and unbeaten until they met their poor neighbours, entertained Leixões in late October, and were beaten 3-2 in a crazy game. Braga, an unheralded midfielder signed from the minnows Leça in the summer, became a hero, scoring a brace, and the town of Matosinhos went out to celebrate the historic victory.

A week later, Leixões became league leaders, and as such they visited Sporting in Lisbon. They beating the Lions 1-0 to remain top. It was a late evening game and by the time the team bus got back to the town after a journey of 300km, it was 2am. Fans were waiting for their beloved players, though, and partied with them on the streets through the night.

By that time, every rumour of a club possibly changing coach in Portugal terrified Leixões who didn't want to lose José Mota to a bigger club. They didn't have to worry for too long, though, as the magical run finally came to an end. The first four games of 2009 all ended in goalless draws, and from March Leixões began to add defeats to their repertoire. The Dragons were especially glad to take revenge with a 4-1 win at the tiny Estadio do Mar. Eventually, Leixões finished sixth, their best placing since 1963, but 25 points behind Porto.

2009-10 was a disaster, with José Mota resigning in February, and Leixões

eventually finished last, winning just five games. They were relegated and have never returned to the top flight.

 UD Levante
2011-12

Sergio Ballesteros outrunning Cristiano Ronaldo. Who could have imagined a 36-year-old journeyman, who had been mocked for his weight problems throughout his career, could outstrip the most expensive player in the world? Levante fans were so jubilant during the magical autumn of 2011 that they started campaigning for their captain to be called into the national team — and the Spanish press went along with them, for these were the most improbable leaders the country has ever witnessed.

It was surreal to see anyone but Barcelona or Real Madrid topping La Liga table anyway, but to have the poorest team of them all, the one that had only marginally avoided both relegation and bankruptcy the previous season, was incredible. Levante, a club from an industrial district of Valencia, are so small that Valencia CF fans never really considered them to be their rivals — many of the city's football lovers support both teams.

The Frogs started the season with two draws, but then managed to beat Real thanks to a goal by Arouna Koné, a loanee from Sevilla who had previously scored just once in 40 league games for the Andalusians. That's where the dream began. The team coached by Juan Ignacio Martínez, recruited from Cartagena of the second division, went on to record seven consecutive wins. Ballesteros became a symbol, but that was not just about him — most of the squad were veterans whom nobody else wanted. In the sensational 3-0 away win at the then-*nouveau riche* Malaga, the average age of Levante players was close to 32. José Barkero, their most talented midfielder had won the Under-20 World Cup alongside Xavi, but was mainly known for his time at Numancia.

Even the players were left stunned, Joselu calling the achievements "a miracle". Spain fell in love with the sensation and Levante stories were told all across the country, including the bizarre case of a fan who buried a copy of the league table in his grandmother's grave.

Eventually, the run came to an end with a 2-0 defeat at Osasuna in late October and Levante lost 14 more games before the season ended. They still finished sixth, 45 points behind the champions Real, and qualified for the Europa League.

During the 2012/13 season, Barkero accused Ballesteros of match fixing and the fairy-tale image disappeared. Nevertheless, Levante comfortably avoided the drop again. 🅱

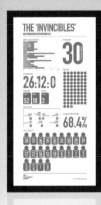

Contributors

The Blizzard, Issue Eleven

Shaul Adar is the author of *Liverpool: Football, Life and Death* (in Hebrew). He writes mainly for *Haaretz* and has been based in London since 2001. Twitter: **@ShaulAdar**

David Ashton is a playwright, TV and film screenwriter; creator of the BBC Radio 4 series *McLevy*. He has written four novels, the latest being *Nor Will He Sleep*. Also an actor, he played Dr McDuff in *Brass* and the father in *The Last King of Scotland*. www.david-ashton.co.uk.

Dion Fanning is the football correspondent of the *Irish Sunday Independent*. He was nominated as Irish Sports Columnist of the Year and Irish Sports Journalist of the Year in 2012 and 2013. He lives in London.

Ian Hawkey is the author of *Feet of the Chameleon, The Story of African Football*, a winner of Football Book of the Year. He writes regularly on African football for *The National* and the Johannesburg *Sunday Times*.

Uli Hesse is the author of *Tor! The Story of German Football* and co-author of *Who Invented the Stepover?* He has also written three German-language football books, is a regular columnist for ESPN, and a contributing editor of *Champions* magazine.

Nicholas Hogg was nominated for the IMPAC literary award for his debut novel, *Show Me the Sky*. Winner of numerous short story prizes, his work has also been broadcast by the BBC. He is co-founder of *The Authors Cricket Club*, an anthology of cricket-playing writers published by Bloomsbury. Twitter: **@nicholas_hogg**

James Horncastle is a European football writer who divides his time between London and Rome. He has written for the likes of *FourFourTwo*, *Champions*, *When Saturday Comes* and the *Observer Sports Monthly*. Twitter: **@JamesHorncastle**

Alexander Jackson is a collections officer at the National Football Museum. He has recently been awarded a PhD for a thesis that used the museum's collections to explore football and childhood between c1880 and c1960.

Sam Kelly writes about Argentinian football for *When Saturday Comes* and ESPN, and writes for English-language Argentinian news website bubblear.com. He is the presenter of *Hand Of Pod*, the internet's only English-language podcast on Argentinian football. Twitter: **@HEGS_com**

Ben Lyttleton covers European football for the *Sports Illustrated* website and Bloomberg TV, and is a regular guest on the *European Football Show*. He is editorial director of *The Global Player* and his book *Twelve Yards: The Art and Psychology of the Perfect Penalty Kick*, will be published in 2014. Twitter: **@benlyt**

Martín Mazur is an Argentinian football writer and deputy editor of the magazine *El Gráfico*. He has made regular contributions to *FourFourTwo* and *Champions*, is *La Gazzetta dello Sport's* correspondent in Argentina. He is the founder of MUNDBØL - www.mundbol.com.

James Montague writes for the *New York Times* and *World Soccer*. He can also be heard regularly on the BBC World Service's *World Football Show*. His first book, *When Friday Comes: Football, War and Revolution in the Middle East* was updated and released this summer. His second, *Thirty One Nil: On the Road With Football's Outsiders* will be out in May 2014. Twitter: **@JamesPiotr**

Firdose Moonda is a writer living in Johannesburg. She writes primarily for ESPNcricinfo on South African and Zimbabwean cricket and ESPNFC, where she runs the Football Africa blog. She also appears regularly on the *Atlantic Post* and runs her own website - www. the-street-seen.com.

Segun Ogunfeyitimi is an award-winning Nigerian photojournalist. He works with supersport.com, goal.com and shengolpixs.

Oluwashina Okeleji is a sports writer and broadcaster for the BBC World Service website, radio and TV. He divides his time between Africa and Europe. He has been writing and reporting on African sport for the BBC since 2004. Twitter: **@oluwashina**

Gunnar Persson is a Swedish author specialising in football. He has written a biography of Lennart 'Nacka' Skoglund as well as club histories on Hakoah Vienna and Hammarby IF. He has recently compiled encyclopaedic overviews of Swedish footballers and their exploits abroad (*Svenska Fotbollsproffs, från Nordahl till Zlatan*) and a short history of the Swedish second tier (*Superettan*).

Igor Rabiner is the author of 16 books including *How Spartak Has Been*

Killed (in Russian), winner at *Knizhnoe Obozrenie's* Sports Book Awards. His latest is *SEx in Sports*, examining the ups and downs of *Sport-Express* and sports journalism in Russia. He has been Russian Football Journalist of the Year four times.

Andi Thomas is a freelance writer based in London. He writes regularly for SB Nation Soccer and Football365, and has written irregularly for ESPN, the Score, Surreal Football and various others. He is the co-author of *A Diary of Love and Hate: The Premier League Season 2012-13*. Twitter: **@andi_thomas**

David Toms is an occasional lecturer in the School of History, UCC. Twitter: **@daithitoms**

Colin Udoh is an award-winning Nigerian football journalist. He was press officer of the Nigerian national team and now works as a studio pundit for SuperSport and ESPN and is editor of KickOffNigeria. com. Twitter: **@ColinUdoh**

Jonathan Wilson is the author of *Inverting the Pyramid*. He writes for the *Guardian*, the *National*, *World Soccer* and *Sports Illustrated*. His latest book is *The Anatomy of Liverpool*. Twitter: **@jonawils**

Richard Winton is the assistant sports editor of *The Herald* newspaper in Glasgow. Twitter: **@richardwinton**

Michael Yokhin is a European football writer with a keen interest in the history of the game. He writes a regular column for ESPN and contributes to the likes of *FourFourTwo* and *Champions*. Twitter: **@Yokhin**

Blizzard Subscriptions

Subscribe to the print version of The Blizzard, *be the first to receive new issues, get exclusive Blizzard offers and access digital versions of all back-issues FREE*

Subscription Options

Set Price for Four Issues

Get a four-issue subscription to *The Blizzard* — for you or as a gift — for a flat fee including postage and packing (P&P):

UK:	£35
Europe:	£45
Non-Euorpe:	£55

Recurring Pay-What-You-Like

Set up a quarterly recurring payment for each edition of *The Blizzard*. The recommended retail price (RRP) is £12, but pay what you like, subject to a minimum fee of £6 plus P&P

See www.theblizzard.co.uk for more

Digital Subscriptions

If the cost of postage is prohibitive, or you just want an excuse to use your new iPad or Kindle, you can set up a subscription to digital versions of *The Blizzard* for just £3 per issue.

See www.theblizzard.co.uk for more

Information for Existing Subscribers

Free Digital Downloads for *Blizzard* Subscribers

Whether you have taken advantage of our set price or pay-what-you-like offer, for the duration of your subscription to *The Blizzard* you are entitled to download every issue FREE.

See www.theblizzard.co.uk for more

We very much value the commitment of our print subscribers and have a policy to make available new issues, special offers and other limited access events and benefits to print subscribers first.

About *The Blizzard*

Distribution & Back Issues
Contact Information
About Issue Eleven

Buy *The Blizzard*

We want as many readers as possible for
The Blizzard. We therefore operate as far
as we are able on a pay-what-you-like
basis for digital and print versions.

Digital Version
(Current & Back Issues)

All issues of *The Blizzard* are available to
download for Kindle, Android, iOS and PC/
Mac at: *www.theblizzard.co.uk.*

- *RRP: £3*
- *Pay-what-you-like minimum: £0.01*

Printed Version
(Current & Back Issues)

Purchase a physical copy of *The Blizzard*
in all its luxurious, tactile, sensual glory
at: *www.theblizzard.co.uk.* If you haven't
felt our rough textured cover-varnish and
smelled the inner genius, you haven't
properly experienced its awesome true
form. Read it, or leave it on your coffee
table to wow visitors.

- *RRP: £12* (+P&P)
- *Pay-what-you-like min: £6* (+P&P)

Contact *The Blizzard*

**All advertising, sales, press and business
communication should be addressed to the
Central Publishing Office:**

The Blizzard
Ashmore Villa,
1, Ashmore Terrace,
Stockton Road,
Sunderland,
SR2 7DE

Email: info@theblizzard.co.uk
Telephone: +44 (0) 191 543 8785
Website: www.theblizzard.co.uk
Facebook: www.facebook.com/blzzrd
Twitter: @blzzrd

About Issue Eleven

Editor Jonathan Wilson
Publisher The Blizzard Media Ltd
www.theblizzard.co.uk
Design Daykin & Storey
www.daykinandstorey.co.uk

Copyright
All content is ©Copyright The Blizzard Media Ltd
and may not be reproduced without explicit
consent. Thanks to Jeanette G Sturis at the Kingsley
Motel, Manjimup, for kind use of Warren Walker's
original sketches of Dog.

WORKSOFARTICLES

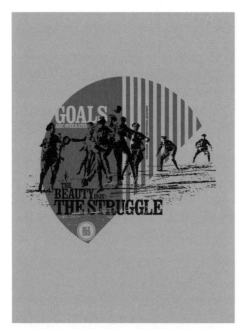

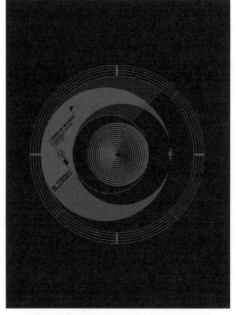

THE BLIZZARD BY GOALSOUL
A PARTNERSHIP BORN OF FOOTBALL

The Blizzard by goalsoul partnership is a commitment to style and substance in equal measure.

Our stunning and original story-inspired artworks are available on stunning, high-quality giclée art prints and boxed canvas'; across a range of sizes. Exclusively available online from www.theblizzard.co.uk, www.goalsoul.net and instore at goalsoul's flagship store in Sheffield.

CLASSIC FOOTBALL SHIRTS.CO.UK

THE MOST EXTENSIVE RANGE OF ORIGINAL SHIRTS ONLINE

HUGE CLEARANCE SECTION FULL OF 1000's OF BARGAIN ITEMS

| GETAFE | FC YOUNG BOYS | LYON TECHFIT | MARSEILLE TECHFIT | VALENC |
| £11.99 | £19.99 | £34.99 | £22.99 | £19.9 |

STOKE CROUCH £29.99 **NAPOLI CAVANI** £49.99 **NAPOLI HAMSIK** £44.99 **SHORTS, SOCKS, BAGS, JACKETS E**